SAGE was founded in 1965 by Sara Miller McCune to support the dissemination of usable knowledge by publishing innovative and high-quality research and teaching content. Today, we publish over 900 journals, including those of more than 400 learned societies, more than 800 new books per year, and a growing range of library products including archives, data, case studies, reports, and video. SAGE remains majority-owned by our founder, and after Sara's lifetime will become owned by a charitable trust that secures our continued independence.

Los Angeles | London | New Delhi | Singapore | Washington DC | Melbourne

ENERGY
ECONOMICS
and the
ENVIRONMENT

Thank you for choosing a SAGE product!
If you have any comment, observation or feedback,
I would like to personally hear from you.

Please write to me at **contactceo@sagepub.in**

Vivek Mehra, Managing Director and CEO, SAGE India.

Bulk Sales

SAGE India offers special discounts
for purchase of books in bulk.
We also make available special imprints
and excerpts from our books on demand.

For orders and enquiries, write to us at

Marketing Department
SAGE Publications India Pvt Ltd
B1/I-1, Mohan Cooperative Industrial Area
Mathura Road, Post Bag 7
New Delhi 110044, India

E-mail us at **marketing@sagepub.in**

Subscribe to our mailing list
Write to **marketing@sagepub.in**

This book is also available as an e-book.

ENERGY ECONOMICS *and the* ENVIRONMENT

Conservation, Preservation and Sustainability

EDITED BY
MOHAMMAD YOUNUS BHAT
HIRANMOY ROY
M. S. BHATT

Los Angeles | London | New Delhi
Singapore | Washington DC | Melbourne

First published in 2020 by

SAGE Publications India Pvt Ltd
B1/I-1 Mohan Cooperative Industrial Area
Mathura Road, New Delhi 110 044, India
www.sagepub.in

SAGE Publications Inc
2455 Teller Road
Thousand Oaks, California 91320, USA

SAGE Publications Ltd
1 Oliver's Yard, 55 City Road
London EC1Y 1SP, United Kingdom

SAGE Publications Asia-Pacific Pte Ltd
18 Cross Street #10-10/11/12
China Square Central
Singapore 048423

Published by Vivek Mehra for SAGE Publications India Pvt Ltd. Typeset in 10.5/13 pt Adobe Caslon Pro by Zaza Eunice, Hosur, Tamil Nadu, India.

Library of Congress Control Number: 2020939371

ISBN: 978-93-5388-310-2 (HB)

SAGE Team: Rajesh Dey, Syed Husain Naqvi, Mahira Chadha and Anupama Krishnan

Contents

List of Figures

List of Tables

List of Abbreviations

AARDO	African–Asian Rural Development Organization
AMC	Augmented marginal cost
AMRUT	Atal Mission for Rejuvenation and Urban Transformation
BAU	Business as usual
BCCL	Bharat Coking Coal Limited
BEE	Bureau of Energy Efficiency
CCO	Coal Controller Organization
CEMDE	Centre for Environmental Management of Degraded Ecosystem
CGWA	Central Ground Water Authority
CHPs	Coal handling plants
CIL	Coal India Limited
CMPDL	Central Mine Planning and Design Institute
CO2P	CO_2 emission per capita
CPCB	Central Pollution Control Board
CS	Consumer surplus
CSR	Corporate social responsibility
CTE	Consent to establish
CV	Component variable
CVM	Contingent valuation method
DJB	Delhi Jal Board
EC	Environmental clearance
EC	Energy consumption
EIRR	Economic internal rate of return
ES	Ecosystem services
ESV	Ecosystem services valuation
ETP	Effluent treatment plant

FAO	Food and Agricultural Organization
FGD	Focus group discussion
FIRR	Financial internal rate of return
FSM	Faecal sludge management
FSSM	Faecal sludge and septage management
Gen	General
GHG	Greenhouse gas
HDI	Human Development Index
HM	Hotelling's model
IEA	International Energy Agency
IGNOU	The Indira Gandhi National Open University
IK	Indigenous knowledge
ILO	International Labour Organization
IPCC	Intergovernmental Panel on Climate Change
ITCM	Individual travel cost method
IUCN	The International Union for Conservation of Nature
JCF	Jharia Coalfield
JMP	Jharia Master Plan
JRDA	Jharia Rehabilitation and Development Authority
JSPCB	Jharkhand State Pollution Control Board
KWS	Kuttanad wetland system
MC	Mohalla committee
MCDR	Mineral Conservation and Development Rules
MCL	Mahanadi Coal Field Limited
MEA	Millennium Ecosystem Assessment
MEC	Marginal extraction cost
MoEF&CC	Ministry of Environment, Forest and Climate Change
MUC	Marginal user cost
NAAQS	National Ambient Air Quality Standards
NAM	Non-aligned Movement
NAPCC	National Action Plan on Climate Change
NoC	No objection certificate

NRSC	National Remote Sensing Centre
OB	Overburden
OBC	Other Backward Class
OC	Opencast
OLS	Ordinary least square
OSPCB	The Odisha State Pollution Central Board
OSS	On-site sanitation
PL&DQ	Purnapani Limestone and Dolomite Quarry
PP	Project proponent
RCP	Representative Concentration Pathway
RI	Respiratory illness
RSPM	Respirable suspended particulate matter
SAAP	State Annual Action Plan
SAIL	Steel Authority of India
SBM	Swachh Bharat Mission
SC	Scheduled Caste
SoB	School of Business
ST	Schedule Tribe
STP	Sewerage treatment plants
TEV	Total economic value
ULB	Urban local body
UN	United Nations
UNFC	United Nations Framework Classification
UGC	University Grants Commission
UNFCCC	United Nations Framework Convention on Climate Change
WHO	World Health Organization
ZTCM	Zonal travel cost method

Foreword

Understanding the complex issues and challenges of energy as well as environmental management is an important component of policy-making. These issues range from energy consumption to the impact of climate change. Therefore, credible and accurate assessments are required so that some of these issues can be addressed. On the one hand, assessment of ecosystem goods and services highlights their importance to the global economic system, while on the other hand, integrating this information into environmental policymaking continues to be an important challenge. In addition, an increase in energy consumption since the last 50 years has been dominated by fossil fuels like coal leading to an increase in global greenhouse gas emissions contributing towards climate change.

This book is a pack of case studies in the field of environment and energy economics. It demonstrates how the information and conclusions drawn from these studies can be used in policy development. It sketches out some of the key issues in environment and energy policy in the Indian subcontinent and provides evidence on preferences connected with policy options. One of the key features of this volume is the diversity and presentation of the book. While going through the text, I found variation both in the methods as well as in the way the results are integrated into policy analysis. This book is for the admiration of readers as researchers have considered innovative approaches both in formulating the problems/issues and presenting or analysing the data.

Dr Deependra Kumar Jha
Vice Chancellor
University of Petroleum and Energy Studies (UPES)
Dehradun, Uttarakhand

Acknowledgements

The editors first and foremost sincerely acknowledge the contribution of the contributors. This industrious, scholarly and distinguished crew's sincere dedication made it possible to take this book from an idea to reality. In addition, there are many others who kept supporting with utmost readiness and affection in making this book possible. In developing this collective work, we had the benefits of advice and guidance from a train of research experts, practising economists and policymakers. The editors are highly grateful to the SAGE, who readily approved the manuscript of this book without delay. We are exceedingly thankful to the SAGE editorial staff and reviewers for their significant suggestions regarding titles and meaningful observations while the book was in the making. We take this opportunity to say thanks in particular to Mr. Rajesh Dey and Mr. Syed Husain Naqvi for their constant help that ensured timely publication of the manuscript. In the end, we sincerely hope this collaborative work will bridge the knowledge gaps as it is meant to be so.

Introduction

The discourse on energy supply erupted globally when in the 1970s a short-term oil energy crisis, triggered by oil embargo, badly hit the high-income economies. The prices of crude oil skyrocketed. Thus, countries across the globe became extremely concerned about energy security. It prompted them to navigate for alternative sources of oil and quest for newer efficient technologies. Simultaneously, the idea of ecosystem goods and services found echo in scientific discourses. In prefatory statement of their collective monumental craft, Ginley and Cahen have brilliantly put that academically and publicly present societies and individuals have become conscious of the fact that demographic increase propels huge demand for energy consumption that radically claims its large-scale cataclysmic effect on natural environment (Ginley & Cahen, 2011). Such a nature of demand for energy, water and food supply is destined to pose severe challenges in the coming times for their end effects on quality of life, economic development and international relations could engender mounting concerns and result in global conflicts. That is why ecosystem services have become part of vibrant scientific discourse. The concept of ecosystem services was proposed by Paul R. Ehrlich in his book *The Population Bomb* (1968) within a purely Malthusian methodological commitment of population biology as all resource economies do. He made a suggestion that among dramatic climatic reverses, the swivelling increase in population would outstrip natural resources by manifold which would lead to long-term mass starvation, severe famines and pandemic diseases among others.

The environmental crisis discourse was globally acknowledged following the 1992 Earth Summit in Rio de Janeiro. It persuaded the governments and policymakers into adoption of sustainable development under Agenda 21 Section II to ensure environment-sustaining diverse life forms. It boasted that poverty, inequality and ecological degradation are interrelated. It called for an integrated approach towards safeguard of fragile ecosystems, conservation of biodiversity, sustainable agriculture and environmentally sound management of hazardous wastes.

Why Study Economics of Energy and Environment?

To set the scene, energy technology development has changed the world landscape in numerous ways leading to a range of mounting environmental dilemmas that threaten the symbiotic relationship between man and environment. Since the beginning of the new millennia, the risks of environmental deterioration have become more ostensibly marked since globally the economic growth concerns have unleashed forces which are sapping the capabilities of diverse ecosystems to sustain and reproduce themselves. Simultaneously, in developing countries, India in particular, extinction and habitat loss of species have tremendously accelerated. Environmental problems have transpired in the form of deracinating ecological biodiversity, global climate changes escalating oceanic acidification, recurring frequency of flash floods and melting of snow glaciers. The onus for ecological crisis is ultimately on a combination of potentially anthropogenic factors including global population growth, severe weather patterns, massive increase in levels of mass consumption, dynamics of unregulated industrial activity, mechanization of agriculture, privatization of energy industry, subsidization of agricultural fertilizers, inefficient regulation of chlorofluorocarbons and transportation vehicles.

It seems fitting to declare positively that energy is increasingly being seen as a basic prerequisite for growth and development of national economies. Vital for satisfying essential human ends and extending our future capabilities, inevitably energy in all of its existing forms is one of the enabling features of human civilization. Energy and human well-being are closely linked to each other which is illustrated in the correlation between energy use per capita and Human Development Index (HDI). A strong correlation exists between energy consumption and the human development index as 80–90 per cent HDI is achieved at approximately 100 gigajoules (GJ)/person/year (Foust et al., 2015). Use of fossil fuels has hazardous consequences as it creates potential damage to the environment. Fossil fuel combustion in vehicles emits carbon dioxide (CO_2) gas including other greenhouse gases (GHGs) leading to significant climate changes because of which as a consequence, the economic growth driven by fossil fuel-based energy consumption has been the main contributor to GHGs, leading to the threat of global warming. The main drivers of sustainable energy policy of any country of the world are energy security, economic well-being and environmental protection.

Estimates suggested that the global human population has reached the 7.6 billion mark in 2019 (https://data.worldbank.org/indicator/SP.POP.TOTL). It demonstrates that the world population has more than doubled in the past 50 years increasing by over 150 people per minute. This growth in population is intensifying the need for more and more energy in the future. However, energy consumption is dominated by fossil fuels leading to further deterioration of environment. Numerous studies have extensively delineated the dynamic linkages between energy consumption and environmental degradation. Against this backdrop, the World Summit on Sustainable Development, 2002, had as a priority reiterated and committed itself to not only boost but also encourage the enhancement of renewable energy resources in order to achieve sustainable consumption and production. It focussed that economic growth must ensure environmental protection as well as improve resource efficiency.

Recurrent and brand new cyclones are natural hazards frequently occurring in India taking away human lives and property. Rising bad air quality in most of the cities too is incurring huge human and financial costs. Forest cover has drastically shrunk for India's largest mangrove forests have declined with extraordinary rapidity. Nevertheless, the green discourse is still to effectively spark off. In the wake of cumulative increase in levels of environmental pollution, which specifies a horrifying reality, there is a need for implementation of comprehensive programmes, quality monitoring strategies and frameworks necessitating a mild hybrid approach in fuel economy regime. What facilitates preservation and conservation of energy and environment is interaction between society and nature. In a nutshell, interventions are needed from key government agencies to mitigate current levels of pollution, health risks, humongous plastic waste generation (25,000 tonnes per day), rapid increase in motorization and widespread destruction of original habitats. Global warming, ceteris paribus, is the most visible form of climate change. According to the CSE Annual Report (2016–2017),

> What is clear is that the most dominant determinant of our future's survival will be our ability to mitigate and to cope with changing climate. There is no doubt already today weather is more variable, extreme and horrendously devastating for the poorest, who live on the margins of subsistence. It is they who today face the intense heat waves; the floods, the droughts and lose their crops and livelihoods to freak weather events.

It is paradoxical that India, though counted among the list of megadiverse nations, has more than four biodiversity hotspots. The Sundarbans mangrove forest canopy, house of the Royal Bengal tiger, is fast withering away. 'Biodiversity is under threat' is currently an open secret in India. In an unregulated manner, several private companies are eliminating wildlife habitats and regularly illegally felling trees in the forests as though clearing away decks to create space for infrastructural projects. Such a lopsided approach to development path has put human civilization on the brink of extreme climate change, threatening our future existence and original habitats of living beings. Rising water level, depleting aquifers, melting of glaciers, and ever-increasing global warming and the current levels of pollution are evidences enough that both short-term and long-term policy measures are required to tackle and mitigate destruction of biological diversity, and at the same time preserve and conserve energy and environment in all forms. In all fairness, the book addresses these issues at length, be it air quality depletion, improper solid waste generation and its disposal, water resource distribution and effective sanitation, limiting the destruction of ecological diversity or recovering the habitat loss threatened with complete extinction.

Topography of the Book

A pack of diverse case studies, this book is a blueprint of the economics of energy and environment. It broadly details various challenges and prospects in the realm of energy efficiency, management and allocation, and conservation and sustainability of environmental biodiversity. It explores a wide spectrum of challenges restricting ecosystem services, their provisioning, regulation, supporting, classification, diverse benefits and multiple dimensions. Being implicitly systemic, forest and aquatic ecosystem goods and services provide fundamentally all the necessary benefits to people which are either directly or indirectly received from an ecosystem. Safeguarding ecosystem health and its diverse ecosystem services is a precondition to sustainable future of life forms. The succeeding discreet case studies persuasively disentangle problems and challenges based on efficient allocation and utilization of natural resources such as water bodies, estimation and valuation of the ecosystem services and goods, the multiple-dimensions of unprecedented global climatic changes with adverse impacts of human energy consumption, sustainability and security of energy resources, low access to clean energy, distribution and management of water-based electricity, scarcity and consumption of water in rural and urban areas, and on top of that the social dimensions associated with local people in mining areas for fossil fuels like coal and their associated negative externalities, and ultimately energy governance in India. Several chapters have addressed issues such as the causation and impact of GHG emissions, energy consumption and the negative environmental externalities on human well-being. In these set of specific studies, the contributors have addressed vulnerabilities associated with global climate alterations limiting direct social and economic benefits from ecosystem goods and services. In its wake, it highlights the drawbacks in accounting ecosystem services—quantification and valuation—critical role of indigenous knowledge concerning forest ecosystem services to maintain a sustainable livelihood. This unique catena of studies approaches the central theme of sustainability— environment, social and economic. Kernel of each and every study addresses accomplishment of the Sustainable Development Goals adopted by the United Nations on 25 September

2015 with the fundamental *telos* to have synergy among energy consumption, environmental and ecosystem safeguarding and eventually socio-economic inclusiveness.

Chapter 1 basically introduces the problem that students of energy economics, environmental economics as well as policymakers need to understand diverse terminologies and methodological approaches associated with non-marketed ecosystem goods and services. What, for instance, do ecosystem services mean? Which are the major ecosystem services provided by different natural and man-made ecosystems? Which ecosystem services are particularly important and how can these be assessed? How to capture the multiple dimensions of ecosystem services? How to quantify and evaluate ecosystem services? What is the role of institutions in ensuring sustainability of ecosystem services? This chapter also addresses the multiple dimensions of ecosystem services, various frameworks for their analysis and assessment, along with a case study of the Kuttanad wetland ecosystem of Kerala. It intends to identify and quantify the bio-physical and socio-economic indicators of ecosystem services provided by the Kuttanad wetlands, and to design and apply economic methods for valuation of wetland ecosystem services.

It analyses the complexity of human–environment symbiotic relationship and broad linkages among energy, environment and its sustainability. Ecosystems directly provide food, medicine, wood and fibre in addition to a wide variety of useful interconnected services which enhance human well-being. Rich biological diversity guarantees diverse ecosystem services. Being highly productive for valuable functions, ecosystems provide a range of services, many of which are of fundamental importance to human well-being for health, livelihoods and survival. Most ecosystems provide joint services, usually hidden in nature, hence leading to them being neglected in national accounting. Human beings draw extensive benefits from ecosystems for their day-to-day activities, livelihood and recreational purposes. Hence, ecosystem health is vital and degradation of these services may certainly worsen human welfare.

We are conscious of the hard fact that the indigenous local people are an integral part of a forest ecosystem. As the authors in Chapter

2 argue livelihood of such indigenous people is associated with their knowledge and decision on allocation of labour among different economic activities as well as for collection of natural resources produced and supplied by forest ecosystem services. Their indigenous knowledge (IK) of resource harvesting always brings sustainable livelihood for them. They know how and from where the resources can be harvested so that ecological resiliency would be possible within a short span of time. But human interventions like mining degrade the ecosystems by attracting large number of migrants for direct and indirect job opportunities. These non-indigenous people also harvest resources from the forests and create population pressure on local forest ecosystems. Because of overexploitation of resources, forest ecosystems are degraded, thus impacting livelihood of indigenous people negatively

Against this backdrop, Chapter 2 summarizes findings of a primary survey conducted by the authors in the Purnapani mined-out area. Authors conducted a primary survey of 1,052 households to analyse the data using statistical tools. They convincingly argue that human intervention without considering indigenous knowledge of resource harvesting leads to the unsustainability of livelihood. According to the authors, in the post-mining period, non-indigenous people go back to their respective place; but as a result of resource scarcity, indigenous people start migrating to other industrial areas in search of jobs and alternative sources of livelihood.

The subsequent Chapter 3 commences with a concise description of different natural capital resource classifications and the interconnection among separate sub-categories. Some important questions addressed in this chapter are:

1. How are resources classified to facilitate effective methods of study and analysis?
2. Is there a unique system of classification or are separate categories based on mutually exclusive criteria?
3. Are existing classifications compatible with the Indian economy?

It also discusses the theoretical framework that is effectively applied in deciding precedence for resource management. Two different approaches are discussed to measure resource scarcity and the diverse scarcity indicators are empirically utilized in the existing literature. Attention has been paid to the major issues of resource exploitation with a focus on constraints posed by limited availability and the assimilative capacity of our planet. This is followed by a discussion on sustainable development, along with different frameworks in the context of sustainable utilization of energy resources. The discussion is enriched by bringing in examples of sustainable strategies at local, national and international levels.

In Chapter 4 an attempt has been made to bring to light an integrated and comprehensive perspective on economics and policies related to bio-energy. It highlights the potential opportunities available as well as the challenges developing countries are grappling with, specifically in the Indian context. It covers a breadth of issues related to economic and policy analysis at local, regional and global levels including crop and feedstock choices, transportation and infrastructure, processing and production, markets and trade, as well as societal implications (welfare effects, agriculture and food) and environmental impacts (climate change and land use).

In Chapter 5 the author has explored an intriguing theme of energy governance, jurisprudence and energy security in post-colonial India. It aims to show that how the control over resources, and governing frameworks and mechanisms in current India gave rise to conflict between energy regime demands and environment. The author upholds that the renewable energy regime adheres to the class characteristics of its own, however, it requires due attention.

In the region-specific study, the author in Chapter 6 takes up the challenge of solid waste management which is lethal to its surroundings if kept untreated. It emits toxic gases such as methane and CO_2. Here the fundamental objective is to test the feasibility of a co-opetition organic waste supply strategy for the waste-based power plant at Pabna where the broker, household and *mohalla* (area) methods are co-existing through the use of the Game Theory approach. Monte Carlo simulation technique and sensitivity analysis have been used by the author to check the efficiency of co-opetition and its comparison with the competition and cooperation strategies. It illustrates in conclusion, while impossible under the other strategies, it is only co-opetition strategy which makes possible the maximum amount of organic waste to maintain the supply chain and bring the highest profits for the households, brokers and energy plant. In addition, the co-opetition strategy maintains the highest equilibrium level of organic waste in terms of quantity and price for power generation, and ensures the highest profit followed by the cooperation and the competition strategies. The findings of this study will provide a robust basis for policymakers to develop a specified policy to lessen the emission of GHGs from organic waste, build a resilient and sustainable waste management technique, and establish a low-carbon society.

Authors in Chapter 7 seek to investigate social issues related to access to water, particularly water sources for household use. For the purpose of analysis, they have used the multinomial logit model to estimate the determinants of household decisions about different sources of water, and the correlation coefficient of error terms among public, private and other sources (tube well and borewell). The results indicate that the households make decisions based on the location of the source and the frequency of water collection from the public and private source. The distance covered to collect water, the time consumed and the frequency of collection are each statistically significant with the public source and other sources. Households make decisions based on the availability of water from public and private sources. Interestingly, a household's decision in determining the water source is primarily based on the water availability in semi-arid regions such as Nuh.

Chapter 8 deals with the hazards that occur in the process of coal mining, the ecosystem and how the new concept of development of eco parks can help in controlling the pollution. Utilizing the empirical data from Coal India Limited (CIL) and its subsidiary Bharat Coking Coal Limited (BCCL), the study deals with the negative externalities that coal mining causes in the ecosystem, and development of eco parks to control the levels of incessant and unwanted pollution.

Since depletable, coal is a non-renewable natural resource—its limited availability makes its optimal allocation, extraction and use necessary. In Chapter 9, the author explores significant negative externalities of coal mining in locality of Angul–Talcher in Odisha. Coal production is treated as a 'dirty industry' as it is treated as the most polluting of all energy sources. Given that coal dust and fly ashes are more contaminating and hazardous in comparison to other minerals, the health outcome of coal exposure is considered to be very critical and demands serious policy intervention. Apart from the direct impact of the occupational hazards to the coal miners, coal mining activities, particularly opencast coal mining, impose highly negative environmental and health externalities (through air pollution) on the communities living in the neighbourhood of the mining region. The authors use the health production function model and attempt to predict the restricted activities days or sick days or work days lost due to severe respiratory illnesses (RI) induced by air pollution in opencast coal belt of Odisha. The study is based on the household survey data in the Angul–Talcher opencast coal mining region of Odisha.

The region records the largest reserve of coal in Odisha and air pollution indicators often exceed the national average by manifolds. They have adopted an OLS regression analysis for estimating work days lost due RI-elated sickness. The result confirms that there is a positive and highly significant relationship between the level of air pollution (RSPM/PM_{10}) and RI-related sick days in the OLS regression model. The positive value of the coefficient of pollution variable depicts that a reduction in air pollution level (PM10 level) causes a reduction in expected number of RI-related sick days.

Chapter 10 is basically an endeavour to capture the global trends in hydropower and review the opportunities and risks linked to hydropower development. Since hydropower projects confront environmental, social, engineering, project management and financial risks, it is imperative to address and mitigate the risks to promote hydropower development. Adoption of new climate resilience guidelines and G-res Tool for estimation of carbon footprint of hydropower projects can assess sustainability of the projects and help mitigate risks.

In Chapter 11, the author takes a long-term view to demonstrate three basic objectives: firstly, man–environment interactions from Holocene epoch when the domestication of plants and animals was undertaken by humans in the Indian subcontinent, secondly, the problem of spread of agrarian expansion into pre-literate and pre-state societies among frontier regions such as Sindh, Tamilkam and Rajasthan. This change is supposed to have occurred after the 6th century CE when newly emerging regional states were extending gracious land grants to Brahmans. Lastly, the author takes up the relations between frontier communities and the early modern and colonial empires such as Mughals and British; ultimately he focuses on the issue of colonial modernity that unleashed ecological watershed in south Asian environmental landscape.

The authors of Chapter 12 have analysed the present status and impact of global climate change, which is taking place at an alarming rate, its economic, environmental and geo-political bearings, and ways to mitigate it. It basically attempts to deliver constructive recommendations towards policy creation to mitigate these wider concerns of humanity especially global climate change and safeguard biological reserves. This study is significant for developing countries and it specially focuses on mitigating policy challenges in achieving sustainable development and advocating the sustainable use of renewables as they are secure, efficient, environmentally justifiable and economically viable.

The Government of India initiated an all-out cleanliness drive, Swachh Bharat Mission in 2014 to make India open-defection free by 2019. In this regard, Chapter 13 seeks to analyse the missing market in the sanitation chain vis-à-vis the management of septage and faecal sludge, and explore the sustainability of the existing urban sanitation model and deliberate upon future possibilities. It also looks at the role which private sector plays in the chain especially when the government fails to provide basic public goods. This missing market not only leads to improper disposal of sludge which contaminates soil and water bodies, and leads to health risks but at the same time also excludes those who are unable to pay for these services. By every definition people's access to basic sanitation is a fundamental right; the recently started Swachh Bharat Mission of the Government of India aiming to achieve universal access to toilets and making India open-defection free is hailed as a crucial step in this regard. However, the policy initiative remains partially addressed unless faecal sludge and septage are systematically managed and disposed safely. Big cities such as Delhi and Mumbai partially run on off-site sewer-based systems with about half the city having access to the sewer network. With increased and uneven urbanization, these cities have now come up with on-site sanitation systems. The improper and unregulated containment, disposal and management of faecal sludge which are carried out in big cities often pose grave health risks and also lead to soil and water pollution.

In Chapter 14 authors' objective is to explore the causality among HDI, CO_2 emission and energy consumption (EC), and impact of CO_2 emission and EC on HDI of Brazil, Russia, India, China and South Africa (BRICS) nations. Using panel regression technique, the resultant findings confirm the existence of negative and significant impact of CO_2 emission on HDI and positive significant impact of EC on HDI of BRICS nations. Increasing energy consumption without considering environmental risks like carbon emissions will adversely affect the HDI.

The concept of water scarcity has been extended to developing countries with its consequences being felt ubiquitously around the globe. The authors of Chapter 15 have tried to bring together physical scarcity of water with the economic, social and environmental aspects to measure water poverty in a region. It is part of global discourse on water scarcity and conservation that across the globe there are several signs that indicate the human use of water has extended beyond sustainable levels. Low river flows, depleting ground water resources, increasing water pollution and environmental degradation are some of the main indicators of water stress in the world. With the dimensions of water scarcity becoming large, the way water scarcity is perceived and measured has seen a change since the late 1990s. The concept of 'water scarcity' has given way to the more comprehensive term 'water poverty', such that the latter covers all aspects of water scarcity, including physical and socio-economic. Water poverty is a people-centric concept and covers all forms of deprivation of water. While water scarcity is a resource-centric term, which only covers the physical estimates of resources available per capita. Among the several indicators of water poverty, the one that has received the maximum attention and seen widespread application is the Water Poverty Index (WPI). The WPI, according to the authors, aims to bring together physical scarcity of water with the economic, social and environmental aspects to measure water poverty in a region.

In Sum

While majority of works are primarily based upon fieldwork, this volume integrates network of diverse disciplines—pedagogic and non-pedagogic. This volume has the potential to offer great value to various groups in research academia, policy formulation, industrial practices, energy education, environmental education and governmental as well as non-governmental organizations since environmental concerns mounting over consecutive decades and depletion of renewable resources have attracted global attention. It is meant to serve as a ready reference for analysts in developed and developing countries working in the area of energy economics, environmental economics, green economics and sustainable development. It will motivate practitioners and managers in industry to deepen and enlarge their theoretical and practical understanding of the prevailing challenges associated with the use of energy consumption, climate change mitigation strategies and restoring biodiversity of environmental resources. Thus, the intention behind is to enthuse practising social scientists, law makers and policymakers, particularly in developing countries, who have to deal with environmental matters and energy concerns on a regular basis. Energy and environmental issues are not at all restricted to pollution of air and water, but other themes and issues are addressed in this book as case studies. Also, economic, mathematical, sociological, legal, statistical and other tools are demonstrated through different case studies as are relevant for practitioners, policymakers and non-governmental organizations. This is a book comprising case studies, doctrinal studies and policy studies, covering various aspects of environmental and energy issues, and introducing appropriate economic, legal, mathematical, statistical and econometric tools and methods. The final emphasis of this volume is on demonstrating the practicality of environmental and energy economics in practical applications and action works.

Each of the chapters is carefully selected to meet specific objectives. This collaborative effort aims at meeting requirements of lawmakers, policymakers, managers of energy and environmentally relevant plans, projects and programmes, and practising social scientists across the disciplinary divides.

References

Centre for Science and Environment. (2016–2017). *Annual report: Knowledge based activism* (p. 1). New Delhi: Author. Retrieved from https://cdn.cseindia.org/userfiles/cse-annual-report-16-17.pdf

Foust, T. D, Arent, D., Macedo, I. D. C., Goldemberg, J., Hoysala, C., Filho., R. M. ,... Somerville, C. R. (2015). Energy security. In *Bioenergy & sustainability: Bridging the gaps*. Retrieved from http://rembio.org.mx/wp-content/uploads/2014/10/bioenergy_sustainability_scope-report.pdf

Ginley, D. S., & Cahen, D. (Ed.). (2011). *Fundamentals of materials for energy and environmental sustainability*. New York, NY: Cambridge University Press.

CHAPTER 1

Ecosystem Services
Concepts, Methods and Synthesis of Valuation Techniques

Sulakshana Rao C. and R. Balasubramanian

Introduction

Ecosystems deliver goods as well as services which support the livelihood of numerous people. 'An ecosystem is a collection of plants, animals, and micro-organisms interacting with each other and with their non-living environment'. Wetlands (coastal and inland), forests, deserts, lakes and agro-ecosystem are some examples. 'Ecosystems are valuable and ecologically sensitive systems that provide useful services to mankind and hence are of vital importance to human well-being, health, livelihood and survival' (Costanza & Folke, 1997; Costanza & Kubiszewski, 2012; Kumar, 2010). Examples include production of direct consumable goods (food, water, timber and fish); habitats for flora and fauna; environmental regulation and stabilization (carbon sequestration and nutrient cycles); and recreational or aesthetic components. The shared services from ecosystems are concealed in nature and hence ignored in growth accounting. However, in 1997 there had been an attempt to assess global ecosystem value and it was more than US$30 thousand billion per annum (in 1995–1996 prices), a much higher value than the global domestic value of product (GDP) at the time (Costanza & Kubiszewski, 2012). Human beings draw extensive benefits from ecosystems for their livelihood and recreational purposes. Hence, ecosystems are of utmost significance to human beings, and ecosystem degradation leads to worsening of human welfare. These pertinent issues are addressed across the globe by various multi-disciplinary researchers. This chapter focuses on diverse terminologies and methodological approaches associated with ecosystem services (ES). What, for example, do ES mean? Which are the major ES delivered by different ecosystems? Which ES are particularly important and how can they be assessed? How to apprehend the multiple dimensions of ecosystems and their services? How to quantify and valuate ES? What is the role of institutions in ensuring sustainability of ecosystems? This chapter also addresses the multiple dimensions of ES, various frameworks for their analysis and assessment, along with a case study of the Kuttanad wetland ecosystem of Kerala. The case study intends to identify and quantify the bio-physical and socio-economic indicators of services provided by the Kuttanad wetlands, and to design and apply economic methods for wetland ecosystem valuation.

Ecosystems and ES

'Ecosystem services (ES) are defined as the benefits people derive from ecosystems—the support of sustainable human well-being that ecosystems provide' (Costanza & Folke, 1997; MEA, 2005). ES remain invaluable in nourishing human life (Costanza, 1997; Daily, 1997). These are services distributed by various ecosystems which assure welfare of people (Daily, 1997). Even though these are life-supporting services, they are largely unrecognized and have non-marketed goods (Proctor, 2001). ES are traditionally divided into product or goods, services (ecological functions) and attributes such as structure or diversity.

Costanza et al. (2014) defined ES as 'the relative contribution of natural capital to the production of benefits in combination with the three other forms of capital'. Costanza et al. (2014) defined ES as 'the relative contribution of natural capital to the production of benefits in combination with the three other forms of capital (categorized as direct-use, option and existence value from the natural capital)'. Ecosystems are multiple-use user systems and exclusion principle is not applicable in these common pool resources. Besides, many of the goods and services except the direct ones are not market traded and hence capturing their total worth is always flawed.

The term 'ecosystem services' got global consideration after the Millennium Ecosystem Assessment (MEA) of 2005. MEA (2005) categorized ES into provisioning, regulating, recreational and supporting services. Provisioning services denote products which are directly obtained from ecosystems such as fish, timber and medicines. Regulating services are concealed activities which contribute to commercial manufacturing or reduced expenses, such as natural drift regulation (comprising flood protection, base flow control and groundwater retention), sediment retention and carbon sequestration. Recreational services include visual appeal, recreation and other amenities obtained from the ecosystem. Supporting services are biological or physical procedures that support other services, and are not included in ecosystem valuation to prevent any multiple counting. Table 1.1 depicts the major ecosystems across the world and major services as labelled in the MEA (2005).

Ecosystems are often considered as free goods and thereby underestimated in their conservation-restoration choices (Kumar, 2010). MEA (2005) brings out that ecosystems and their goods and services are threatened globally, and demand conservation measures. Numerous researchers such as Costanza and Folke (1997), and Sukhdev (2008) opined that one reason for the trend is the non-inclusion of their value in decision-making. This has also paved way for ecosystem degradation due to overexploitation of ecosystem resources. In this line, the major challenge now is to include the multi-user benefits of ES while they are categorized as public goods (Costanza, 2008; Ehrlich & Pringle, 2008). The challenges to ecosystems are perceived to be manifold given the burgeoning population and its rising demand as well the existing climate change scenario. Biodiversity and associated ES are certainly not free goods and are exhaustible, thereby highlighting the necessity for proper accounting of the true value to the human beings.

Table 1.1 *Relative Availability of Goods and Services from Different Ecosystems*

Ecosystem Service	Crop land (agro-ecosystem)	Forest	Agro-forestry	Coastal wetlands	Marine	Mangroves
Provisioning Services						
Water		+	+	+		
Food	+++	+	++	++	++	
Firewood and fibre	+	+++	+++			+
Supporting Services						
Bio-diversity support	+	+++	++	++	+++	++
Regulating Services						
Carbon sequestration	++	+++	++	+		++
Nutrient cycling	+	+++	+++	+	+	+
Quality of air and climatic management	+	+++	++	+	+	++
Hazard management	+	++	++	++	+	+++
Recreation Services						
Cultural and recreation	++	++	+	+++	++	+

Source: Pal et al. (2019).

Note: The number of + indicates relative availability of the service.

Ecosystem functions and services are now receiving growing recognition but are being overlooked in decision-making; yet the free good consideration leads to their overexploitation. Hence, the trade-off between conservation-restoration and exploitation of ES for human activities has to be made with an enhanced knowledge about the potential conflicts in interest among the beneficiaries. Understanding economic value is necessary to decide the trade-offs and also to compare different categories of services with each other. Portraying ecological, economic and sociocultural aspects of ecosystem is complex as these are incomparable to each other as such. Anthropocentric choices of conservation or restoration of ecosystem demand improved knowledge on sustainability versus development trade-off. The effective way to compare these aspects is to express the relative importance to policy makers through monetary terms.

Monetary value of ES guides policy makers in understanding user preferences and the nominal values that the current generation places on these services. Monetary value also facilitates making decisions on allocating resources among competing uses which are non-marketed and are neglected. Furthermore, assessment of monetary value of ES is important to provide incentives and generate expenses for restoration and management, for example, the concept of payments for ES. The underlying premise of the monetary valuation of ES is that assignment of proper values helps policy makers to make better informed decisions.

ES and Their Valuation

'Valuation of ecosystem services has become one of the fastest growing areas of environmental research (Turner et al., 2003)'. 'Economic valuation of ecosystem refers to the assessment of ecosystem services and its contributions in sustainable human well-being with the equitable distribution principles' (Liu, Weinbauer, Maier, Dai, & Gattuso, 2010). 'Ecosystem services valuation (ESV)' is defined by the MEA (2005) as 'the process of expressing a value for a particular good or service in terms of something that can be counted, often money, but also through methods and measures from other disciplines (sociology, ecology and so on)'. 'Economic valuation can be defined as the attempt to assign quantitative and monetary values to goods and services provided by environmental resources or systems, irrespective of the availability of market prices' (Balmford et al., 2002).

ESV is one way to understand the benefits received by people through which environmental investment could be determined

(Barbier, Acreman, & Knowler, 1997). Lambert (2003) opined that people are not always informed of the ecosystem value. Finlayson, Bellio and Lowry (2005) discussed that majority of the ecosystems are underrated and overexploited due to divergent interests and the exploitation of some services by stakeholders. Sustainability regarding multi-beneficiary use of ecosystems is ecologically stable and economically beneficial both to local communities and society as a whole (Balmford et al., 2002).

Methods in Ecosystem Valuation

Economic valuation is neither an easy nor a non-conflictive exercise. Ecosystem resources are complex, hidden and multi-functional, and disaggregating their effect on human welfare is quite complex. 'The total economic value (TEV) of ecosystem is defined as the total amount of resources that individuals would be willing to forego for increased amount of ecosystem services' (Turner et al., 2000). The TEV is divided into different components as given in Figure 1.1 and Table 1.2. Theoretically, Total economic value (TEV) is broadly categorized into use and non-use value. Firstly, the use value may be either direct use-consumptive/non-consumptive (crop output, water, fish etc.) or

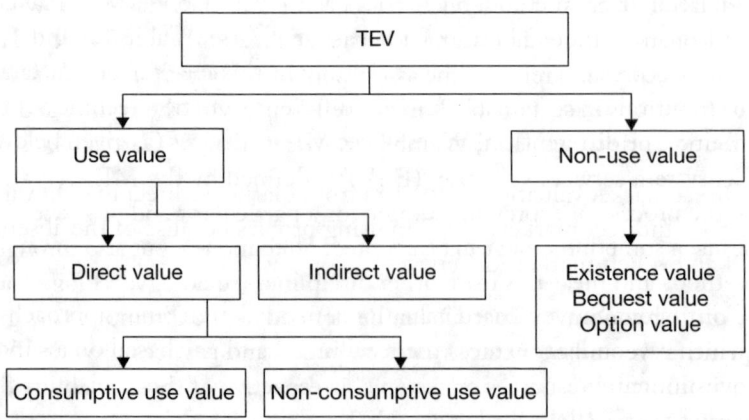

Figure 1.1 *Ecosystem Valuation: The Taxonomy*

Source: Adapted from Ghosh (2017); Rao, Ranjith, & Pal (2018).

Table 1.2 Components of Total Economic Value

Total Economic Value	
Use Values	
Direct use values	Benefits such as food, water, farming, timber, cultural amenities, energy, essential oils and dyes
Indirect use values	Indirect welfare from the ecosystems such as nutrient retention, flood prevention, defence from storm, microclimate and shoreline stabilization
Option value	Benefits from assurance of availability of resource in the future
Non-use Values	Non-use values such as existence value and bequest value are derived from assurance that a resource is maintained

Source: Author.

indirect use (for example aesthetic value from backwaters) with respect to its tangibility. Secondly, non-use value includes existence value and bequest value derived from assurance that a resource is maintained.

Ecosystem Service Valuation (Monetary Terms)

Monetary ESV methods are of four basic types. Monetary or financial valuation methods fall into three basic types (see Table 1.3 and 1.4) (de Groot et al., 2006). The case study in this chapter on Kuttanad wetland valuation uses all the four different valuation techniques for each of the different categories of ecosystem services (as given below).

Direct market valuation: Uses data from market indirect market valuation: Indirect market valuation using proxies because of the absence of an explicit market for services

Contingent/Survey-based valuation: A stated preference approach in which respondents express their willingness to pay based on a survey questionnaire.

Benefit-transfer method: When there is time and resource constraints, monetary values from previous studies focusing on a different region or time period. This is called 'benefit transfer'.

Table 1.3 *Methods in Monetary Valuation of Ecosystem Services*

Type	Explanation	Examples
Market-based valuation: direct	Exchange value that ES have in markets	Market price method in goods such as fish, food, raw materials and factor income methods for change in income due to some services
Market-based valuation: indirect	In absence of markets for services, indirect market valuation is used	Avoided cost method (flood control), Replacement cost method (groundwater recharge) and hedonic pricing (clean air or aesthetic views)
Contingent valuation	A survey questionnaire is used and respondents express their willingness to pay (often used for non-use attributes) for the services	Mainly for non-use values like biodiversity conservation
Benefit-transfer method	Uses values from similar ecosystems to reach the value of a given service in the study site when time and resources are scarce	For resource consuming estimation of process such as sediment retention, erosion control and carbon sequestration

Source: De Groot, Stuip, Finlayson, & Davidson (2006).

Valuation of Global Ecosystems

MEA (2005) and numerous studies on economics of ecosystems have recognized the crucial role of ESV in achieving the UN Sustainable Development Goals (SDGs). ESV studies are globally being conducted every year and different methods of valuation are employed such as production function method (Kundu & Chakraborty, 2017; Ramachandra & Rajinikanth, 2005), factor income method (Schuyt, 2004), revenue approach (Costanza & Folke, 1997), individual travel cost method (ITCM) and zonal travel cost method (ZTCM; Anoop, Suryaprakash, Umesh, & Amjath Babu, 2008; Dehlavi & Adil (2011); Lamsal, Sawagaki, Watanabe, & Byers, 2016), opportunity cost (Barbier, 1994; Sathirathai & Barbier, 2001), cost of alternatives/replacement (Emerton & Kekulandala, 2002; Gren, Folke, Turner, & Batemen, 1995) and contingent valuation method (Bateman, Mace, Fezzi, Atkinson, &

Table 1.4 Ecosystem Valuation Methods, Features and Examples

Method		Description	Limitation	Examples
Direct market valuation	Market price	Marginal productivity-based exchange value	Distortion of market prices due to market imperfections and policy interventions	Goods (e.g., fish, timber)
	Factor income method	Loss or gains in earnings/productivity	Double counting needs to be accounted	Natural water quality improvements leading to better catch and income
Indirect market valuation	Avoided cost method	Costs avoided due to presence of services	Assumption: avoided cost match the original benefit.	Flood mitigation
	Replacement cost	Replacement costs with man-made systems		Groundwater recharge—substitute costs.
	Mitigation or restoration cost	Cost of restoration		Preventive expenditures e.g., flood barriers
	Travel cost method	Cost incurred to visit the recreational site	Over-estimation issue	Lakes/parks
	Hedonic pricing method	Prices people pay for associated marketed goods reflect the value of service	Willingness to pay captured	Clean air and aesthetic amenities and real estate prices
Surveys	Contingent valuation method (CVM)	WTP for ecosystems	Bias in the interview techniques	Non-use values: biodiversity
Benefit transfer	Benefit transfer	Results from other, similar area used	Values are site and context dependent	Resource-intensive surveys

Source: Adapted from De Groot et al. (2006), Barbier et al. (1997).

Turner, 2011; Chopra et al., 1997; Ghosh, 2017; Siew, Yacob, Radam, Adamu, & Alias, 2015). The choice of ESV method is based on the type of service being valued (Freeman, 2003; MEA, 2005).

De Groot et al. (2012) and Costanza and Kubiszewski (2012) estimated the ESV of different ecosystems as well as the global flow of services in monetary terms, respectively (Tables 1.5 and 1.6). De Groot et al. (2012) estimated the ecosystem value of various main ecosystems (marine and coastal, wetlands and freshwater, forests and grasslands) through globally distributed local case studies. Marine and coastal ecosystems valued around $0.38 million per hectare per year. Value of wetlands and freshwater ES was around $0.22 million per hectare per year, while forests and grasslands around $12 thousand per hectare per year. Regulating services provided by marine and coastal biome was 50 per cent of the total value to be $0.19 million per hectare per year. Wetlands and freshwater systems provide regulating and supporting services with one-fourth of the total ecosystem value. As per Costanza and Kubiszewski (2012), the global ESV increased by 4.4 times from 1997 to 2011 (Table 1.6). Marine ecosystem noted highest growth in value terms followed by wetlands and agro-ecosystems.

Role of Institutions in Ensuring Sustainability of ES

The Chapter 2 of the Brundtland Report of the UN World Commission on Environment and Development suggests that 'the goals of economic and social development must be defined in terms of sustainability across the world'. And we must reach a consensus about the concepts of sustainable development and the strategy to achieve it (Brundtland et al., 2006). The key for sustainable development is to strike a long-term balance between natural resource exploitation for socio-economic development, and conservation of ecosystems and their services for societal well-being. Since the benefits from ES are passively perceptible, a crucial understanding of how they contribute to the societal well-being and livelihoods, and how ecosystem degradation affects the various stakeholders is necessary.

Table 1.5 Ecosystem Services Valuation of Different Services under Different Ecosystems ($/ha/yr, 2007 Prices)

S. No.	Ecosystem Services	Marinend Coastal Ecosystems[a]	Wetlands and Fresh Water[b]	Forests and Grasslands[c]
1	Provisioning	58,222	6,571	4,057
	Food	3,154	1,831	1,743
	Water	0	3,433	278
	Raw materials	21,548	783	488
	Genetic material	33,048	10	14
	Others (medicine and ornamental resource)	472	114	32
2	Regulating	197,390	35,066	3,230
	Climate regulation	1,732	553	2,243
	Waste treatment	162,210	3,208	82
	Erosion prevention	182,511	2,622	62
	Nutrient cycling	0	1,758	96
	Others (include air quality and water flow regulation, pollination and biological control)	16,991	14,891	727
3	Habitat	16,590	19,593	3,392
	Nursery services	194	11,935	1,289
	Genetic diversity	16,395	7,658	2,102
4	Cultural (recreational and aesthetic)	109,456	8,562	2,057
	Total economic value (1+2+3+4)	382,557	223,794	12,736

Source: De Groot et al. (2012).

Notes:

[a] Marine and Coastal ecosystems includes marine ecosystems, coral reefs and coastal systems.

[b] Wetlands and fresh water ecosystems include freshwater, inland and coastal wetlands.

[c] Forests and grassland ecosystems includes tropical and temperate forests, woodlands as well as grasslands.

Table 1.6 Total Global Flow Values of Ecosystems during 1997–2011 (in $/year)

Ecosystems	Value of Ecosystem Services ($/year)		
	1997	2011	Change
Marine	796	1,368	572
Open ocean	348	660	312
Coastal	5,592	8,944	3,352
Others (includes estuaries and coral reefs)	66,119	410,081	343,962
A. Marine and coastal ecosystems	72,855	421,053	348,198
Terrestrial	1,109	4,901	3,792
Forest	4,524	12,319	7,795
Grassland/rangeland	321	4,166	3,845
B. Forests and grasslands	5,954	21,386	15,432
Wetlands	20,404	14,0174	119,770
Tidal/marsh/mangroves	13,786	193,843	180,057
Swamps/floodplains	27,021	25,681	-1,340
Lakes/rivers	11,727	12,512	785
C. Wetlands and freshwater	72,938	372,210	299,272
D. Cropland	126	5,567	5,441
Total economic value (A+B+C+D)	151,873	820,216	668,343

Source: Costanza et al. (2014).

Ecosystems such as marine, coastal, wetlands, grasslands, lakes and mangroves are common or shared resources across the world. Hardin's tragedy of commons[1] applies to the ecosystem scenario and due to its inevitability in the rising rational resource users. Neo-institutional efforts and research are the keys to develop ideas and new directions in the conservation and restoration of commons in ecosystems to attain the sustainability objective. The UN Sustainable Development Agenda

[1] Hardin's tragedy of commons in the simplest conceptual definition describes situations in which a shared resource is progressively degraded by the rational users for their short-term interests.

of SDGs (SDG 15) makes a clear emphasis that protection of the global commons is essential for achieving development ambitions. For understanding ecosystems in a holistic manner, due emphasis should be given to multi-functionality characteristics of various ecosystems as well as economic, ecological and social dimensions.

Monetary valuation of ES provides an understanding of relative value or consumer surplus (CS) human beings keep on ES. These monetary values aid to understand the relevance of ecosystems to human beings and user preferences, and to decide on allocation of resources among divergent uses. Underpinning the rational human behaviour, institutions and policy makers should focus on determining incentives that provide benefits to stakeholders to favour cooperation to conserve and restore ecosystems.

ESV: A Case of Kuttanad Coastal Wetlands of Kerala

Wetlands are globally valued and ecologically sensitive systems that deliver goods and services globally, and substantially improve human welfare. Contrary to their significance, these lands are always considered to be wastelands. The associated resources and services are overexploited by stakeholders leading to persistent degradation across the globe. The non-excludable public good nature of the wetlands resulted in their undervaluation and inconsiderate use. Despite being a source of livelihood to vulnerable groups such as farmers and fishermen, their multi-use character is undervalued and neglected. Most of the valuation techniques are focused on visible market-based direct benefits and narrowly focused. The overall benefits and potential use of these coastal wetlands is narrowly understood and undervalued in the cost–benefit approach of ESV. A broad-based and holistic approach in ESV is quintessential in policy making and financial assistance of wetland restoration.

With this background, the case study intends to provide a profound comprehension of the multiple—yet unrecognized—direct and indirect services of coastal wetland ecosystems to the present and future generations, and to quantify these benefits. The broad objective of the present research is the economic analysis of Kuttanad coastal wetland ecosystem of Kerala, and its conservation and management. The specific objectives are: (a) to identify and quantify the bio-physical and socio-economic indicators of ES provided by the coastal wetlands and (b) to design and apply economic methods for valuation of coastal wetland ES.

The study was conducted in the Kuttanad wetlands which are spread across the districts of Alappuzha, Kottayam and Pathanamthitta. A representative area of the wetland ecosystem was selected from different agro-ecological and socio-economic environments in Kuttanad. The major stakeholders are rice farmers, fishermen, neighbourhood residents living in the vicinity of the wetlands, and tourists visiting the wetlands for recreational activities. A random sample of rice farmers, fishermen and neighbourhood residents (120 samples each) were selected from six villages (20 samples each) namely, Alleppey, Muhamma, Thanneermukkom, Champakulam, Ramankary and Neelamperoor. The tourist stakeholders were interviewed at the tourist boat hub at Alleppey. The personal interview method was adopted using structured, pretested interview schedule along with direct observation. The major analytical methods used for data analysis were market price method, cost of alternatives/replacement method, ITCM, benefit transfer method, contingent valuation method (CVM), choice experiments and conditional logit model.

The major stakeholders of Kuttanad wetlands are paddy farmers, fishermen, local residents and the public/tourists. All the stakeholders depend directly or indirectly on the wetlands for their living or for some services. Rice farmers are the dominant stakeholders of the Kuttanad wetlands. With a net return of around ₹60,000 per hectare and benefit–cost ratio of 1.7, rice farming was a profitable venture in Kuttanad. Average income per day of the fishermen was approximately ₹1,600. The net income from fishing activity is ₹89,000 per annum.

Kuttanad Wetland Ecosystem: ES and Economic Benefits

Kuttanad wetland system (KWS) delivers an array of ES. ES identified in the study area are briefed in Table 1.7. Out of the

Table 1.7 Ecosystem Services in Kuttanad Wetland System

Ecosystem Service	Relative Importance	Socio-economic Indicators
Provisioning Services		
Food and raw materials: rice, fish, vegetables, ducks, lotus, edible plants and medicinal plants	**	Value of output
Water for agricultural production	**	Area irrigated, duration of water supply, quantity and value of water used in agriculture and value of output
Potable freshwater	*	Duration of water use and replacement cost of providing alternative sources
Supporting Services		
Biodiversity regulation	**	Number of flora and fauna supported by the ecosystem
Regulating Services		
Carbon sequestration	*	Quantity of carbon sequestered
Nutrient cycling	*	Wetland nutrient removal (in tonnes or %)
Air quality and climate	*	Water quality in aquatic systems
Natural hazard regulation	**	Flood prevention/mitigation, storm protection
Cultural Services		
Cultural and amenity	***	Amount of tourism earnings

Source: Key informant interview and Primary survey by author.

Note: Number of asterisk indicate strength of the service.

22 ES identified, there were nine provisioning, two supporting, four regulating and seven cultural or aesthetic services which were estimated through different bio-physical indicators and economic methods of valuation.

The major stakeholders of Kuttanad wetlands are paddy farmers, fishermen, local residents and tourists. All the stakeholders depend in a direct or indirect way on the wetland for survival. They are affected by the changes in the wetland ecosystem which are either due to natural or anthropogenic factors. Focus group discussions with resident communities revealed that the highest ranked service was rice farming followed by fishing, tourism, water for irrigation and habitats for biodiversity. One of the important ES upon which the stakeholders depend on a day-to-day basis is water. Water from canals is used for irrigating rice fields, and also for washing and bathing purposes by the residents. The wetlands also provide services such as erosion control and also act as a habitat for biodiversity. The 10 important services along their ranking and details on their use by residents are shown in Table 1.8.

Total Economic Value of Kuttanad Wetlands

In this study, the authors estimated the TEV of KWS to be around ₹51.27 billion per annum at 2017 price levels. KWS is worth ₹0.316 million per hectare per annum and distributed across an overall area of 162,125 hectares. The direct and indirect values (in monetary terms) from the KWS are summarized below under various headers.

Economic Value of Wetlands from Direct Services

Rice Cultivation

Dominant stakeholders of the KWS were rice farmers. Rice farming (provisioning service) was valued by direct market valuation method. The value of KWS from rice was ₹60,079 per hectare per year. The total monetary value of Kuttanad wetlands per annum based on paddy farming was ₹3.04 billion (estimated by multiplying area of wetlands under paddy and the net returns per hectare).

Fishing

Fishing, the tangible resource from KWS valued to around ₹5.4 billion per annum. The net income from fishing activity is ₹89,103 per annum. This was then multiplied with the number of active fishermen to estimate total monetary value of Kuttanad wetland fishery.

Table 1.8 Ecosystem Services: Use, Valuation Methods and Ranking by the Stakeholders

Rank	Ecosystem Services and Category	Uses	Remarks	Valuation Technique Used
1	Rice farming (provisioning)	Food and market value	70% of the population depends on rice farming as a source of income	Market price method
2	Fishing (provisioning)	Food and market value	More than 60,000 active fishermen in the area. Average income of ₹1,600 per day during peak seasons	Market price method
3	Recreational (cultural)	Employment and global recognition	Important tourist destination. Average inflow of tourist is more than two lakh per annum	Individual travel cost method
4	Water (provisioning)	Irrigation and household purposes	Daily dependence by stakeholders for irrigation, washing and bathing purposes	Cost of alternatives method
5	Sediment retention (regulating)	Protect and stream banks against erosion action	Act as buffer against run off, also provide drainage and natural irrigation	Benefit transfer approach
6	Habitat for biodiversity (supporting)	Global recognition and biodiversity conservation	Diverse species of wild flora and fauna have been identified	Contingent valuation
7	Fish nursery (supporting)	Breeding ground for fishes	High fish diversity	method

Source: Primary survey by author.

Domestic Water Supply

Even though the water from wetlands is non-potable, the domestic residents depend on it mainly for washing and bathing. With an average water consumption of 285 litres per month, the total water use by the residents was 1.1 billion litres per annum (58.3% dependency on the water). The water charges applied as alternative costs were the standard tariff rates of the Kerala Water Authority. The yearly value of local water supply from KWS was around ₹6.2 million.

Economic Value of Wetlands from Indirect Services

Two major indirect services, namely recreational services and sediment retention services were valued by ITCN and benefit transfer method respectively.

Recreational Services from KWS

Tourists are those stakeholders who reside far away from the wetlands and visit the place for the recreational purposes. Kuttanad wetlands are major tourist destination globally. Average tourist visit to KWS was about 0.306 million per annum. CS was estimated by the absolute value of the reciprocal of coefficient of travel cost. CS is the surrogate of net benefit received by stakeholders from the recreational services. The CS per visit was around ₹769.23. Total recreational value was ₹0.24 billion.

Sediment Retention by KWS

Erosion control through sediment retention by KWS was estimated by benefit transfer method. The per hectare value of coastal wetlands from sediment retention was US$3929 per ha per year (value derived from De Groot et al., 2012 and Costanza et al., 2014). Total value from sediment retention was estimated to be ₹40.76 billion per ha per annum. It could be observed that the indirect value constitutes 79.96 per cent of the TEV of KWS.

Table 1.9 *Total Economic Value from Kuttanad Wetland System*

S. No.	Ecosystem Services	Total Value in ₹ Billion per Year
A. Direct values		
1	Rice farming	3.04
2	Fishing	5.4
3	Domestic water supply	0.0062
Total		**8.45 (16.47%)**
B. Indirect values		
4	Recreational services	0.235
5	Sediment retention	40.76
Total		**40.99 (79.96%)**
C. Non-use values		
6	Biodiversity conservation	**1.83 (3.57%)**
Total economic value (₹ billion per year)		**51.27 (100%)**
Area of wetlands (in hectare)		162,125
Total economic value (₹million per ha/per year)		**0.316**

Source: Based on secondary data (from National Wetland Atlas Kerala, SAC ISRO, 2010) and field survey data.

Non-use ES

The non-use values are directly or indirectly used by stakeholders. CVM was employed to calculate the benefits of KWS from non-use services. The average Willingness to Pay (WTP) per annum was ₹1,088, ₹1,226, ₹1,328 and ₹4,760 for farmers, fishermen, local residents and tourists, respectively. TEV from non-use services of KWS was estimated to be ₹1.83 billion per annum.

Thomson (2003) used CVM to estimate the non-use values from estuarine biodiversity in Kerala (₹546.994 lakh per annum). Kakuru et al. (2013) estimated the non-use value from western Ugandan wetlands to be around US$298.14 million per annum.

The TEV of KWS was estimated to be ₹51.27 billion yr⁻¹ which was 1.1 per cent of the state's gross state domestic product which highlights the economic significance of Kuttanad wetlands in the Kerala economy. Table 1.9 indicates that the value of indirect ES is five times the estimates of direct provisioning services. The per hectare economic value of Kuttanad wetlands was ₹0.316 million yr⁻¹. Keeping this value in mind, the study recommends conservation and restoration of the KWS owing to the declining land resources and rising population.

Conclusion

Ecosystems are valuable and ecologically sensitive systems which play a significant role in delivering ES globally. Tangible goods and services such as food, fish, raw materials and water are economically important, however, various intangible services such as climate stabilization, carbon sequestration, air purification, biodiversity conservation services are significant to human well-being. This chapter has summarized diverse terminologies and methodological approaches related to ecosystems, and their services and valuation. We also reviewed ES, their relevance to livelihood, and economic values for wetlands, forests, grasslands, agro-ecosystems and lakes.

Direct use values from ecosystems are estimated using market price method and factor income approach, while indirect use services are estimated by cost of alternatives method, benefit transfer method and so on. Recreational value provided by ecosystem was estimated mainly using ICTM and ZTCM, and non-use values using CVM. The synthesis of estimates of economic value of various ecosystems from various valuation studies across the globe in the study illustrates the degree of economic significance of ecosystems over and above their ecological significance. The estimated values intend to raise awareness among policy makers and other stakeholders about the economic relevance of the ecosystems and how would their sustainable management benefit the society. Furthermore, the role of institutions in striking a balance between natural resource exploitation for socio-economic development and conservation of ecosystem is identified.

The estimates from the two major global valuation studies reviewed here indicate that the value of indirect ES (regulating services) is three times the direct provisioning services (De Groot et al. 2012, Costanza et al. 2014). Similar results were also observed in the case study on valuation of Kuttanad wetlands ecosystem of Kerala where the indirect use values (sediment retention and ecotourism) were five times the total direct use values. The results indicate that the value of ecosystems possess value far more than that merely based on the exchange or utility viewpoint. There is a need to include economic value of ES in policy making. An ecosystem inventory and accounting of ecosystem in national development estimates are recommended. Mainstreaming ES in the development process is the need of the hour for which institutional mechanism for incentivizing practices for conserving ecosystems and enhancing their services for existing and forthcoming generations is necessary.

References

Anoop, P., Suryaprakash, S., Umesh, K. B., & Amjath Babu, T. S. (2008). Economic valuation of use benefits of Ashtamudi Estuary in South India. In M. Sengupta & R. Dalwani (Eds.), *Proceedings of the taal 2007: The 12th world lake conference* (pp. 1822–1826). Retrieved from https://pdfs.semanticscholar. org/3ba4/3880c8684376ea15a794d2213a15309c549c.pdf

Balmford, A., Bruner, A., Cooper, P., Costanza, R., Farber, S., Green, R. E., & Munro, K. (2002). Economic reasons for conserving wild nature. *Science, 297* (5583), 950–953.

Barbier, E. B. (1994). Sustainable use of wetlands valuing tropical wetland benefits: Economic methodologies and applications. *Geographical Journal, 159,* 22–32.

Barbier, E. B., Acreman, M., & Knowler, D. (1997). *Economic valuation of wetlands: A guide for policy makers and planners*. Gland: Ramsar Convention Bureau.

Bateman, I. J., Mace, G. M., Fezzi, C., Atkinson, G., & Turner, K. (2011). Economic analysis for ecosystem service assessments. *Environmental Resource Economics, 48* (2), 177–218.

Brundtland, G., Khalid, M., Agnelli, S., Al-Athel, S., Chidzero, B., Fadika, L., ...Singh, M. (1987). *Report of the world commission on environment and development: Our common future*. Retrieved from http://www.un-documents. net/our-common-future.pdf

Chopra, K., Kadekodi, G., Bathla, S., Subbarao, D. V., Sharma, S., Pandey, P., & Agarwal, M. (1997). *Natural resource accounting in the Yamuna basin: accounting for forest resources*. New Delhi: IEG Monograph.

Costanza, R., de Groot, R., Sutton, P., van der Ploeg, S., Anderson, S. J., Kubiszewski, I., & Turner, R. K. (2014). Changes in the global value of ecosystem services. *Global Environmental Change*, *26*, 152–158.

Costanza, R., & Folke, C. (1997). Valuing ecosystem services with efficiency, fairness and sustainability as goals. In Gretchen C. Daily (Ed.), *Nature's services: Societal dependence on natural ecosystems* (pp. 49–70). Washington, DC: Island Press.

Costanza, R., & Kubiszewski, I. (2012). The authorship structure of 'ecosystem services' as a transdisciplinary field of scholarship. *Ecosystem Services*, *1* (1), 16–25.

Daily, G. (Ed.). (1997). *Nature's services: Societal dependence on natural ecosystems*. Washington DC: Island Press.

De Groot, R., Stuip, M., Finlayson, M., & Davidson, N. (2006). *Valuing wetlands: guidance for valuing the benefits derived from wetland ecosystem services* (IWMI Research Reports, No. H039735). Colombo: International Water Management Institute.

De Groot, R., Brander, L., van der Ploeg, S., Costanza, R., Bernard, F., Braat L., ...van Beukering, P. (2012). Global estimates of the value of ecosystems and their services in monetary units. *Ecosystem services*, *1* (1), 50–61.

Dehlavi, A., & Adil, I. H. (2011). *Valuing the recreational uses of Pakistan's wetlands: An application of the travel cost method*. Kathmandu: SANDEE.

Ehrlich, P. R., & Pringle, R. M. (2008). Where does biodiversity go from here? A grim business-as-usual forecast and a hopeful portfolio of partial solutions. *Proceedings of the National Academy of Sciences, 105* (Supplement 1), 11579–11586.

Emerton, L., & Kekulandala, B. (2002). *Assessment of the economic value of Muthurajawela wetland*. Colombo: IUCN—The World Conservation Union.

Finlayson, C. M., Bellio, M. G., & Lowry, J. B. (2005). A conceptual basis for the wise use of wetlands in northern Australia—linking information needs, integrated analyses, drivers of change and human well-being. *Marine and Freshwater Research, 56* (3), 269–277.

Freeman, A. M., III. (2003). Economic valuation: What and why. In Patricia A. Champ, Kevin Boyle & Thomas C. Brown (Eds.), *A primer on nonmarket valuation* (pp. 1–25). Netherlands: Springer.

Ghosh, P. K. (2017). Valuing the attributes of wetlands in coastal areas of south Asia: Incorporating the economic value into policy making. In B. Anjan Kumar Prusty, Rachna Chandra & P. A. Azeez (Eds.), *Wetland science: Perspectives from South Asia* (pp. 347–367). New Delhi: Springer.

Gren, M., Folke, C., Turner, K., & Batemen, I. (1995). Primary and secondary values of wetland ecosystems. *Environmental and Resource Economics, 4* (1), 55–74.

Kakuru, W., Turyahabwe, N., & Mugisha, J. (2013). Total economic value of wetlands products and services in Uganda. *The Scientific World Journal, 2013* (1). doi: 10.1155/2013/192656

Kumar, P. (2010). The economics of ecosystems and biodiversity: Ecological and economic foundations. In P. Kumar (Ed.), *Earthscan, London and Washington*.

Kundu, N., & Chakraborty, A. (2017). Dependence on ecosystem goods and services: A case study on east Kolkata wetlands, West Bengal, India. In B. Anjan Kumar Prusty, Rachna Chandra & P. A. Azeez (Eds.), *Wetland science: Perspectives from south Asia* (pp. 381–405). New Delhi: Springer India.

Lambert, A. (2003). Economic valuation of wetlands: An important component of wetland management strategies at the river basin scale. *Conservation Finance Guide, Washington*. Retrieved from http://www.unepscs.org/ Economic_Valuation_Training_Materials/06%20Readings%20on%20 Economic%20Valuation%20of%20Coastal%20Habitats/07-Economic-Valuation-Wetlands-Management.pdf

Lamsal, D., Sawagaki, T., Watanabe, T., & Byers, A. C. (2016). Assessment of glacial lake development and prospects of outburst susceptibility: Chamlang South Glacier, eastern Nepal Himalaya. *Geomatics, Natural Hazards and Risk, 7* (1), 403–423.

Liu, J., Weinbauer, M. G., Maier, C., Dai, M., & Gattuso, J. P. (2010). Effect of ocean acidification on microbial diversity and on microbe-driven biogeochemistry and ecosystem functioning. *Aquatic Microbial Ecology, 61* (3), 291–305.

Millennium Ecosystem Assessment (MEA). (2005). *Ecosystems and human wellbeing: wetlands and water synthesis*. Washington, DC: Author.

Pal, S., Rao C. S., & Chand P. (2019). Agriculture and ecosystem services: Introduction and synthesis of the issues. *Proceedings of the National Seminar on Agriculture and Ecosystem Services*, held at ICAR-National Institute of Agricultural Economics and Policy Research, New Delhi, May 28–29.

Pal S., Rao, S., & Ranjit, P. C. (2018). Valuation of ecosystem services: A review of methods and evidences. In: S. Pal (Ed.), *Agriculture and Ecosystem Services*. ICAR-National Institute of Agricultural Economics and Policy Research, New Delhi.

Ramachandra, T. V., Rajinikanth, R., & Ranjini, V. G. (2005). Economic valuation of wetlands. *Journal of Environmental Biology, 26* (2), 439.

Rao, C. S., Ranjith, P. C., & Pal, S. (2018). Valuation of ecosystem services: A review of methods and evidences. *Proceedings of the National seminar on Agriculture and Ecosystem Services*, held at ICAR-National Institute of Agricultural Economics and Policy Research, New Delhi, May 28–29.

Sathirathai, S., & Barbier, E. B. (2001). Valuing mangrove conservation in southern Thailand. *Contemporary Economic Policy, 19* (2), 109–122.

Schuyt, K. D. (2004). Economic consequences of wetland degradation for local populations in Africa. *Ecological Economics, 53* (2), 177–190.

Siew, M. K., Yacob, M. R., Radam, A., Adamu, A., & Alias, E. F. (2015). Estimating willingness to pay for wetland conservation: A contingent valuation study of Paya Indah Wetland, Selangor Malaysia. *Procedia Environmental Sciences, 30*, 268–272.

Sukhdev, P. (2008). *The economics of ecosystems and biodiversity* (pp. 15–25). Retrieved from http://ec.europa.eu/environment/nature/biodiversity/economics/pdf/teeb_report.pdf

TEEB Foundation. (2010). *The economics of ecosystems and biodiversity: Ecological and economic foundations.* London & Washington, DC: Earthscan.

Thomson, K. T. (2003). Economic and social management of estuarine biodiversity in the west coast of India. *Cochin University of Science and Technology, Cochin,* 1–282.

Turner, M. G., Collins, S. L., Lugo, A. L., Magnuson, J. J., Rupp, T. S., & Swanson, F. J. (2003). Disturbance dynamics and ecological response: The contribution of long-term ecological research. *AIBS Bulletin, 53* (1), 46–56.

Turner, R. K., van den Bergh, J. C. M, Soderqvist, T., Barendregt, A., van der Straaten, J., Maltby, E., & van Ierland, E. C. (2000). Ecological-economic analysis of wetlands: Scientific integration for management and policy. *Ecological Economics, 35,* 7–23.

Online Sources

CBD. 2015. Convention on Biological Diversity, Retrieved from https://www.cbd.int/

GoK. 2015. Government of Kerala, Retrieved from https://kerala.gov.in/economic-review

GoK. 2016. Government of Kerala, Retrieved from http://www.ecostat.kerala.gov.in/index.php/reports/agricultural-statisitcs/ /181.html

SANDEE. The South Asian Network for Development and Environmental Economics, Retrieved from http://www.sandeeonline.org/

TEEB. 2010. The Economics of Ecosystems and Biodiversity, Retrieved from http://www.teebweb.org/

Indigenous Knowledge for Ecological Resilience from Pre-mining Period of a Mined-Out Area

Narendra Nath Dalei and
Yamini Gupt

Introduction

Indigenous people in a forest ecosystem depend on some form of ecological service to sustain themselves. They are an integral part of a forest ecosystem. Livelihood of such indigenous people is associated with their knowledge and decision on allocation of labour among different economic activities as well as for collection of natural resources produced and supplied by forest ecosystem services. Their indigenous knowledge (IK) of resource harvesting always brings sustainable livelihood for them. They know how and from where the resources can be harvested so that ecological resiliency would be possible within a short span of time. But human interventions like mining degrade the ecosystems by attracting large number of migrants by providing direct and indirect job opportunities. These non-indigenous people also harvest resources from the forests and create population pressure on local forest ecosystems. Because of overexploitation of resources, forest ecosystems are degraded, thus impacting livelihood of indigenous people negatively. During post-mining period, non-indigenous people go back to their respective places; but resource scarcity in the region forces indigenous people to migrate to urban areas to earn their livelihood.

Indigenous communities successfully self-organize to govern the resources in a sustainable manner. Factors like human intervention in terms of urbanization, agricultural practices, commercial harvesting and mining activities affect resource-use patterns. Communities of different habitats under specific ecosystem services have different resource harvesting practices, which are based upon their specific IK. For example, communities residing in and around a rainforest ecosystem would have a very different practice of resource harvesting than communities residing in a dry deciduous forest ecosystem. IK plays an important role in bringing better agricultural practices, health care services, educational opportunities and other similar services (Warren, 1991). Article 8(j) of the Convention on Biological Diversity (CBD) focuses on preservation of IK and practice, and gives due importance to provide respect to such knowledge and practice. Management and preservation of natural resources through IK and practice play an important role in livelihood sustainability of indigenous communities. Overexploitation of resources by the growing population has resulted in environmental degradation, thus impacting human well-being negatively. Deforestation has resulted in land degradation, soil erosion, landslides, floods and droughts. Ecological resilience based upon indigenous resource management practice is considered as an unbiased practice and often ensures livelihood sustainability of the local resource-dependent communities.

IK System

IK is specific and unique to every community of the world. This knowledge and its practice of resource harvesting are important components of the global IK system. IK differs from community to community, hence the practice of resource harvesting of these communities also differs. However, each indigenous community uses its knowledge to harvest resources and its harvesting practice always brings sustainable livelihood for them.

IK system has evolved from the prehistoric period when humans were residing in the forest. To meet their daily food consumption, these people started adopting various practices such as hunting, firewood harvesting, planting trees, harvesting medicines, and collecting fruits and nuts from the natural forests (IIRR, 1996; Subba, 2009). While harvesting these forest products they used their knowledge in a way that brought sustainable management of biodiversity. Over a period of time this knowledge became a part of the IK system. This knowledge is based upon the experiences of a large number of indigenous communities. The knowledge they gained is derived from a complex system of acceptance, rejection, arguments and selection of large number of practices of specific activities (Arce & Long, 1992; Nakashima et al., 2000). IK varies from community to community and culture to culture, and therefore it is unique to every community or culture (Wiersum, 2000). It reflects how much the specific community understands the socio-ecological culture to preserve the ecosystems (Tanyanyiwa & Chikwanha, 2011; Warren, 1991).

The Study Area

We have selected Purnapani, Gattitangar, Bhojpur and Karkatnasa villages of Purnapani area of Odisha state, which falls between latitudes 22° 24' 38" and 22° 24' 52" north and longitudes 84° 51' 42" and 84° 54' 23" east. The area consists of one mined-out area and one reserved forest with a total geographical area of 1,552 hectares, 10.77 hectares of forestland, 230.53 hectare of mined-outland and 1,310.7 hectares of cultivated area. The location map of Purnapani area is shown in Figure 2.1.

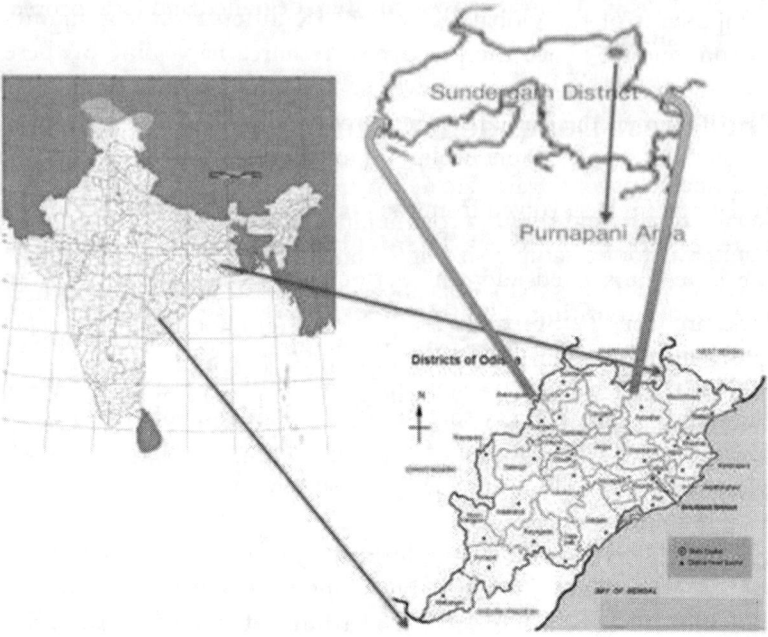

Figure 2.1 *Purnapani Area*
Source: Authors.

The Mining Activities and Resource Harvesting

Purnapani Limestone and Dolomite Quarry (PL&DQ), a mining company of Rourkela Steel Plant (RSP) of Steel Authority of India (SAIL) started its mining activities in September 1958. The mining activities were undertaken on 569.64 acres of agricultural land of local indigenous people against some amount of compensation. After closure of mining activities in 2003, all the people including the local people working in the mines lost their jobs.

However, during the mining period the mining activities created direct and indirect job opportunities and attracted large number of migrants, thus increasing population pressure in the area. These migrants used unsustainable forest resource harvesting practices and as a result the local forest ecosystems were degraded and local people lost their livelihood.

The Forest-Dependent Community

The inhabitants of the area are mostly tribal people of Munda, Oram, Badaik, Khadia and Bhuinya communities, and other non-tribal communities. From a sample size of 78 households, 56 were identified as Scheduled Tribes (ST), 10 as Scheduled Castes (SC), 5 as Other Backward Class (OBC) and 7 as General (Gen) households prior to mining operation. During mining period, 56 were ST, 17 were SC, 3 were OBC and 2 were Gen households out of total sample size of 78 households. During post-mining period, 52 were ST, 15 were SC, 5 were OBC and 6 were Gen households out of total sample size of 78 households.

ST households being the indigenous forest-dependent community contribute 71.79 per cent to the total sample size during pre-mining and mining period and 66.67 per cent during post-mining period. The remaining 28.21 per cent and 33.33 per cent are contributed by non-indigenous other forest-dependent communities (SC, OBC and Gen) during pre-mining and mining and post-mining period respectively.

IK of the Forest-Dependent Community in Resource Harvesting

The forest-dependent communities of Purnapani area are of the view that resiliency of ecosystem is possible if the following harvesting practices are followed: Only dry wood should be collected from the forest. Whenever necessary to cut a tree, permission should be taken from the village committee and cutting fee per tree should be deposited. Harvesting of dry wood and non-timber forest products should not be undertaken from a particular forest cluster again and again. Grazing of animals should not be allowed in a specific cluster of forest again and again. Live branches of tree should not be cut. Roots of the trees should not be removed and should be left in the forest in order to help the trees to grow again.

Resource Harvesting Practice and Ecological Resiliency

The indigenous people harvest resources using their traditional knowledge in such a way that ecological resiliency becomes possible in a limited span of time. Thus, people decide when, where and how much to harvest, giving enough scope to species to regenerate and contribute to ecological resiliency in a given period. However, human intervention in terms of mining activities degrades the ecosystem by limiting its multiple functions. During pre-mining period due to low population pressure and sustainable resource harvesting pattern (as a consequence of use of traditional and IK), livelihood become sustainable. The sustainability of livelihood is a result of sustainable resource harvesting which is because of traditional and indigenous practices by these indigenous communities. But during mining period because of heavy population pressure being experienced by inward migration, resource harvesting becomes unsustainable. This unsustainability of resource harvesting is because of the harvesting practices of migrants who always ignore the traditional and IK of resource harvesting. As a result, over harvesting of resources leads to degraded ecosystems leading to unsustainability of livelihood (Table 2.1).

Table 2.1 *Impact of Resource Harvesting Practice*

Period	Resource Harvesting Practice	Forest Ecosystem	Livelihood	Impact
Pre-mining	Indigenous	Natural	Sustainable	a. Self-sustained economy b. Resilient ecosystem
Transition	Indigenous	Natural or close to natural	Sustainable	a. Self-sustained economy b. Resilient ecosystem
Mining	Modern	Degraded	Unsustainable	a. Resiliency is impossible b. Out-migration is alternate coping strategy
Post-mining	Modern	Degraded	Unsustainable	a. Resiliency is impossible b. Out-migration is alternate coping strategy

Therefore, during pre-mining period, there are no mining activities. The forest-dependent communities use indigenous harvesting practices so that resiliency of ecosystem is possible and livelihood is sustainable. During transition period, the local economy moves from being forest dependent to mining dependent. During this period mining is not so significant. So during this period also the forest-dependent communities use indigenous harvesting practices so that resiliency of ecosystem is possible and livelihood is sustainable.

During mining period because of heavy population pressure due to migrants, the forest ecosystem is degraded. This degradation is because of modern and scientific resource harvesting practices undertaken by migrant people. As a result, and because of over harvesting, resiliency of ecosystem becomes impossible, leading to unsustainability of livelihood and out-migration of the local people. Again, during post-mining period, forest ecosystem remains degraded due to abandonment of mines and overburden dump. So resource scarcity is inevitable, livelihood is unsustainable and out-migration becomes a continued phenomenon.

Research Methodologies

The research methodologies of this study consist of selecting the primary survey area, preparing the sampling design and using econometric tools for data analysis.

The Primary Survey Area

Purnapani area of Sundargarh district is selected for this study because migrants being attracted by mining activities degraded the local forest ecosystem (because of their unsustainable resource harvesting practice), which has affected the local livelihood pattern to a great extent. In this area a primary survey was undertaken to collect required data.

Primary survey was conducted in the four villages—Purnapani, Gattitangar, Karkatnasa and Bhojpur, one abandoned mine-spoilt area and a degraded reserved forest adjacent to it. Table 2.2 shows that out of the total geographical area of the survey area of 1,552 hectares

Table 2.2 *Land Use Pattern of the Study Area (in Hectares)*

Village	Total Geographical Area	Cultivated and Other Area	Forest Area	Mining Area
Purnapani	855	621.7	3.42	229.88
Gattitangar	193	188.77	4.23	0
Bhojpur	419	415.88	3.12	0
Karkatnasa	85	84.35	0	0.65
Total	1,552	1,310.7	10.77	230.53

Source: Census of India (1991), PL&DQ (1998).

0.69 per cent is forest area, 14.85 per cent is mine-spoilt area and the remaining 84.46 per cent is cultivated and other land area.

The Time Period and State of Ecosystem

Pre-mining, transition, mining and post-mining are considered as the four periods of entire mining activity in this study. The mining operation in Purnapani area ended in the year 2003 as the lease period was over and further mineral production was not economically viable.

The period prior to 1955 is considered as the 'pre-mining period' when there was no human intervention like mining. We assumed the period from 1955 to 1960 as transition period due to the fact that the nature-based local economy started shifting to mining-dependent local economy. During the period from 1960 to 2003 the mining activities were in full swing and therefore this period is known as the mining period. The post-mining period started just after 2003 when there was closure of mining operations.

This study is based upon the fact that the pre-mining period is a period of natural state of ecosystems whereas the mining and post-mining periods are periods of degraded ecosystems.

Table 2.3 Household Distribution

Sector	Age > 70	Age 60–70	Age < 60	Total Households	Selected Households (30%)
Primary	54	60	240	354	106
Secondary	25	78	405	508	152
Tertiary	16	37	137	190	57
Total	95	175	782	1,052	315

Source: Primary survey by author.

The Sampling Design and Econometric Tools

A pre-designed questionnaire survey was undertaken in and around the mined-out Purnapani area of Sundargarh district, Odisha. A sampling frame of 1,052 households was prepared by listing each household. Then the households were classified based upon their principal occupation and age of senior member as shown in Table 2.3.

It was found that a total of 354, 508 and 190 households were dependent upon primary, secondary and tertiary sectors, respectively, for their livelihood out of 1,052 households. From each sector 30 per cent of households were taken into account. Then from various age group (age > 70, 60–70 and <60) in each sector these 30 per cent were first taken from age group greater than 70 years and the remaining households were taken from lower age groups. The households from each sector were selected by following circular systematic random sampling method for detailed enquiry.

Taking these data the IK being a binary variable is estimated using logit and probit models.

Descriptive Data Analysis

This section provides analysis of the data generated by primary survey conducted in and around Purnapani area of Sundargarh District of the state of Odisha.

Ecosystem Divergence

The variables, which are the determinants of ecosystem divergence, are explained in the following sections with their descriptive statistics presented in Table 2.4.

Number of trees (Timber): It was extracted from the reserved forest since the pre-mining period. The mean amount of timber collected

Table 2.4 *Descriptive Data Analysis: Ecosystem Divergence*

Species Type	Species/Ecological Products	Pre-mining	Transition	Mining	Post-mining
Plant	TIMBER	4.45	3.96	1.73	2.23
	FHLD	79.73	75.28	38.72	37.29
	FRTKG	66.9	38.96	11.9	4.79
	NUTKG	86.37	31.15	6.14	5.72
Mammals and reptiles	Rabbits	0.99	0.86	0.68	0.95
	Wolves	0.99	0.79	0.63	0.82
	Bears	0.49	0.41	0.35	0.29
	Wildcats	0.6	0.38	0.24	0.28
	Wild goats	0.46	0.28	0.01	0.01
	Squirrels	0.5	0.06	0.04	0.04
	Mongooses	0.65	0.17	0	0.05
	Foxes	0.64	0.06	0.04	0.01
	Snakes	0.96	0.41	0.08	0.04
Birds	Parrot	1	1	0.88	0.99
	Eagle	1	1	0.88	0.99
	Cuckoo	0.99	0.97	0.88	0.95
	Owl	0.74	0.41	0.32	0.36
	Vulture	0.56	0.05	0	0

Source: Primary survey by author.

Note: Timber, number of trees; FHLD, number of head load of firewood; FRTKG, mean value of the fruits; NUTKG, mean value of the nuts.

from the forest has decreased by 11 per cent during transition, 61 per cent during mining and 50 per cent during post-mining period as compared to the mean amount during the pre-mining period.

Number of head load of firewood (FHLD): The mean value of the number of head load of firewood (FHLD) collected by the household was 79.73 per annum during the pre-mining period, which declined continuously and reached a minimum average head load of 37.29 during the post-mining period. One head load is around 10 to 20 kg. But the tribal people were not able to give the correct amount in metric measurement. So 'head load' was taken as the unit of measurement in the primary survey to gather information pertaining to amount of firewood collected by the indigenous people from the nearest reserved forest. The variable FHLD represents the plant species yielding firewood.

Fruits collected from the reserved forest (FRTKG): The mean value of the fruits (FRTKG) collected by the household was 66.9 kg per annum during the pre-mining period, which declined continuously and reached a minimum average of 4.79 kg per annum during the post-mining period.

Nuts collected from the reserved forest (NUTKG): The mean value of the nuts (NUTKG) collected by the household were 86.37 kg per annum during pre-mining period, which declined continuously and reached a minimum average of 5.72 kg per annum during post-mining period.

Practice of IK for Resource Harvesting and Sustainable Livelihood

The variables representing ecological, economic and social dimensions, which are the determinants of resource use practice and livelihood sustainability are explained in the following sections with their descriptive statistics presented in Table 2.5.

Ecological Dimension

In the ecological dimension, two component variables (CVs) are chosen for estimation of practice of IK. The CVs for ecological

Table 2.5 Descriptive Statistics of Component Variables (Mean±SD), $n=312^{a}$

Dimensions	Variables	Pre-mining Period (Before 1955)	Transition Period (1955–1960)	Mining Period (1961–2003)	Post-mining Period (After 2003)
Ecological	FHA (n=78) (kg/year)	5.44±7.03 (0–30)	2.81±4.67 (0–20)	1.67±6.44 (0–50)	2±4.78 (0–20)
	HWA (n=78) (kg/year)	1.47±2.23 (0–8)	0.54±1.35 (0–5)	0.10±0.66 (0–5)	0.14±1.04 (0–9)
Economic	TLO (n=78) (in acres)	11.22±12.72 (0–40)	3.29±4.33 (0–19)	1.84±5.67 (0–33.95)	1.89±4.15 (0–27.95)
	PDQ (n=78) (quintals/year)	18.95±32.62 (0–250)	10.28±15.34 (0–65.6)	5.05±14.99 (0–99.3)	4.09±9.62 (0–64)
Social	HEL (n=78) (in years)	2.83±3.70 (0–14)	3.47±3.93 (0–15)	6.69±4.81 (0–15)	6.38±4.83 (0–18)
	PSA (n=78) (in Rs)	98.04±1.65 (93.67–100)	97.53±2.64 (89.73–100)	69.54±12.99 (45–96)	64.96±16.42 (32.12–98.94)

Source: Primary survey by author.

Note: 'Ranges' are given in the parentheses and 'n' is the sample size; FHA, harvesting fish from the agricultural field during rainy season; HWA, hunting wild animals from the forest; TLO, total land owned by the household; PDQ, annual paddy production; HEL, highest education level of the members of the household; PSA, percentage of income spent for performing social activities.
[a] $n=312$ is the overall sample size of the entire time period and $n=78$ is the sample size in a specific sub-period.

dimensions are (a) harvesting fish from the agricultural field during rainy season (FHA) and (b) hunting wild animals from the forest (HWA).

The people of Purnapani area harvest fish from the agricultural field during rainy season to support their livelihood. They also hunt wild animals such as wild chicken, wild goat, wild pig, rabbit, snake and other reptiles from the forest to support their livelihood. Other things remaining constant, households try to maximize fish harvesting from the agricultural field during rainy seasons and hunting wild animals from the forest. Availability of fish in agricultural field in rainy season and wild animals in the forest depends on existence of the ecological conditions suitable for growth of these species in their respective habitats. More harvesting and hunting depend upon more availability, which in turn depends upon the ecological condition for growth of these fish and wild animal species in their respective habitats. Therefore, harvesting fish from the agricultural field during rainy season (FHA) and hunting wild animals from the forest (HWA) are taken as two representative CVs for ecological dimension.

While fish harvesting is undertaken independently, wild animal hunting is undertaken collectively. After hunting, the wild animals are slaughtered and the total meat is distributed equally among the participants of the hunting mission. During the pre-mining period, the households of Purnapani area had harvested on an average 5.44 kg of fish from the agricultural field during rainy season and 1.47 kg of meat by hunting wild animals from the forest with a range of 0 to 30 kg and 2 to 8 kg per annum, respectively. During transition period the mean amount of fish harvested had declined to 2.81 kg and meat to 0.54 kg with a range of 0 to 20 kg and 0 to 5 kg per household per annum, respectively. Similarly, the mean amount of harvesting fish had further declined to 1.67 kg and meat to 0.10 kg with a range of 0 to 50 kg and 0 to 5 kg per household per annum respectively during mining period. However, the mean amount of harvesting fish had increased to 2 kg and meat to 0.14 kg with a range of 0 to 20 kg and 0 to 9 kg per household per annum respectively during post-mining period.

Economic Dimension

In the economic dimension two CVs are chosen for estimation of practice of IK. The two CVs are (a) total land owned by the household (TLO) and (b) annual paddy production (PDQ).

Agriculture is the major economic activity in Purnapani area. Households of Purnapani area own four categories of land for agriculture, namely, high land, medium land, low land and forestland converted for agriculture. Elevated or mountainous land is high land, where pulses are cultivated in Purnapani area. A low, flat land relative to the surrounding area is low land, where paddy and other cereals are cultivated in Purnapani area. In between high land and low land the medium land is situated, where paddy, other cereals and vegetables are cultivated in Purnapani area. Households of Purnapani area have encroached and converted some amount of forestland for agriculture purpose. Agricultural activities mainly depend upon monsoon rain in Purnapani area. Paddy is the major crop, which is mainly cultivated during kharif season (July–October) in this area. Thus, cultivation of paddy is the major economic activity undertaken on the land owned by the households in Purnapani area. Therefore, total land owned by the households (TLO) and total paddy production (PDQ) are taken as two CVs for economic dimension.

During pre-mining period, the households of Purnapani area had owned on an average of 11.22 acres of land and produced 18.95 quintals of paddy with a range of 0 to 40 acres and 0 to 250 quintals per annum, respectively. During transition period the mean amount of land owned declined to 3.29 acres and paddy production to 10.28 quintals with a range of 0 to 19 acres and 0 to 65.6 quintals per household per annum, respectively. During mining period the mean amount of land owned further declined to 1.84 acres and paddy production to 5.05 quintals with a range of 0 to 33.95 acres and 0 to 99.3 quintals per household per annum respectively. During post-mining period the mean amount of land owned increased to 1.89 acres and paddy production had declined to 4.09 quintals with a range of 0 to 27.95 acres and 0 to 64 quintals per household per annum, respectively.

Social Dimension

The two CVs in social dimension are (a) highest education level of the members of the household (HEL) and (b) percentage of income spent for performing social activities (PSA) which include expenditure on food, social functions—namely—marriage, religious functions and other social traditions, and other miscellaneous activities such as travelling to market and visiting relative's house.

Education level of a household determines the extent of decision-making in various social activities. Higher the level of education of members of households better is assessment and understanding of social phenomenon happening in everyday life. Better living standard of households depends upon the knowledge and skill of its members, which in turn depend upon the attainment of education level. Therefore, other things remaining constant, higher education level of the members of the households leads to better living standards. The social status of the household seems to be better if it could able to spend more income on social activities rather than on health. Other things remaining constant more the expenditure on health of the members of the households less income would be available for meeting social expenditure. Therefore, less expenditure on health indicates socially healthy households having capacity to perform social activities better. Therefore, highest education level of the members of the household (HEL) and percentage of income spent for performing social activities (PSA) are considered as two component variables for social dimension.

The highest education level is considered based upon the attainment of vertically highest years of schooling of any member of the household in Purnapani area. During pre-mining period the highest education level attained by the members of the households of Purnapani area was 2.8 years on an average with a range of 0 to 14 years of education. During transition period the same increased to 3.5 years with a range of 0 to 15 years of education. During mining period the highest education level further increased on an average to 6.7 years with a range of 0 to 15 years of education; however, the same declined to 6.3 years with a range of 0 to 18 years of education during post-mining period. The household average income spent on social activities was 98.04 per cent with a range of 93.67 to 100 per cent during pre-mining period as against 97.53 per cent with a range of 89.73 to 100 per cent, 69.54 per cent with a range of 45 to 96 per cent, and 64.96 per cent with a range of 32.12 to 98.94 per cent during transition, mining and post-mining period, respectively.

Response Variable

It is observed from the primary survey that livelihood was more sustainable, and state of ecosystems was in natural or close to natural state respectively during pre-mining and transition period when people were using IK for resource harvesting. So during this period resource harvesting practice (RHP) is coded as 1 (use of IK) relative to resource harvesting practice during mining and post-mining period where it is 0 (otherwise) in and around Purnapani area. Hence, RHP being binary is taken as a response variable in our resource harvesting model. The detailed frequency distribution of response variable is presented in the Table 2.6.

The frequency of response variable RHP is 156 for mining and post-mining period taken together. The frequency of response variable RHP is also 156 for pre-mining and mining period taken together.

Table 2.6 *Frequency Distribution of Response Variable*

Period	RHP (1 = use of IK, 0 = otherwise)	Freq.	Percent	Cum.
Mining and Post-mining	0	156	50.00	50.00
Pre-mining and Transition	1	156	50.00	100.00
Total		312	100.00	

Source: Primary survey by author.

Note: RHP, resource harvesting practice.

Results and Discussions

Ecosystem Divergence/Resilience

Plant species population and number of individuals in each species are generally taken into account for estimating the divergence. But because of data limitation, total number of trees, amount of fruits, nuts and firewood collected by the indigenous people are taken as proxies for representing variables on plant species.

The number of trees, amount of firewood, fruits and nuts were harvested from the reserved forest since the pre-mining period. In Purnapani area indigenous and other forest-dependent people use timber for construction, repair and maintenance of their houses, and firewood for cooking and heating purpose. This timber is collected by cutting down tree species such as sal (*Shorea robusta*) and tamarind (*Tamarind usindica*) from the forest. Therefore, timber is used as a proxy for plant species yielding materials for construction, repair and maintenance of houses. Fruits such as mango, tendu, jackfruit, guava, Aegle marmelos (bel), tamarind and kusum are collected by the tribal people. Nuts such as char, cashew nut, ber (*Ziziphus nummularia*) and kusum nut are collected by the tribal people. From the descriptive data analysis, it is observed that the amount of timber and firewood, fruits and nuts collected from the forest has been declining since pre-mining period. This is because of unsustainable practice, use of modern technique and negligence of IK of tree cutting from the forest.

The mammals and reptile population, and number of individuals in each species are taken into account for estimating the species divergence. But because of data limitation, number of people who saw these species during various time periods are taken as proxies for representing variables on mammal and reptile species. The number of mammals and reptiles has been declining since pre-mining period except post-mining period. During the post-mining period number of rabbits, wolves, wildcats and mongooses increased, wild goats and squirrels remained constant, and bear and fox are declined.

The bird population and number of individuals in each bird species are also taken into account for estimating the species divergence. But because of data limitation, only number of people sighted these species during various periods are taken as proxies for representing variables on bird species. The population of parrot, cuckoo and owls has been declining since pre-mining period except post-mining period when it increased substantially. The vulture population has been declining since pre-mining period and got extinct during mining and post-mining period.

The increasing number of population of some mammals and birds during post-mining period is because of ecological restoration work initiated in the area by Centre for Environmental Management of Degraded Ecosystem (CEMDE), University of Delhi in collaboration with Department of Biotechnology, Government of India. In case of some other mammals and birds, their population size has declined as their habitat being has not been fully restored.

Practice of IK for Resource Harvesting and Sustainable Livelihood

Heavy population pressure due to mining activities leads to unsustainable resource harvesting (using modern technique) from the local forest. As a result, forest ecosystem is degraded in the Purnapani area. The livelihood of the local forest-dependent people became unsustainable due to degradation of forest ecosystem services. Using logit and probit model the analysis of data are explained below, presenting the result in Table 2.7.

With collecting one more kilogram of meat by hunting wild animals from the forest (HWA), the predicted probability of use of IK in favour of households belonging to pre-mining and transition period relative to mining and post-mining period was expected to rise significantly. That means use of IK was significantly more likely to be practiced for hunting wild animals during pre-mining and transition period as compared to mining and post-mining period. Because of use of IK during pre-mining and transition period, resiliency of forest ecosystem was possible, keeping it in natural state. Adequate

Table 2.7 Probit and Logit Model of Resource Harvesting Practice (1 = Using IK, 0 = Otherwise)

| Variables | Probit Model | | Logit Model | |
	Coef.	dF/dx	Coef.	Odds Ratio
FHA	0.026015 (0.0421842)	0.0001305	0.0444953 (0.080747)	1.0455
HWA	0.6918315[a] (0.2472977)	0.0034717	1.211314[a] (0.4422867)	3.357896
TLO	0.0102064 (0.0377717)	0.0000512	0.0194556 (0.0717681)	1.019646
PDQ	0.0268123 (0.0204073)	0.0001345	0.0491638 (0.0376848)	1.050392
HEL	–0.1113646[a] (0.0376305)	–0.0005588	–0.2002068[a] (0.0692756)	0.8185615
PSA	0.3045789[a] (0.062048)	0.0015284	0.529622[a] (0.1150929)	1.69829
_cons	–28.32255 (5.977752)		–49.23228 (11.05402)	

Note: [a]Significant at 1 per cent level.
Source: Author's own estimation.

amount of resource harvesting during these periods led to sustainable livelihood.

With increasing one more year of education of the member of the household having highest level of education (HEL), the predicted probability of use of IK in favour of households belonging to pre-mining and transition period relative to mining and post-mining period was expected to decline significantly. That means IK was significantly less likely to be practiced by members of household having highest level of education. This indicates that more educated members were less likely to use IK.

With increasing one per cent of income spent for performing social activities (PSA), the predicted probability of use of IK in favour of households belonging to pre-mining and transition period relative to mining and post-mining period was expected to rise significantly. That means use of IK was significantly more likely to be practiced if the households were spending more percentage of income on social activities than on health. This indicates that use of IK brings resiliency to forest ecosystem, which was possible during pre-mining and transition period. Natural state of forest ecosystem during these periods was impacting health and well-being of the people positively so that less percentage of income was spent on health and more on social activities.

Harvesting fish from the agricultural field during rainy season (FHA), total land owned and annual paddy production are not significant predictors of resource harvesting practice.

Conclusion and Policy Implication

The result and analysis reveal that the amount of timber, firewood, fruits and nuts collected from the forest has been declining since pre-mining period, indicating divergence of ecosystem from its natural state to degraded state. This is because of unsustainable practice, use of modern technique and negligence of IK in resource harvesting from the forest.

The increasing number of populations of some mammals and birds during post-mining period is because of ecological restoration work initiated in the area by CEMDE, University of Delhi in collaboration with Department of Biotechnology, Government of India. In case of some other mammals and birds, their population size has declined as their habitat has not been fully restored.

Heavy population pressure due to mining activities leads to unsustainable resource harvesting (using modern techniques) from the local forest. As a result, forest ecosystem is degraded in Purnapani area. The livelihood of the local forest-dependent people became unsustainable due to degradation of forest ecosystem services.

Therefore, IK is very much important in conserving forest ecosystem services, which will help in keeping livelihood sustainable. Policy makers and planners of mining activities should think seriously while granting mining lease to any government or private agency and should ensure conservation of ecosystem services, which is possible by following sustainable resource harvesting practices such as use of IK.

Acknowledgements

The authors thank the Department of Biotechnology, Government of India for financial support to carry out this study through the project entitled, *Environmental Biotechnology Restoration Ecology* sanctioned to the CEMDE, University of Delhi. The authors are grateful for the support provided by CEMDE for research and analysis, and the logistic support provided by PL&DQ SAIL to carry out the primary surveys. The authors acknowledge that they are responsible for the views expressed in this study, and Department of Biotechnology, SAIL and CEMDE are no way responsible for any kind of inference drawn out of this study. The authors appreciate the valuable comments of the anonymous referees.

References

Arce, A., & Long, N. (1992). The dynamics of knowledge-interfaces between bureaucrats and peasants. In N. Long & A. Long. (Eds.), *Battlefields of knowledge: The interlocking of theory and practice in social research and development* (pp. 278–295). London: Routledge.

Chakravorty, C., & Singh, A. K. (1991). Household Structures in India. Census of India 1991. Occasional paper, 1.

International Institute of Rural Reconstruction (IIRR). (1996). *Recording and using indigenous knowledge a manual.* Cavite: Author.

Nakashima, D., Prott, L., & Bridgewater, P. (2000). Tapping into the world's wisdom. *UNESCO Sources, 125* (July–August), 12.

Orissa State Pollution Control Board. (2006). *State of environment Orissa 2006.* Retrieved from http://orienvis.nic.in/index1.aspx?lid=28&mid=1&langid=1&linkid=26

PL&DQ (1998). *Mining plan* (Vol. 1). Ranchi: CET, SAIL.

Subba, J. R. (2009, January). Indigenous knowledge on bio-resource management for livelihood of people of Sikkim. *Indian Journal of Traditional Knowledge, 8* (1), 56–64.

Tanyanyiwa, V. I., & Chikwanha, M. (2011). The role of indigenous knowledge systems in the management of forest resources in Mugabe area, Masvingo, Zimbabwe. *Journal of Sustainable Development in Africa*, *13* (3), 132–149.

Warren, D. M. (1991). *Using indigenous knowledge in agricultural development* (Discussion Paper No. 127). Washington, DC: World Bank.

Wiersum, K. F. (2000). Forestry, forest users and research: New ways of learning. In A. Lawrence (Ed.), *European Tropical Forest Research Network (ETFRN) Publication Series* (Vol. 1). The Netherlands: Wageningen.

World Commission on Environment and Development. (1987). *Our common future*. Oxford, NY: Oxford University Press.

CHAPTER 3

Natural Resources
Classification, Scarcity and Management

Jaweriah Hazrana

Background: A General Classification of Resources

The cumulation of all physical, biological and social assets surrounding human beings collectively constitute the environment. Natural resources are generally defined as constituents of the environment that aid in the functioning of living organisms, populations and ecosystems, and contribute positively to human welfare (Bhattacharya, 2001). The natural resource base is diverse and integrates an element of dynamism. Due to its diversity, resources are used to satisfy different wants. While some resources such as air, soil, water, plants and animals are essential for the survival of all living organisms, many others, such as minerals and fossil fuels, enable man to satisfy material needs and desires. In this context, the concept of resource dynamism is relevant as it indicates that what is perceived as a natural resource depends on the technological, economic and social circumstances prevailing in the society. Over the past century several new resources have been added to the existing base due to an improvement in environmental knowledge, such as wetlands, which were not classed as resources few decades ago. For example; forest area (including tangible goods such as wood and intangible services such as habitat functions), land, water bodies, marine resources, metals (such as copper and chromite), mineral resources, non-mineral energy sources (solar, tidal, wind and so on) and the waste-assimilative capacity of the environment systems.

Some important questions concerning natural resources are:

1. How do we classify resources to facilitate effective methods of study and analysis?
2. Is there a unique system of classification or are separate categories based on mutually exclusive criteria?
3. Are existing classifications compatible with the Indian economy?

To address these questions, we first define different classification systems of natural resources, along with their applications and implications for decision-making. We end the discussion by defining the case study of resources in the Indian economy and their various classes.

It is a challenging but essential task to segregate resources into separate sets on the basis of their distinctive features to facilitate an effective study and analysis. The most common approach is to identify common physical properties and the time scale of the relevant adjustment processes. On the basis of physical features resources are divided into biological, energy, non-energy and environmental resources. Biological resources are largely reproducible and comprise biological species such as fish, wildlife, insects and vegetation. Energy resources are those that are mostly utilized to derive other forms of energy (such as heat energy) and include solar radiation, timber and natural gas. Non-energy resources consist of minerals such as iron ore, salt and soil. Finally, environmental resources are those that cater to recreational consumption, as opposed to material consumption, such as air, water, forests, the ozone layer or a virgin wilderness.

Holding the time scale as an anchor, resources can be categorized as expendable, renewable or depletable. Renewable resources demonstrate a natural rate of regeneration within a time frame that is relevant to human exploitation and yield a continual flow of services. The rate of renewal causes the resource base to adjust rapidly to depletion and augments resource flow over subsequent time periods. For example, though felling a tree or fishing marine species will lead to a decrease in the present base, their natural self-renewal mechanism will lead to replenishment of the resource (provided their population has not fallen below the critical threshold). However, the continual flow of many renewable resources is not a certainty. Instead their continual availability is dependent on the rate of utilization due to which they are further classified into two sub-categories. In the first case, resource availability does not depend on the rate of use and consumption in one time does not have consequences in subsequent periods, for example, solar energy. In the second case, resources can be exploited to the level of exhaustion if the rate of consumption exceeds the rate of natural replenishment. For example, excessive fishing reduces the stock of fish, over pollution and destruction of habitat damage the regenerative capacity of fauna species, and overutilization causes soil to lose its natural fertility. In all these cases there is a reduction in the concerned resources beyond their critical zone. A further distinction in renewable resources can be made on the basis of whether they can be stored or not. For storable resources intertemporal allocation is facilitated to achieve optimal resource management. Examples are food grains, solar energy (in the form of biomass) and the use of dams to store water. For other resources storage is not possible. Storage is possible even for depletable resources as surplus can be stocked for use during durations of deficit and serve to extend the economic life of resources. Depletable resources exhibit a very slow adjustment speed spread over such a long period that it is not economically meaningful. The slow rate of formation for these resources compromises their renewability in any reasonable frame of time. As the feedback loop is effectively ignored, the supply of depletable resources is rendered fixed. For example, in principle, oil resources can be generated, but their formation requires millions of years due to which they are considered to exist in a fixed stock. Other examples include crude oil, virgin wilderness and endangered species. Depletable resources can further be divided into recyclable and non-recyclable. A recyclable resource is one that exists in a form that allows its mass to be recovered once a specific use is fulfilled (such as most metals). In comparison, many resources once combusted convert into other forms of energy and dissipate rendering their recoverability zero (such as fossil fuels—coal, oil and gas). Finally, expendable resources are those for which the adjustment speed is so fast that the impact on the resource in one time period has little or no effect in subsequent periods such as solar radiation and agricultural production.

Table 3.1 demonstrates the two dimensional categorization supplemented by examples of each class and sub-class. The resource classes depicted in Table 3.1 are not mutually exclusive and can be combined to highlight their interrelation and connection. For example, while most non-energy resources (such as iron ore and bauxite) are depletable, others are expendable such as salt as its evaporation does not impact the total availability of seawater. Similarly, biological resources (such as endangered species) are depletable, while others (such as forest products) are renewable and some (such as agricultural products) are expendable.

Resource Taxonomy

In addition to the multiple classifications discussed above, another popular distinction among resource categories is to group them based on their stage of development. This method is applied specifically to exhaustible resources and is based on three important concepts namely: current reserves, potential resources and resource endowment. Current reserves consist of proven deposits that that are known to exist and can economically be harvested at the prevailing prices and state of technology. The magnitude of current reserves is efficiently expressed as an absolute number. In contrast, potential reserves are those that have been acknowledged to exist but are not economical to extract in the present time period. Potential resources are most accurately defined as a function relative to a number and can further be segregated into para-marginal or sub-marginal resources. Para-marginal resources do not meet the criteria of economic extraction. They are characterized by economic uncertainty and/or failure to meet the criteria which define economic reserves. With a change in economic or technological factors they will move to economic reserves. Similarly, sub-marginal resources are also not economical to harvest. They require considerably higher market prices or cost-reducing advancement in technology to render

Table 3.1 Categorization of Natural Resource

	Biological	Non-energy Mineral	Energy	Environmental
Expendable	Agricultural products such as grains and pulses	Salt	Solar radiation, hydro-power and ethanol	Noise pollution, non-persistent: air pollution (NOx, SOx, par-ticulates) and water pollution
Renewable	Forest products, marine culture, live-stock and insects	–	Wood as fuel, hydro-power and geothermal	Ground water, air, water pol-lution: carbon dioxide, toxics and forests
Depletable	Endangered species such as the Indian Bengal tigers	Minerals such as gold, iron ore, bauxite, salt and topsoil	Petroleum, natural gas, coal, uranium and oil shale	Virgin wilderness, ozone layer and selected aquifers

Source: Author's own examples.

them economic. Whether or not a resource is feasible to extract is an economic concept as a resource involves a cost to bring it under effective use. The amounts of reserves that are obtainable are reliant on the price that can be demanded for those resources and with a higher price potential reserves will be larger. Finally, the resource endowment represents the natural occurrence of resources in the Earth's crust. This concept is significant as it highlights that there is an upper limit on the availability of terrestrial resources. Moreover, prices do not influence the size of resource endowment due to which this is a geological concept relative to an economic one.

The three concepts discussed above can be combined to reflect the total resource situation in an economy at any given time period. The current reserves in isolation reflect the usable portion of resource endowment. These can be combined with potential reserves to illustrate the maximum potential reserves that are available in an economy under feasible conditions. The inclusion of entire resource endowment highlights the portion that can be made available as potential reserves at a feasible price. The entire resources base consists of discovered reserves and those which can possibly be discovered and brought under-utilization. Being a geological concept, it highlights the upper limit to the availability of terrestrial resources.

The above discussion highlights that reserves can be categorized as *economic* and *physical*. In this context, an effective system of classification is the McKelvey diagram that was initially developed a by the U. S. Geological Survey (2013; USGS). It incorporates both economic and geological dimensions to show the composition and changes in reserves. A change in reserves takes play due to the impact of economic factors such as:

1. A reduction in extraction cost due to technological improvement such as reduced energy requirement for processes such as transportation and extraction.
2. An expansion of reserves due to discovery of new deposits and a change in the economic condition.
3. A fall in the price of inputs required or an increase in price of a resource. For example several oil deposits in the North Sea became

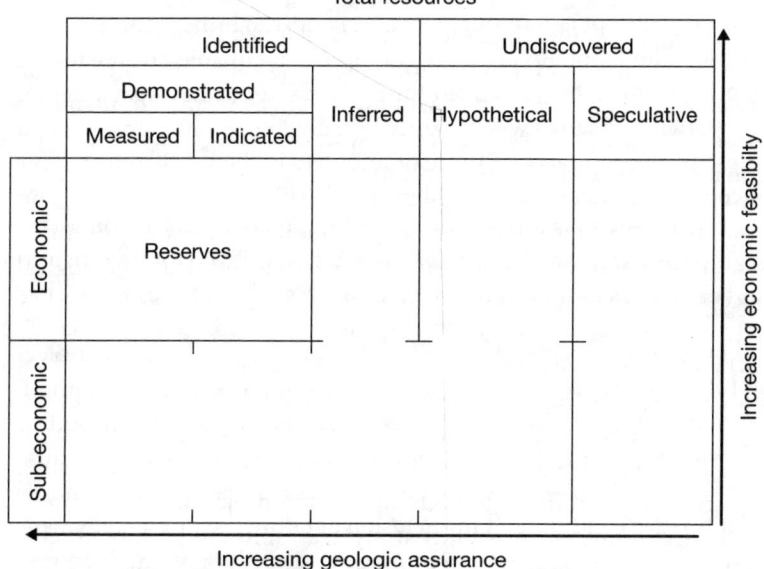

Figure 3.1 *Categorization of Resources*
Source: U.S. Geological Survey (2013).

economically exploitable post the price increase in the 1970s. Conversely, it is also possible that price reduction of a resource renders deposits, which were previously under exploitation, uneconomical. Even if the price of inputs falls deposits can be rendered economical.

The McKelvey diagram is illustrated in Figure 3.1. A downward movement represents a shift from cheaply obtainable resources to those extracted at substantially higher costs. By comparison, a rightward movement signifies rising geological uncertainty about the size of the resource base.

Examples from the Indian Economy

Over the past several decades, India has undergone several stages of resource classification. From 1970 to 1999 few categorization systems were considered. However, with the advent of globalization and privatization in 1999 India implemented the United Nations Framework Classification (UNFC) System of representation.[1] The benefit of this action was that it permitted natural resources in the country to be presented on a universally accepted scale and integrated flexibility to enhance international communication.

The UNFC has a three-dimensional procedure based on a three digit code system. This includes the method utilized for investigation and evaluation of mineral reserves/resources. These codes are geological assessment (G), feasibility assessment (F) and economic viability (E) and are depicted on three axes. Geological assessment includes four sub-stages that represent a pre-specified degree of geological assurance. These are: reconnaissance, prospecting, general exploration and detailed exploration. The second one is feasibility assessment which is a precondition to build up mining projects. It comprises of geological study, pre-feasibility study, feasibility study/mining report and measuring economic viability of resources. Economic viability is indicated in the first digit, feasibility in the second and geological assessment in the third. All classes are denoted by the codes 1, 2 and 3 and follow a decreasing order. The same pattern is also shared by the three classes in feasibility study. In the case of geological assessment there are four phases (detailed exploration, general exploration, prospecting and reconnaissance) denoted by four codes. The National Mineral Inventory is organized by the Indian Bureau of Mines. The complete resource inventory was recorded on 1st April 2010. It included 70 minerals and more than 18,000 deposits/blocks (excluding atomic and fuel minerals). Table 3.2 contains selected resources from the complete list (Indian Bureau of Mines, Government of India, 2013). An interim update was recorded on 1st April 2013 in the case of 25 minerals. Table 3.2 presents reserves of selected exhaustible resources in India.

---

[1] The UNFC was adopted in the Geneva Conference of United Nations Economic Commission of Europe (UNECE).

Table 3.2 Reserves/Resources of Minerals in India as on 1.4.2010

Mineral	Unit	Reserves				Remaining Resources								Total Resources
		Proved	Probable		Total (A)	Feasibility	Pre-Feasibility		Measured	Indicated	Inferred	Reconnaissance	Total (B)	A+B
		STD 111	STD 121	STD 122	(A)	STD 211	STD 221	STD 222	STD 331	STD 332	STD 333	STD 334	(B)	A+B
Barytes	Tonne	29,557,972	90,844	1,935,312	31,584,128	179,447	4,288,189	2,608,562	207,384	1,269,214	32,491,229	105,721	41,149,746	72,733,874
Bauxite	'000 Tonnes	321,258	89,223	182,457	592,938	105,894	245,091	274,165	655,673	431,006	1,155,570	19,283	2,886,682	3,479,620
Chromite	'000 Tonnes	31,652	7,165	15,153	53,970	1,371	1,407	4,431	31,787	36,525	52,497	21,359	149,376	203,346
Copper Ore	'000 Tonnes	133,388	127,100	133,884	394,372	15,781	21,323	12,429	147,989	224,976	741,588	0	1,164,086	1,558,458
Copper Metal		1,604.73	1,508.36	1,655.24	4,768.33	213.01	223.01	23.45	1,453.04	1,686.84	3918.99	0	7,518.34	12,286.67
Iron Ore (Hematite)	'000 Tonnes	5,982,024	1,173,324	938,180	8,093,546	515,353	756,190	494,738	540,188	1,197,539	3,942,673	2,341,870	9,788,551	17,882,098
Iron Ore (Magnetite)	'000 Tonnes	15,973	3,672	2,111	21,755	189,478	1,714	50,816	1,513,168	1,984,566	6,313,583	568,980	10,622,305	10,644,060
Lead & Zinc Ore	Tonnes '000	20,215	87,569	1,196	108,979	129	1,077	3,983	21,433	221,601	325,051	3,340	576,614	685,593
Lead Metal		398.42	1,817.89	28.7	2245.01	0	34.32	50.95	427.37	2,915.7	5,831.04	0	9,304.38	11,549.39
Zinc Metal		1,938.37	1,0460.72	54.17	12,453.26	5.2	4.71	86.91	1,168.96	9,607.12	13,237.09	101.65	24,211.64	36,664.9
Lead and Zinc Metal		0	0	0	0	0	0	0	0	0	118.45	0	118.45	118.45
Manganese ore	'000 Tonnes	97,425	1,1590	32,962	141,977	23,529	27,594	51,074	5,732	23,726	151,704	4,644	288,003	429,980
Tin Ore		4,404	1,015	1,713	7,131	22,592,692	2,326	31,330,000	168,622	561,080	29,064,345	0	83,719,066	83,726,197
Tin Metal		925.75	189.76	16.92	1,132.43	32,222.43	652.89	54,032.8	894.91	231.63	13,107.75	0	10,1142.41	10,2274.84

Source: Indian Bureau of Mines, Government of India (2013).

Measures of Resource Scarcity

One of the most important questions in the scarcity debate is whether resources are moving towards exhaustion. Rising scarcity is analogous to a reduction in the availability or quality of the resource which causes a decline in economic well-being. There are two fundamental approaches used to classify scarcity: *use scarcity (productive scarcity) and exchange scarcity.* These terms differentiate between the classical concepts of use and exchange value. Use scarcity is the difficulty in production of a natural resource commodity based on the balance between productivity and availability of the resource stock, and given state of technology (Cleveland & Stern, 1993). It is generally measured by estimating the units or quantity of factors other than the scarce resource required to generate a unit of output. Exchange scarcity refers to the exchange value of the resource and is applicable to both factor and output markets (Stern, 1996).

These concepts of scarcity are important as they govern the selection of scarcity indicators. The classical viewpoint considers scarcity as a concern of resource productivity which captures the capacity of resource assets to generate use value. A classic example is the unit cost measure by Barnett and Morse (1963). Its underlying rationale is that with inferior and decreasing resource quality (such as land), more labour would be required to produce a given output. Unit cost is generally measured by production factors per unit of output (i.e., unit extraction cost) and is applicable to stocks as compared to commodities. The neo-classical viewpoint focuses on exchange scarcity and is founded on Hotelling's theory of optimal depletion. According to Hotelling's model (HM), resource owners maximize the discounted profits from resource extraction and sale. Furthermore, the solution to HM results in two scarcity indicators: price and rent (Fisher, 1979). In other words, exchange scarcity is the opportunity cost of acquiring a resource and is generally estimated though the utilization of real price or scarcity rent. In the simplified HM both these indicators rise monotonically with an increase in resource scarcity.

A scarcity measure is expected to indicate growing scarcity of the concerned resource so that producers and consumers are alerted, and can adjust their consumption in accordance and implement required measures. Tietenberg (1996) proposed that the major criteria for choosing between diverse indicators of scarcity can be summarized into three points-:

1. **Foresight:** An ideal scarcity indicator should not only describe past trends but should also project future scarcity. This indicates that it should integrate factors such as future demand for the resource, possibilities of substitution and changes in extraction costs.
2. **Comparability:** An indicator should allow comparison among scarcity levels for different resources and their substitutes in order to identify seriousness of the problem.
3. **Computability:** Data collection and method of computation should be reliable and straightforward.

Scarcity measures can be broadly classified as physical and economic indicators.

Physical Indicators of Scarcity

Physical indicators are also known as quantity indicators. They are based on the rationale that activities such as consumption and production impact physical abundance of resources and a comparison aids to estimate the state of scarcity. They mostly consist of supply side measures or comparison between reserve base and physical quantity or consumption. Popular physical indicators are: existing reserves, proved reserves, crustal abundance, ratio of utilization rate to remaining resources, economical deposits, reserves-to-production ratio and geological deposits.

Reserves

Resources can be categorized as current reserves, potential reserves and resource endowment. Current reserves are proven deposits that are economical to harvest given current prices and state of technology. Potential reserves refer to those that have been identified, but are not economical to extract. They may be para-marginal or sub-marginal. These are expressed as a function relative to a number. If the price for them will be higher, more of these resources will be available.

Resources consist of discovered reserves and those which can possibly be discovered and utilized. It is a geological concept relative to an economic one and places an upper limit on the availability of terrestrial resources. The above definitions highlight the distinction between physical and economical resources.

Reserves are the most popular measure of physical scarcity and are defined in terms of economic recovery. The absolute amount of reserves is insufficient to estimate scarcity due to which it is always expressed in comparison to a depletion measure. An example is the reserve-to-consumption ratio which calculates the number of years for which the present level of consumption can be sustained given known deposits. Several studies have utilized measures such as the reserve-to-consumption ratio to demonstrate that reserves are dangerously low with very short estimated life spans. For example, Nordhaus (1974) estimated the reserve-to-yearly consumption ratio and established a limited lifetime for resources. However, these pessimistic predictions were far from realized due to the dynamic nature of reserves.

There are few important factors which cause uneconomical deposits to move to the resource category. The first is reduction in extraction cost (due to technological improvement such as reduced energy requirement for processes such as transportation and extraction). The second factor is expansion of reserves due to discovery of new deposits. The third reason is a change in the economic condition. This happens when there is a fall in the price of inputs required or an increase in price of a resource. For example, several oil deposits in the North Sea became economically exploitable post the price increase in the 1970s. Conversely, it is also possible that price reduction of a resource renders deposits which were previously under exploitation uneconomical. Even if the price of inputs falls, deposits can be rendered economical.

Crustal Abundance and Other Measures

Crustal abundance is the entirety of minerals that are present on earth. It represents the resource material that is present in minute concentrations in rocks on the earth's crust based on the optimistic notion that it can all be recovered in nature. Crustal abundance is always larger than cumulative extraction. Of the total crustal abundance, a very meagre quantity exists in non-silicate forms (such as oxides and sulphides). In the case of some minerals non-silicate form is especially rare and Skinner (1976) referred to them as geochemically scarce (examples include lead, copper and mercury). An important factor is that energy requirement for per unit of extraction of geochemically scarce resources increases in leaps at the threshold level. On the other hand, for geochemically abundant resources energy requirement for per unit of extraction rises gradually with a fall in ore quality. This leads to the prediction that the former will be substituted for the latter with rising resource utilization.

An important factor is that energy requirement per unit of extraction for geochemically scarce resource increases in leaps at the threshold level. On the other hand, for geochemically abundant resources energy requirement per unit of extraction rises gradually with a fall in ore quality. This leads to the prediction that the former will be substituted for the latter with rising resource utilization. Figure 3.2 shows this.

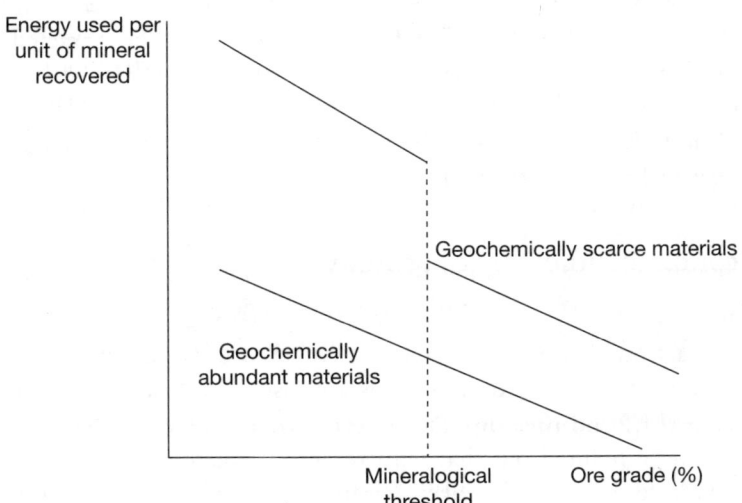

Figure 3.2 *Mineralogical Threshold*
Source: Skinner (1976).

Crustal abundance of a resource can be compared with reserves to estimate scarcity. Nordhaus (1974) compared the reserve-to-consumption ratio and crustal abundance-to-consumption ratio. For the former, life span was 10 years while for the latter it was 85 million years. This implies that both these measures represent two extreme viewpoints. While crustal abundance suffers from over-estimation and fails to account for difficulties that prevent mining the entire resource stock, the resource-to-consumption ratio underestimates by failing to account for positive changes in reserves. An intermediate measure would be more representative of present and future scarcity. Based on this the proposition of mineralogical threshold was suggested by Brobst (1979). Below this level minerals are chemically bonded to silica, i.e. they are silicates (Hanley et al., 1997). Mineralogical threshold shows concentration in the range of 0.01 per cent and 0.1 per cent. If a metal is found to occur below the lower limit of 0.01 per cent, then it is in the atomic structure of silicate mineral and cannot be considered as a mineral on its own. Harvesting metal from that state would involve exorbitant costs due to high material requirement to segregate the required metal. For copper, the mineralogical threshold is 0.1 per cent and it is anticipated that approximately 0.01 per cent of it is in this concentration. The final resource that can be extracted is 0.01. The concept of ultimate recoverable resources (URR) is also an intermediate one. It is a function of technology and prices. However this measure is also highly uncertain as it relies on estimation regarding future techniques and prices.

Economic Indicators of Scarcity

There are three economic measures of scarcity popularly utilized. The first one is unit extraction cost (value of factor inputs per unit of extractive-industry output). It is a measure of Ricardian scarcity. Classical (David Ricardo) and neo-classical (Stanley Jevons) economists have pointed out that with resource depletion, costs will rise to indicate scarcity. Moreover, Ricardo proposed that in the case of agricultural land a rise in demand would bring land of inferior quality under cultivation thereby generating rent and increasing costs. The second measure is real resource prices (ratio of an extractive-industry price index to an overall price index). Prices are popularly utilized in conventional microeconomics as measures of scarcity and are favoured by the neo-classical economists. The third measure is resource rent (marginal value of unextracted resource). It is the best indicator of scarcity from a theoretical viewpoint.

Unit Cost

Barnett and Morse (1963) used the extraction cost of mining a single resource unit as a measure of scarcity. This measure is termed as unit cost. It reflects the Ricardian viewpoint that a growing amount of inputs (capital and labour) would be required to obtain rising agricultural output. As such it is based on classical viewpoint of the law of diminishing marginal returns and restricted resource deposits. It proposes that with a rise in scarcity of a natural resource, factors of production (for example labour and capital of homogenous quality) used alongside it will be employed more extensively. Each time period the quality of resource utilized in production declines, putting pressure on other factors and causing unit cost to rise. The opposite, however, does not hold due to irreversibility of deposits. Unit cost was initially defined by the following formula to include two factors of production (Barnett & Morse, 1963):

$$\text{Unit cost} = \frac{(\alpha L + \beta K)}{Q}$$

The above formula is essentially a weighted average of the mentioned inputs where L and K are labour and capital (excluding natural resources) respectively, α and β are factor weights and Q is output. Obviously this specification excludes several other inputs that are required in the production process and impact costs. For example, a more inclusive measure would be where the entirety of inputs is included in the index along with costs of transportation (Brown & Field, 1978).

Despite being used in one of the most influential books on resource scarcity, unit extraction costs suffer from several defects which have highly constrained their utilization in later studies. These are listed below:

1. Mainly a supply side measure, unit cost is impacted by demand (through rising production) and frequently used for goods which are largely dependent on some natural resource input. The employment of unit cost is founded on the underlying principle that extraction is a Ricardian process. It commences with utilization of superior quality resource (ore or land) and gradually proceeds towards relatively inferior quality resources leading to an intertemporal rise in unit costs. The assumption that due to perfect knowledge resources will be utilized in an ascending order based on extraction cost is not always true. Norgaard (1990) refers to this as the Mayflower Problem and points out that it took several decades for agriculture in the American economy to move from the east coast to the mid-west and derive benefits of the more fertile land (Hanley et al., 1997). Moreover unit costs also assume that techniques of production are stationary and an increasing amount of inputs to be utilized to acquire similar outputs in the future. This assumption is faulty as technical progress increases efficiency and causes a fall in input requirements. Also, due to lack of perfect knowledge resource utilization is not strictly in descending order of quality and discoveries can lead to falling costs through resource augmentation.

2. Unit costs are ambiguous and have a tendency to misrepresent advancement in technology. They are prejudiced towards accommodating growing scarcity when it might be the lowest (as in the case of substitution). For example technological advancements in processes of mining, transportation and alteration into final products lead to increased resource utilization. However, these factors also cause costs to fall and unit cost demonstrate falling scarcity when it may be at its maximum. Addition to existing absolute resource stocks in the form of discovery can also cause a decline in marginal costs of harvesting a resource unit which is not reflected in unit extraction costs.

3. An empirical limitation of unit costs is that they are not readily available and have to be calculated utilizing production inputs. This generates two important issues. Firstly, as argued by neo-classical economists, unit cost excludes several inputs that are essential to

production processes (such as fuel) and hence presents a narrow view. To increase representativeness of results, all inputs must be accounted for. Although this defect can be rectified, it is difficult to acquire data for every input. Secondly, inputs such as capital lack homogeneity which causes measuring and combining complexity. This leads to the additional requirement of formulating several assumptions regarding the most suitable method to measure inputs, capital depreciation, assignment of weights and final output.

4. Unit costs do not consider development of substitutes and improvement in techniques leading to false impression of scarcity mitigation.
5. Unit costs are also difficult to be calculated for any particular manufacturing stage.
6. Unit costs are impacted by prices of inputs and output leading to distortions of scarcity trends.
7. Unit costs are quite complex to measure in cases where industries present a high degree of integration. In such a case segregation of resource extraction cost from others such as transport and processing is difficult.
8. Unit costs have a tendency to underestimate futures scarcity. They capture only the extraction characteristics of those deposits that are known.
9. Unit costs do not reflect the environmental cost of resource utilization.

Real Prices

Real prices consist of extraction costs and scarcity rent. Their direction is governed by both marginal extraction cost (MEC) and marginal user cost (MUC). With constant MEC, price in real terms is a positive function of interest rate and will grow in accordance (analogous to MUC). This demonstrates that cumulative extraction will lead to a reduction in absolute resource quantity and generate growing opportunity cost.

$$P_t = MEC_t + MUC_t$$

$$P_{t+1} = MEC_{t+1} + MUC_{t+1},$$

where t is present and t+1 is subsequent time period.

$$P_t = P_{t+1}$$

$$MEC_t = MEC_{t+1}$$

$$MUC_t < MUC_{t+1}$$

So,

$$P_t < P_{t+1}$$

It is a simple exercise to stretch the above example to multiple time periods and establish a monotonically rising price curve. With a stable and linear demand function and constant MEC the absolute amount of resources mined is equal to the value of resource, and marginal net benefits are identical for all time periods. This provides an incentive to increase extraction in present time period (due to a lower MUC) and decrease it in future time period (due to higher MUC). However, if MEC rises intertemporally, then extraction rate will decline and ultimately cease. With declining MUC or MEC (or both) extraction will rise till declining costs persist. It is possible that post a certain point extraction will begin to decrease.

Prices reflect both direct (extraction cost) and indirect (scarcity rent) cost of resource utilization. They incorporate both supply (such as improvement in techniques, enhancement of resource base, and firm's decisions and constraints) and demand (such as consumer choices, economic growth of consuming countries resulting in increasing demand and growth of indigenous industries) side influences along with future anticipations. They can easily be utilized to stretch projections regarding scarcity into future time periods, and gesture present and future availability of resources.

Despite these positive aspects, prices too are subject to certain drawbacks.

1. Market prices only indicate private scarcity. In the presence of market imperfections or market failures, social indicators of scarcity will diverge from private indicators.

2. The choice of deflator can influence price trends. The preference of deflator is subjective to purpose of the study and can impact the conclusion derived. As advanced by Brown and Field (1979) a consumer might choose a retail price index as opposed to a producer who might select an input price index.

3. Another major limitation is that prices demonstrate high susceptibility to market related factors such as cartels, government interventions and rate of interests. At times price rise is in response to one of these factors instead of scarcity. An appropriate example is the oil price hike of the 1970s which was caused by collusive action of OPEC countries rather than any scarcity alert.

4. With the availability of substitute goods product price undervalues resource scarcity. This is because the rise in price is lesser than that of scarcity rent. The predisposition of prices to vary from scarcity rent is inversely related to resource share in output.

5. For resource prices to accurately reflect scarcity externalities should be absent.

Scarcity Rents

Scarcity or economic rent is the value of the resource *in the ground* and is defined as the amount accruing to the producer for an extra unit of resource. It is represented as the difference between price and the MEC, and captures reduction in the value of the resource stock when a single unit is extracted. The term 'rent' was initially propounded by Ricardo (1817) who defined it to be the difference between returns to inferior and superior quality agricultural land, and applicable to agricultural land. However, Ricardo pointed out that it could be applied to mineral deposits also due to grade differences. The dynamic behaviour of rent is theoretically the most representative indictor of scarcity and is favoured by several studies (Brown & Field, 1978; Halvorsen & Smith, 1984; Pindyck, 1978). It is inclusive of inability of regeneration of a renewable resource and forgone future use of a non-renewable resource, along with any contribution that the resource stock makes to the net benefit of extraction: for example, a more abundant resource stock may decrease extraction or harvest cost (Krautkraemer, 2005).

Theoretically scarcity rent is the best indicator as it exists entirely because of scarcity. However it suffers from several limitations.

1. Scarcity rents are plagued by the presence of unrealistic factors such as access to perfect and holistic information regarding resources, future expectations and market alterations.
2. It relies completely on past information and data without integrating any new factor.
3. It is influenced by factors other than resource scarcity. For example rising rents may easily be attributable to alteration in the rate of interest, demand and demand prospects, government policy and economic forecasts.
4. Scarcity rents can fall to zero with diminution of resource if a low grade backstop substitute is available.
5. Fisher (1979) showed that a rise in scarcity rents in accordance to the interest rate is conditional to the absence of positive stock effects. Only if positive stock effect is non-existent, there will be equivalence between rent and interest rate, or else rent will be smaller than interest rate and may even be negative.
6. Insufficient or non-existent data makes utilization of rents difficult. Utilizing a proxy (such as investment undertaken for explorative activities) is fraught with peril. For example, it is often the case that extractive, milling and refining procedures are joined through vertical integration of firms. In such a situation data will not be authentic.
7. The utilization of rents as scarcity indicators is based on the erroneous assumption that firms follow optimal depletion paths of extraction.
8. There can be situations when rent may not rise to indicate growing scarcity. For example, if a resource is facing rapid depletion but has a substitute it is no longer scarce from the economic viewpoint.
9. According to Fisher (1979), scarcity rent is not a well behaved indicator of scarcity as it does not tend to increase with resource exhaustion.

Economic Approaches to Natural Resource Management

Natural resources are often referred to as the foundation of human existence and civilization. Their basic contribution converts into two main functions: (a) source function which includes provision of material inputs for production processes and environmental services (b) sink function which indicates the reception of wastes by the environment. Figure 3.3 summarizes these functions. Perceptibly, the depletion or degradation of the resource base of society will lead to a curtailment of these fundamental services causing a decline in production and consumption patterns, and ultimately in the quality of human life. These factors render resource management as a fundamental requisite for utilizing resources within the framework of sustainability. Natural resource management refers to the sustainable utilization of major natural resources such as land, water, air, minerals, forests, fisheries, flora and fauna.

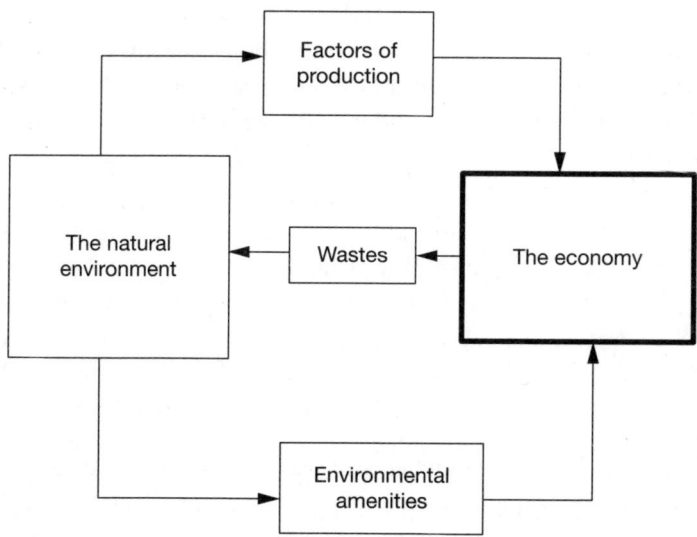

Figure 3.3 *Dependence between the Economy and the Environment*

Source: Author's own example.

Resource management is concerned with depletion in the context of both non-renewable resources (where by definition use will lead to a reduction in the total stock) and renewable resources (where human activities may lead to over-exploitation). The emphasis on the threat posed by resource exhaustion emerged with the Club of Rome in 1972 which proposed inevitable exhaustion of several major exhaustible resources within decades. However these claims remained far from realized mainly due to the impact of scarcity mitigating factors such as discovery of deposits, technological advancements and discovery of substitute goods. Another important factor is resource degradation. The waste from consumption and production activities can degrade natural resources and reduce their ability to provide physical and environmental services.

The Case of Exhaustible Resources

The chief distinguishing feature of an exhaustible resource is that it cannot be duplicated and is available in a fixed supply indicating that a positive rate of extraction rate poses the threat of depletion. The key question in the management of the existing resource base concerns establishment of an optimal rate of consumption.

Whether or not the consumption rate is high depends on what is popularly termed as the optimal rate of extraction. It can be elaborated with the employment of few straightforward concepts (borrowed from the theory of depletion) and certain necessary conditions over the selected time period. The requisite for an optimal extraction path arises as the resource owner is guided by profit-maximizing motives leading to mandatory deviation from standard economic theory. The customary rule for the latter indicates that production will reach a point where equality between marginal cost (incremental cost of production of an extra unit of output) and price will be attained. However, in the case of exhaustible resources the owner deviates from this equilibrium as such a path will require more extraction than is available to the firm due to constrains of the limited resource base and inability of duplication. Management over a given time horizon is constrained as the total availability is limited by the size of the stocks. This generates an opportunity cost (popularly referred to as user cost) of the current extraction and consumption. The present rate of consumption implies that there will be less to consume in the future, that is, the value that might have been obtained for that time at some future date. A resource owner that seeks to maximize profits will take this opportunity cost into account when selling the extracted resources. The existence of opportunity cost is one of the singular most important aspects in the study of exhaustible resources. It exists only in the case of exhaustible resources and is absent for conventional reproducible goods. This is because consumption of the latter now does not reduce the quantity that can be consumed in the future in comparison to a deposit of a certain metal, say copper, extracted today cannot be rediscovered anytime in the future. Thus, the decision of whether to mine a resource or to wait till subsequent time periods depends not only on the cost of extraction but also the cost incurred in foregoing the highest return that could have been earned if the resource had been extracted and sold in the future. When marginal cost includes the opportunity cost component it is referred to as augmented marginal cost. It is specified in terms of its two components namely marginal cost of extraction (MC) and the user cost (UC) as follows:

$$P = MC + UC$$

The above equation is popularly referred to as the primary condition of optimal depletion and its implications are fundamental to managing exhaustible resource deposits. It implies that extraction in the present time period will be lower relative to the case of a non-exhaustible good due to the inclusion of opportunity cost. The first implication is that the current extraction rate by a private owner of a natural resource depends not only on the current price, as in the standard theory, but also on expectation about future prices. These price expectations determine the opportunity cost of additional current extraction. Secondly a competitive supplier that expects future prices to be sufficiently low compared with the current price may extract and sell intensively in the current period, judging the opportunity cost of additional extraction to be small. But if future prices are expected to be sufficiently high, the same current price may induce no extraction whatsoever today. This point is illustrated with the aid of Figure 3.4. Given the exhaustible nature of the resource R, a price-taking

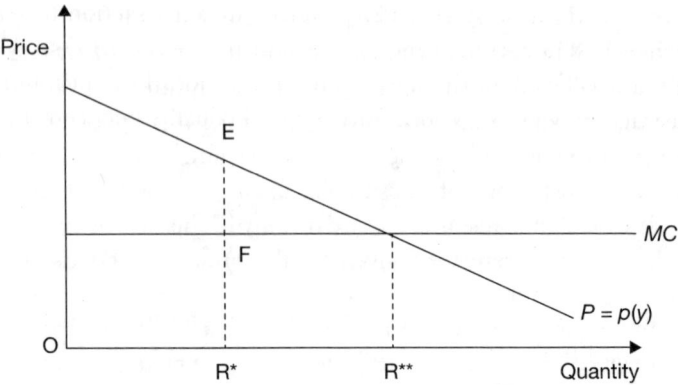

Figure 3.4 *Optimal Extraction of an Exhaustible Resource*
Source: Author's own example.

firm will decide to extract R^* units relative to R^{**} to achieve efficient extraction over time. The distance between the two points E and F is the opportunity cost.

Consider a case where mining activity covers two time periods. The firm is a price-taker faced with fixed extraction costs (C) and can either mine and sell the resource in the present time period, that is, period 1 at the prevailing price P_1 or retain it in the ground until the next period 2 and sell it at price P_2. However, by definition the resource is fixed and any extraction in the first time period leads to a decrease in the absolute quantity of the resource in the second time period.

The net revenue in the initial time period is given by P_1-C, that is, price less revenue of the subsequent time period P_2-C. Integrating the discount rate (r) in the first we get $P_1-C/(1+r)$. Hence, his gain from selling a single unit of the resource in the current time period will be given as:

$$\frac{(P_1 - C) - (P_1 - C)}{(1 + r)}$$

The opportunity cost of mining and selling the resource today is given by $P_2-C/(1+r)$. In the case that $(P_1 - C)/(1+r) > (P_2 - C)/(1+r)$

the owner will have an incentive to enter into transaction to sell the resource in the current time period and if $(P-C)/(1+r)<(P_2-C)/(1+r)$, he will wait for the subsequent time period. The optimum level of extraction will take place at the point of equality between $(P_1-C)/(1+r) = (P_2-C)/(1+r)$

$$P_1-C=(P_2-C)/(1+r) \tag{1}$$

$$P_1=C+(P_2-C)/(1+r) \tag{2}$$

The above stated condition indicates that the prevailing resource price under conditions of optimal mining is equivalent to the MC and the UC. The component of UC is specific to non-renewable resources as in the case of reproducible resources. Production in each time period is targeted to meet demand and there is an absence of carry over between different time periods rendering the optimum output as $P_0 = C$. Equation 2 can also be specified as

$$P_2-C=(P_1-C)(1+r)$$

The above equation was initially proposed by Hotelling (1931). It is the second condition for following an optimal path of extraction. It indicates the optimal exhaustion trajectory where the resource owner will be indifferent between extracting the resource and leaving it unextracted in the mine. Over such a trajectory the net of MEC, i.e., user cost will rise in accordance to the discount rate. Therefore, along the optimum extraction trajectory the price of a resource will rise in accordance to the discount rate. If the discount rate is higher, then the increase in price will be more as the higher discount rate will stimulate extraction by reducing user cost. In actuality extraction costs can't fall to zero and positive costs will cause the price to rise by more than the interest rate.

The discussion so far has considered the question of optimal depletion of an exhaustible resource in the absence of any exogenous influence impacting extraction decisions of the owner. However many factors can impact the management of an exhaustible resource such as possible substitutes for the resource, technical advancement, exploration and discovery of new resource deposits. It is implicitly assumed that the stock of an exhaustible resource under exploitation is known and limited. In reality perfect knowledge regarding all existing deposits is not present and resource reserves prove to be much larger than original estimates. Moreover they are enhanced due to exploration and discovery of new deposits. While the chief reason to undertake exploratory activities is reduction in price level (due to the decrease in opportunity cost), it also impacts resource management. In the case that the initial resource base is small and the cost of extraction is high, the amount of the resource mined will be low and the prevailing price will be high. This condition will lead to exploration of new deposits and add to the absolute quantity of the resource. The increased resource base serves to drive down prices thus controlling the rise in augmented marginal cost.

In practice the impact of technical progress has often led to a reduction in input requirements and increased the lifetime of resources. Invention of cost effective techniques to extract previously uneconomical deposits also leads to an increase in reserves. Substitute goods serve to meet a portion of the resource demand. However, the substitute in question should not face the problem of exhaustion and must be analogous to a backstop technology, that is, it should be available in an unlimited amount at a constant MC. For example if a substitute is available at a constant MC, it would impact the optimal depletion of an exhaustible resource and the AMC of the latter would not exceed the former as demand will always shift towards the resource that is cheaper. The AMC of the substitute good will provide an upper limit for the AMC and P. To conclude, there are several economic factors that impact resource exhaustion. While studying resource management these influences should be included to provide a holistic picture.

Examples from the Indian Economy

The above analysis holds importance for economic management and the discussed concepts can be applied to practical policy applications. For example, consider the case of a developing country that is net exporter in the global market of a resource (such as coal or baryte). While undertaking exports the important question is whether to extract the resource to the point where the MC of extraction equals the global price or to halt mining at a point while more of the resource can still be extracted profitably (as the MC is lesser than the price of a single unit). This problem can be analysed by focusing attention on the opportunity cost of current extraction and the variation that takes place in the costs due to the implementation of a new policy. For instance, increasing production of the resource in the short term by finding equivalence between MC of mining the resource and the prevailing market price is excessive as it does not account for the future net return (profit) that will be sacrificed due to extracting an extra unit of the resource. In addition, if the opportunity cost is very high, extraction in the current time period should be foregone even if the present price is in excess of the present MC of extracting the first unit.

A notable factor is that individual owners aim to maximize profit from mining activities. In such a case the government can intervene to restrict extraction activities for those resources which are regarded highly valuable in the economy (for example gold and aluminium in the Indian economy) or to curb pollutants produced in the process of extraction (for example pollutants form mining activities which uses mercury or arsenic).

The Case of Renewable Resources

Renewable resources are important constituents of the self-regulating process of our planet. Using some trees, fish, groundwater, forage or oxygen will not result in permanent destruction of the resource stock. As such these resources typically pose a different set of management issues relative to non-renewable resources. Existence of growth rate does not indicate that harvesting levels are not subject to a limit. On the contrary, renewable resources may in principle be utilized indefinitely over an economic planning horizon only as long as the use does not exceed the regeneration rate.

The existing stock is the determining factor for sustainable resource availability in future time periods. The size at any point of time is subject to the influence of biological factors (such as diseases, predator population, habitat conditions, pollution and climate) and human actions (exploitation) which affect the resource. Due to the impact of the latter, resource flow is not purely a natural phenomenon and needs to be utilized subject to optimal conditions to ensure a sustainable flow in subsequent time periods. Analogous to exhaustible resources the primary economic question in the management of renewable natural resources is: How much of a resource should be harvested during the present versus future time periods? The time period is generally the plan horizon of a single owner and the economic analysis of how to manage natural resources will depend on the renewable resource in question, for example in the case of fishes it refers to harvest per season and for forest resources it is the length of time between optimal duration (rotation). Notably the harvesting rate determines the balance between current and future benefits and costs, and much of the consideration is to maintain a harvesting rate that does not cross the point of the critical threshold, that is, the minimum level required to ensure the replenishment of the resource.

Biological Dimension: Growth Curves

A renewable resource can be utilized sustainably if the stock is maintained above the critical minimum size. The total stock refers to the absolute resource that is in existence at any given time period while flow is the rate at which the resource is regenerated or replenished. The precise definition depends on the resource under consideration, for example in the case of fishes it is reproduction and for trees it is rate of growth. As the rate of replenishment is not infinite, harvesting activities face an upper limit. This is referred to as the critical threshold and beyond this limit exploitation of the resource is unsustainable as it will compromise resource flow leading to eventual exhaustion. An important benchmark in utilization of natural resources is the maximum sustainable yield, which is the highest harvest that can be maintained indefinitely without decreasing the stock and negatively impacting its existence. The maximum sustainable yield can be defined in terms of a physical quantity of a given resource at a given time period. Exploitation of any amount below this will cause the resource population to rise and any amount above will cause the resource population to decrease

Resource availability over multiple time periods is illustrated in Figure 3.5. The vertical and horizontal axes show the growth and level

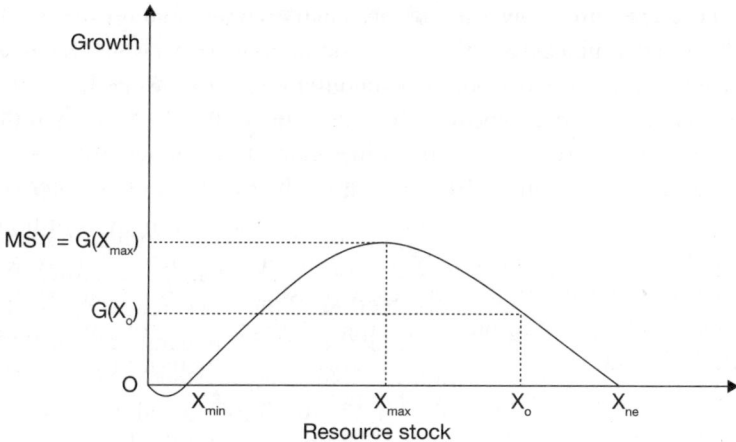

Figure 3.5 *Biological Growth Curve*
Source: Bhattacharya (2001).

of a resource stock. The net growth function (i.e., birth less mortality) is depicted in terms of the growth curve. In the absence of human activities, the renewable resource will attain its natural equilibrium point i.e. X_{ne} which denotes a stable equilibrium. If the stock declines below this level (due to deaths or out-migration etc.) the decline will be exactly offset (due to births, or in-migration etc.) by countervailing forces. For example, if the stock falls to point X_o in one time period it will recover and move towards X_{ne} in subsequent periods because for all stock levels below X_{ne} the growth is positive. In the first year it will increase by $G(X_o)$, and in the second year the population level (i.e. $X_o + G(X_o)$) will grow at a rate lower than $G(X_0)$. This growth process will continue till point X_{ne} is reached. Conversely if the stock exceeds X_{ne}, countervailing forces (such as deaths or out-migration) would increase until it reaches X_{ne}.

Conversely, point X_{min} denotes the minimum population level which is required for the resource to be sustained. Below this point birth rate is lower than death rate. Another important concept is of the maximum sustainable yield denoted by point X_{max} i.e. the maximum quantity of a resource that can be extracted in any given time period without impacting its long-term sustainability. Harvesting beyond point X_{max} leads to overexploitation. Each period's addition is assessed by the difference between growth and harvest. If harvest constantly surpasses the growth rate, then the renewable resource will decline. Similarly, if growth constantly surpasses the level of harvest, then the renewable resource will expand. The steady state is where the level of harvest is precisely equivalent to the growth in every extraction period.

Despite the effectiveness of the concept of maximum sustainable yield, in reality there exists lack of perfect knowledge regarding the absolute stock in existence and its flow. This unawareness integrates ambiguity leading to deviation from the point of maximum sustainable yield. Moreover, modification in biological processes governing the resource can also lead to a shift in the maximum sustainable yield as resources at any given time period are determined by biological factors along with human influences. Another important aspect is that renewable resources are severely threatened by overuse under conditions of open access and ill-defined property rights. This gives individuals an incentive to maintain resource exploitation as long as it is profitable. So there is a lack of interest for conserving the resource, for example, through protective investments or a reduction in the level of utilization. Such unregulated harvesting levels lead to inefficient use of the resource and possibly extinction.

The absence of property rights and open access poses the requisite for some form of government intervention to promote a more socially desirable use of these resources. However, there is a lack of consensus whether (a) such an intervention should promote management of environmental and natural resources under private property regimes and (b) the kind of instruments (whether market based or command and control) that should be used to promote a more socially desirable utilization of resources.

Major Issues in Resource Exploitation

Natural resources form the backbone of every economy and are largely considered indispensable inputs to achieve economic growth and development, along with being instrumental in building capital stocks for the present and future generations. The role natural resources play in human lives has intensified continuously over time. However, a well-documented fact is that the availability of natural resources and the assimilative capacity of our planet are limited. Many of the problems that threaten human survival result from increased consumption of natural resources such as energy, raw materials, water, land and marine resources. Current patterns of resource use suggest that the likelihood that future generations will have access to their fair share of scarce resources is precariously endangered. Moreover, the consequences of excessive resource use may serve to induce serious damages that go beyond the carrying capacity of the environment. While there are controversies or disagreements about the best way forward in recent years there has been a consensus about the importance of sustainability in consumption and production patterns of resource use.

Sustainability and Natural Resources

One of the most popular concepts of present times is of sustainable development. It was defined by the Brundtland Report as 'development that meets the needs of the present without compromising the ability of future generations to meet their own needs' (Brundtland, 1987). Its primary purpose is to ensure an improved quality of life for current and the future generations. Though relatively simple the concept of sustainable development is more than an environmental concept. The general consensus highlights two important requirements for sustainable development to exist. Firstly, development should be based on a multidimensional approach. Such an approach will ensure that development maintains equilibrium between all the factors that contribute to the overall quality of life and include an economic, a social and an environmental dimension. Secondly, development should be carried out in view of the fact that the present generation has an obligation to leave sufficient stocks of social, environmental and economic resources for future generations to enjoy levels of welfare at least as high as our own.

Sustainable development is a multidimensional concept and highlights the requirement to integrate sustainability in resource consumption. In the case of natural resources, the focus is on the latter aspect where exploitation of resources should be managed in such a manner that future generations have the ability to attain at least the present level of welfare utilizing social, environmental and economic resources. This aim poses the requisite to maintain constant stocks of natural capital. However, capital stock can be segregated into man-made and natural capital. While man-made capital pertains to physical assets that include machinery and infrastructure, natural capital constitutes of the stock of natural or environmental assets such as soil, forests areas and biodiversity.

On the basis of the degree of substitutability, between man-made and natural capital, two broad perspectives can be defined. These are weak and strong sustainability. The former is often employed and propounded by economists while the latter by ecologists. Weak sustainability proposes that in order to implement sustainability, the stock of total capital (man-made and natural) should be kept intact. It mandates a high level of substitutability between man-made and natural capital, and assumes that the former can substitute the latter. This can be done when a sufficient share of the benefits of resource use are put back to build man-made capital. So even though natural capital cannot be replaced by man-made capital substitution is possible and as scarcity would increase so would the marginal rate of substitution. In contrast, strong sustainability assumes that a complementary relation exists between man-made and natural capital, and substitution between them is absent in most production functions and the former should be conserved independent of man-made capital.

The applicability of weak and strong sustainability has often been debated, specifically with rising ambiguity about the determination of environmental limits and the precise constraints they present for economic development. However, the recent consensus has been that the maintenance of the total quantity of natural capital is not governed by either of these two extreme viewpoints and instead requires further qualifications. Firstly, some degree of substitution among natural capital and man-made capital must be permitted in the absence of which utilization of non-renewable resources will be totally compromised as any use will reduce the existing stock. Strong sustainability fundamentally focuses only on the need to maintain critical levels of environmental services.

In the case of several non-renewable resources extraction is nearing a peak. Industrial development in the past 200 years was primarily facilitated by the availability of low-priced raw materials (such as fossil fuels). The last decade has seen an increase in prices of raw materials and energy, principally due to increasing demand from emerging countries such as India and China. However, prices remain low and do not reflect the real costs of current levels of resource use. In the case of marketable resources (such as fossil fuels, metals and minerals) economic indicators (such as real prices) do not suggest any substantiation of scarcity through increasing trends. Moreover, factors such as discovery of new deposits, substitution and technological progress have mitigated the impacts of finite availability on the relative scarcity of resources. This suggests that for several non-renewable resources for which markets exist (such as metals and fossil fuels) there does not seem to be any particular need for absolute targets based on some notion of impending scarcity. However, defining actual resource limits post careful analysis is a requirement as the market cannot promote a proper use.

The issue of sustainability assumes specific importance in the case of non-renewable and renewable environmental resources that provide fundamental service to support existence on the planet and generate amenity value. Given the open access and public good nature of these resources and services, market interventions are necessary to prevent inefficient use of these resources. The fact that such environmental resources are likely to be used inefficiently in the absence of market intervention does not automatically suggest that the resources are used inefficiently today. A host of regulation and management schemes are in place for most environmental resources but their efficacy is not well established.

Conclusion

The aim of the above chapter has been to provide a condensed and concise discussion of different resource classifications and the interconnection between separate sub-categories, different measures of resource scarcity, the economic approach to resource management and sustainability in the context of resource utilization.

In the context of measuring whether resources are growing scarce there exist two diverse approaches: exchange and productive scarcity. However, a reliable scarcity indicator should reflect both the direct and indirect cost of resource use. Unit cost exhibits ambiguity and fails to reflect the worth of future consumption by excluding *in situ* value (indirect cost) and focuses instead on implicit (average) cost. In contrast, scarcity rent does not consider direct cost and can effectively be considered the inverse of unit costs. Scarcity rent also suffers from lack of data availability. In contrast resource prices have readily available data, but their efficiency is subject to the choice of deflator and can be distorted by scarcity mitigating factors. A common defect in all scarcity indicators is the failure to factor in social cost utilizing open access resources. No single indicator is an ideal one.

Economic analysis is based on a consistent theoretical framework which is an important building element for sustainable and resilient resource use. This approach to resource management provides an analytical structure for gauging whether available resources are being efficiently utilized, highlights the principles of efficient utilization and can be extended to suggest policies to promote optimal resource use.

The issue of sustainability should not be seen as an isolated question of resource use, but should be seen in the context of sustaining human welfare and as a prerequisite to maintain present patterns of consumption. The weak sustainability paradigm specifies that this can be ensured by maintaining the total value of capital (man-made and natural capital) constant. Conversely, the strong sustainability paradigm proposes a complementary relation between natural and man-made capital. Both these approaches present extreme viewpoints, but can be combined to decide what should be done to promote sustainable resource use.

References

Barnett, H. J., & Morse, C. (1963). *Scarcity and growth: The economics of natural resource availability*. Baltimore, MD: Johns Hopkins Press for Resources for the Future.

Bhattacharya, N. (2001). *Environmental economics: An Indian perspective*. New Delhi: Oxford University Press.

Brobst, D. A. (1979). Fundamental concepts for the analysis of resource availability. In V. Kerry Smith (Ed.), *Scarcity and growth reconsidered* (pp. 106–159). Baltimore, MD: Johns Hopkins University Press for Resources for the Future.

Brown, G. M., & Field, B. C. (1978). Implications of alternative measures of natural resource scarcity. *Journal of Political Economy, 86* (2), 229–243.

Brundtland, G. (1987). *Report of the world commission on environment and development: our common future* (United Nations General Assembly document A/42/427). New York: United Nations.

Cleveland, C. J., & Stern, D. I. (1993). Productive and exchange scarcity: An empirical analysis of the U.S. forest products industry. *Canadian Journal of Forest Research, 23*, 1537–1549.

Fisher, A. C. (1979). Measures of natural resource scarcity. In V. Kerry Smith (Ed.), *Scarcity and growth reconsidered*. Baltimore, MD: Johns Hopkins University Press for Resources for the Future.

Halvorsen, R., & Smith, T. R. (1984). On measuring natural-resource scarcity. *Journal of Political Economy, 92* (5), 954–964.

Hanley, N., Shogren, N. J., & White, B. (1997). *Environmental economics in theory and practice*. Basingstoke: Macmillan Press.

Hotelling, H. (1931). The economics of exhaustible resources. *Journal of Political Economy, 39* (2), 137–175.

Indian Bureau of Mines, Government of India. 2013. *National mineral inventory—an overview*. New Delhi: Author.

Jevons, W. S. (1865). *The coal question: An inquiry concerning the progress of the nation, and the probable exhaustion of our coal-mines* (2nd ed., 1866). London: Macmillan.

Krautkraemer, J. A. (2005). *Economics of natural resource scarcity: The state of the debate* (Discussion paper 05–14). Washington, DC: Resources for the Future.

Nordhaus, W. D. (1974). Resources as a constraint on growth. *American Economic Review, 64* (2), 22–26.

Pindyck, R. S. (1978). The optimal exploration and production of nonrenewable resources. *Journal of Political Economy, 86* (5), 841–861.

Ricardo, D. (1817). *The principles of political economy and taxation*. London: John Murray.

Skinner, B. (1976). A second iron age? *American Scientist, 64*, 258–269.

Stern, D. I. (1996). *The theory of natural resource scarcity indicators: Towards a synthesis* (CEES Working Papers 9603). Boston, MA: Center for Energy and Environmental Studies Boston University.

Tietenberg, T. (1996). *Environmental and natural resource economics* (4th ed). New York, NY: Harper Collins.

US Geological Survey. (2013). *Metal prices in the United States through 2010*. Reston, VA: Author.

CHAPTER 4

Economics of Bioenergy in India

Mohammad Younus Bhat and Arfat Ahmad Sofi

Introduction

Bioenergy is defined as renewable energy that is derived from newly living organic material, or biomass (Williams, Dahiya, & Porter, 2015). It is considered as a larger transition towards a bio-economy (Van Meijl, Smeets, & Zilberman, 2015). As far as development and drivers of bioenergy are concerned, much of the current focus is on capturing issues such as energy security, energy independence, and perceived opportunities for economic growth and development. Additionally, there are various concerns such as energy security, high oil prices, declining oil reserves and global climate change that are fuelling a swing towards bioenergy as a renewable alternative to fossil fuels (Khanna, Scheffran, & Zilberman, 2010). Against this backdrop, there is a natural tendency to increase and enhance national capacities to produce biofuels through public policies and private investments around the globe. Various studies have brought to limelight some serious concerns and issues, and have asked for suitable policy arrangements to address them. For instance, with global population reaching seven billion, there is a tendency for increasing demand for both food as well as biofuels (Pimental, 2012). This increase will further exaggerate the scarcity of both food and fuel. Presently, biofuel production requires about four hundred million tons of food per year. Therefore, production of ethanol or biodiesel to replace fossil fuels using food raises significant nutritional as well as ethical concerns (Pimentel, 2012). Since more than 70 per cent of the seven billion world population is malnourished, there is a critical need for food grains and basic food. Studies have estimated that biofuel production has led to doubling or tripling of some food prices like that of bread (Msangi, Ewing, & Rosegrant, 2010; Msangi, Sulser, Rosegrant, & Valmonte-Santos, 2007). According to United Nations Food and Agricultural Organization's report, using food crops for biofuel production has the tendency to increase hunger worldwide (Food and Agriculture Organization of the United Nations, 2008; Pimentel, 2012). Since the beginning of new millennium policy decisions across nations have mandated increased biofuel production and consumption. For instance, fuel producers in USA are required to use 36 gallons of biofuels by 2022 according to the Energy Independence and Security Act of 2007. Such policy decisions would require all biomass produced in each country every year including crops. Therefore, increased use of biofuels replacing fossil fuel will damage not only the global environment but also the world food system which in turn will enhance global food insecurity. According to some studies, biofuels which were assumed to diminish dependence of countries on fossil fuels actually have increased their dependence (see Pimentel, 2012, for details). Figure 4.1 shows that global biofuel production between 2000 and 2017 has increased from 9.176 billion to 84.121 billion metric tons of oil equivalent worldwide.

There is a tendency of increasing demand for all sources of energy including energy from biofuels. Projections at the global level for increase in energy demand associated with increasing demand for food will have greater stresses on world food systems and the ecosystems they support. Different parts of the world are observing

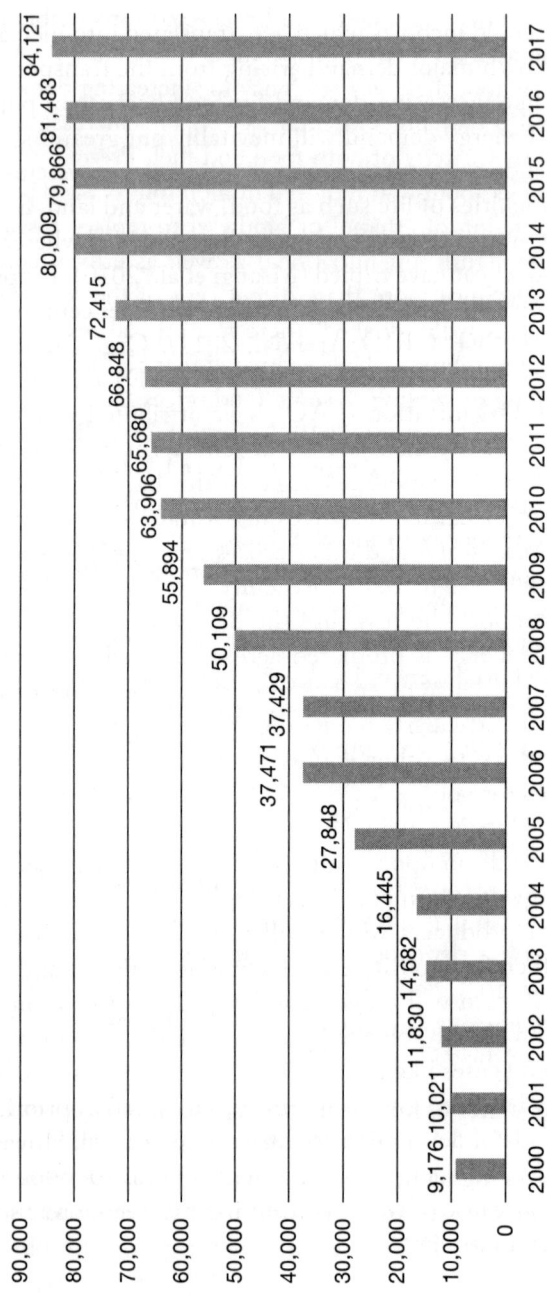

Figure 4.1 Global Biofuel Production from 2000 to 2017 (in 1,000 Metric Tons of Oil Equivalent)

Source: IEA (2019).

increase in household incomes which gets translated into increase in energy demand with major demand arising from the transportation sector. Trends like increasing demand for food because of population growth and energy demand will inevitably put greater stresses as well as demands on natural resources affecting ecosystems that provide basic amenities of life such as food, water and land. Studies have found that prices of basic food grains have doubled whereas the prices of rice and wheat have tripled (Msangi et al., 2010). Empirical estimations of some studies have suggested a 10–15 per cent increase in food prices (UNEP GRID Arendal, 2011). Organization for Economic Cooperation and Development (OECD) and the Food and Agriculture Organization (FAO) have attributed production of biofuels as one of the main drivers of long-term increase in the prices of agricultural commodities. Against this backdrop, sustainable management of natural resources necessitates conservation of biological resources, water and other ecosystems services (Elobeid, Carriquiry, Secchi, & Yu, 2013). Recently there is an increase in bioenergy consumption both within the developed and the developing world. Bioenergy is promoted across the world as a means to enhance independence of energy resources, promotion of rural development and particularly reduction in greenhouse gas (GHG) emissions. Contrary to other energy sources, biofuels have the potential benefits for poor or lower-middle income countries. First, developments in bioenergy would not only reduce fossil fuel dependence but also provide an opportunity in enhancing energy security. Second, bioenergy developments in developing countries can create new markets for producers which will lead to new employment opportunities, therefore, positively affecting agricultural and rural incomes which in turn will reduce poverty and enhance economic growth. Third and notably, bioenergy development can contribute in mitigating harmful gases like carbon dioxide (CO_2) emissions. That is why bioenergy has been given supreme place as well as priority as far as policy agenda of developing countries is concerned. However, as discussed above, bioenergy is critical for economic development but it also can be a cause of worry concerning their economic social and environmental viability.

Bioenergy Market: Some Recent Economic Developments

The key drivers of bioenergy and the emergence of bio-economy are the policies and energy prices in the current world. More than 50 countries across the world have adopted biofuel blending targets or mandates and some others are in the process of biofuel quota implementation and consideration (REN21, 2013). Biomass use is increasing at a great pace because it brings down GHG emissions, enhances energy security and improves economic development in rural areas. According to International Energy Agency (IEA), global demand for bioenergy has shown an increasing trend which was 1,277 Mtoe in 2010 and is expected to increase to 2,235 Mtoe in 2035 as per the 450 Scenario (IEA, 2012). Available literature shows that bioenergy developments are considered transitional towards an economy that is dependent upon renewable sources aiming to mitigate the impact of global warming. For example, IEA, 2012 shows that increase in bioenergy demand is limiting climate change thereby restricting average global temperature to 2 degrees Celsius. As a traditional source of energy, biomass has been used in the form of wood as well as dung. However, technological advancements in engineering and biology have helped modern biofuel industry to produce fuels for transportation and energy.

Employment Generation and Investment Trends in the Case of Bioenergy

One of the main policy objectives/targets for the establishment of a sustainable bio-economy is to enhance economic growth as well as create jobs. Bioenergy promotion is, therefore, expected to enhance economic growth and create jobs, though the impacts of bio-economy at the macro level are not well known. It may be considered valuable as far as job creation is considered because it is characterized as being labour intensive compared to its fuel equivalent. Figure 4.2 shows employment in renewable energy sector. It shows that the share of biofuel jobs in total employment has increased from 2,398 thousand in 2012 to 3,054 thousands in 2017.

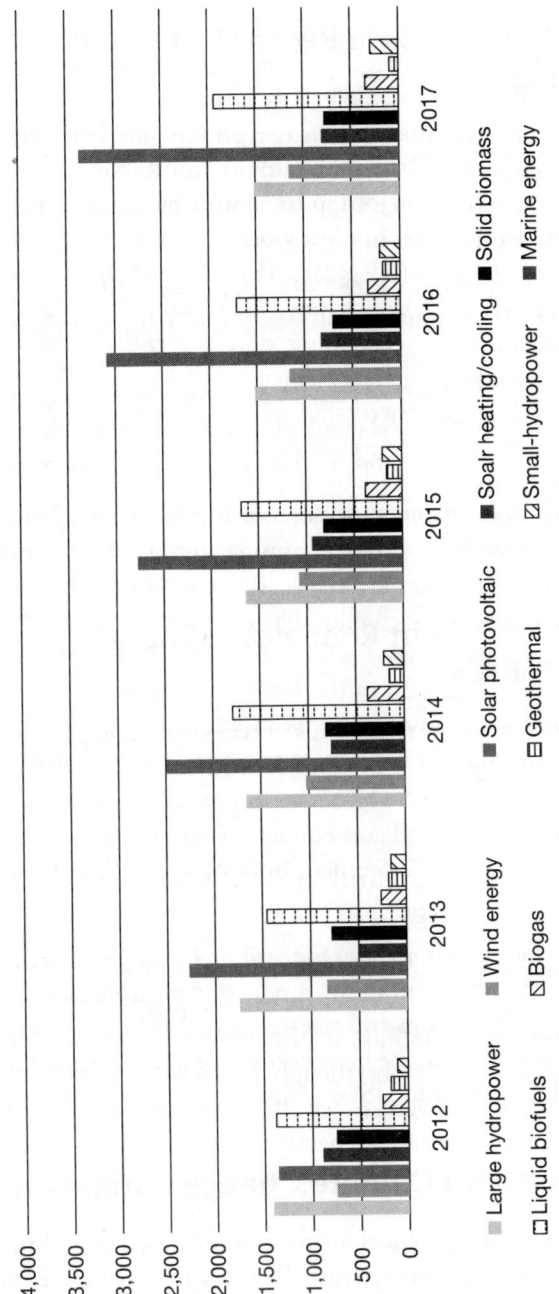

Figure 4.2 *Employment in Renewables (Thousands) by Source*

Source: IRENA (2019).

Figure 4.3 shows employment figures in the renewable energy sector of some leading and emerging economies of the world. It shows that China (43% of all renewable energy jobs) and India (7% of all renewable energy jobs) alone account for 50 per cent jobs in the renewable energy sector. In 2017, the renewable energy sector was able to provide more than 7.2 million jobs in India whereas at the same time USA, Japan and European Union lost jobs.

Modern bioenergy choices such as biomethane, producer gas and agro-processing have a multiplier effect in local jobs, and therefore expand local economics in terms of a higher level of value addition to locally generated biomass products as well as energy carriers. Figure 4.4 provides an overview on the total employment figures in the bioenergy sector (biogas, liquid biofuels and solid biomass) from 2012 to 2017.

It shows that jobs in bioenergy sector have increased from 2.40 million in 2012 to 3.06 million in 2017, almost an increase of 28 per cent.

Investment Trends in Renewable Energy: Global and Indian

Figure 4.5 shows the investment trends of renewable energy in India. As can be seen, it reached a peak of US$13 billion in 2011 and decreased to US$10.9 in 2017. Figure 4.6 shows global investments in renewables such as solar, wind and biofuels. Total global investment has increased from mere US$45 billion in 2004 to a peak of US$320 billion in 2015.

Bioenergy as a secure alternative to fossil fuel energy in particular has led to increased investment in the production of sustainable feedstocks, technology, innovations and research, and development. Figure 4.6 shows that investments in the bioenergy sector have decreased since 2004 from US$12.4 billion to US$6.7 billion.

Bioenergy Use and Climate Change Mitigation

Warming of the climate system is unambiguous as well as anthropogenic. GHG emissions are enormously likely to have been the main

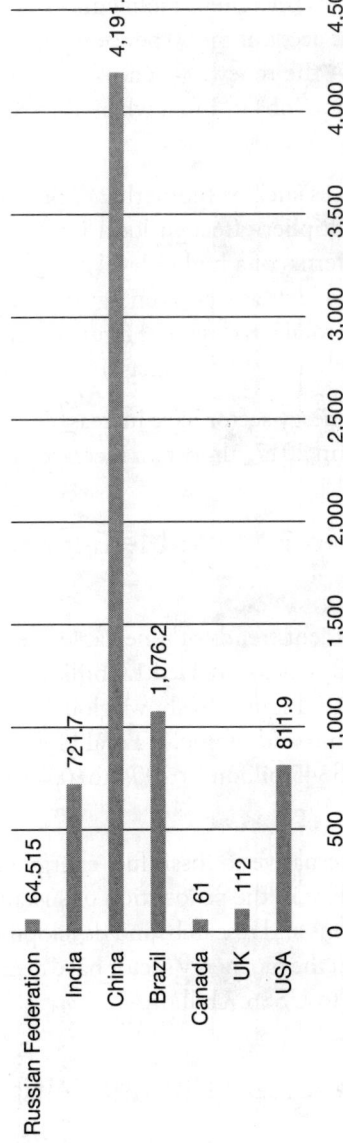

Figure 4.3 *Jobs in Renewable Energy Sector, 2017 (Thousands)*

Source: IRENA (2019).

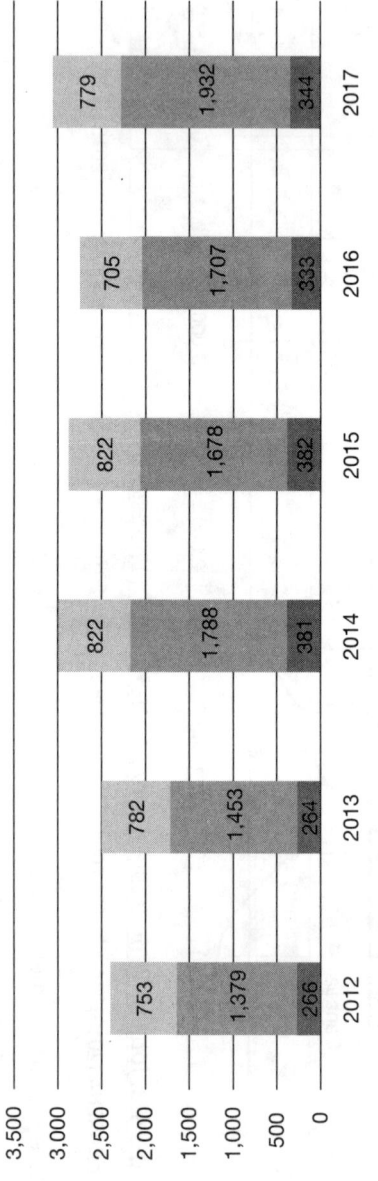

Figure 4.4 Jobs in the Bioenergy Sector, 2012–2017 (Thousands)

Source: IRENA (2019).

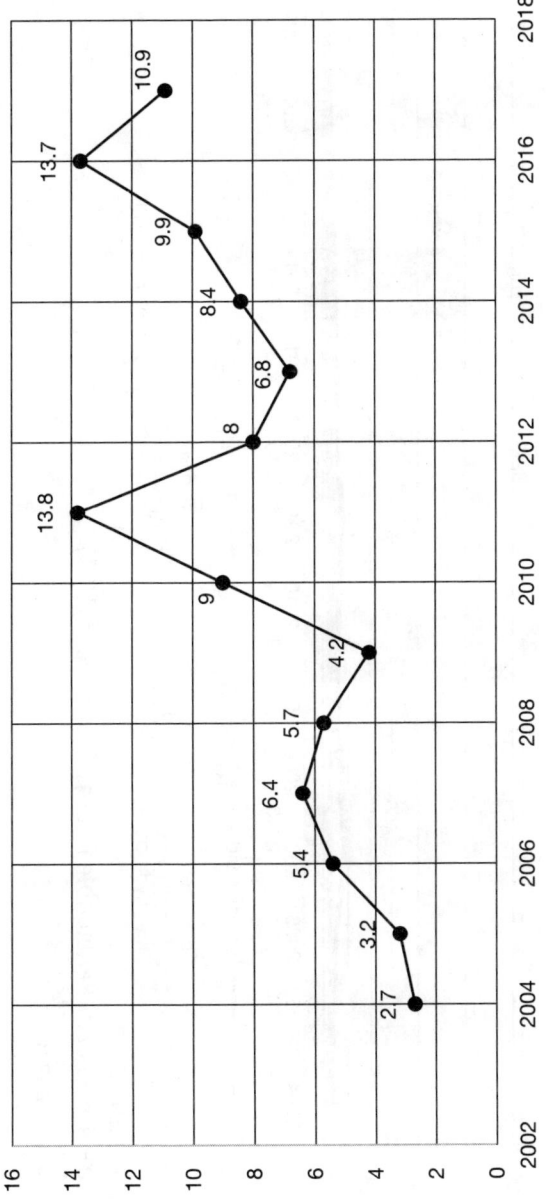

Figure 4.5 Investment Trends in Renewable Energy in India (US$)

Source: IRENA (2019).

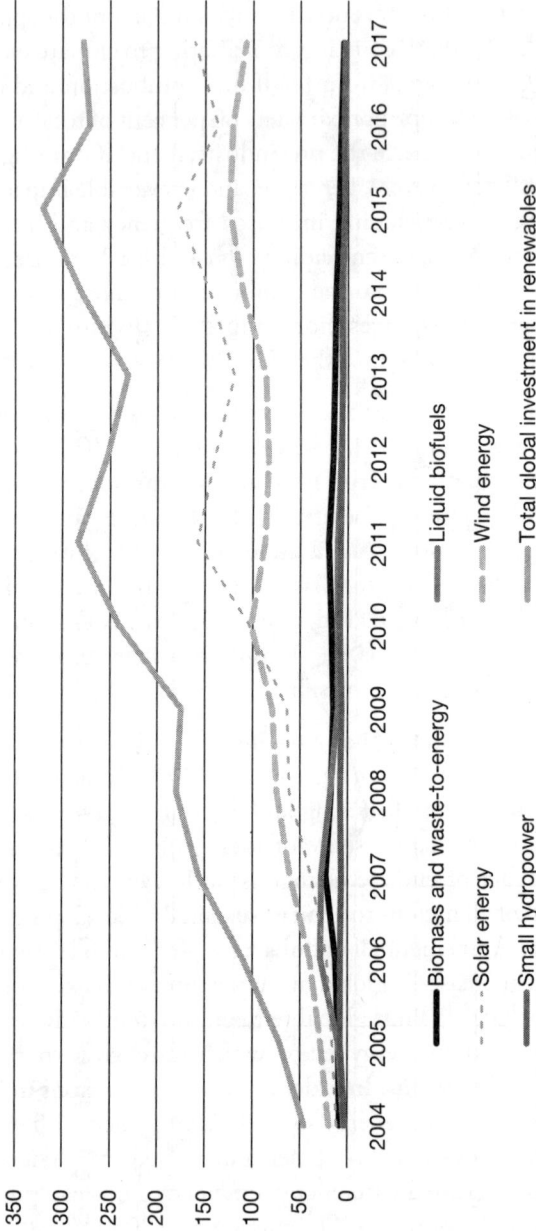

Figure 4.6 Global Renewable Energy Investment (US$)

Source: IRENA (2019).

cause of the observed warming. CO_2 emissions are critical in augmenting atmospheric CO_2 concentrations which account for approximately two-thirds of radiative forcing contributing to climate change. Furthermore, CO_2 emissions from fossil fuel combustion and other industrial processes make up approximately 60 per cent of total anthropogenic GHG emissions since the pre-industrial era. If unmitigated, climate change will have 'severe, pervasive, and irreversible impacts for people and ecosystems', including increased frequency and intensity of extreme weather events, ocean acidification and sea-level rise. CO_2 emissions have increased due to the combustion of more fossil fuels making environmental resources more vulnerable. Figure 4.7 shows the global emissions of CO_2 since the 1960s to 2014.

Total emissions in 1960 were 392.48 metric tonnes which increased to 1218.72 metric tonnes in 2014. Therefore, reducing CO_2 emissions from fossil fuel combustion is crucial for abating the adverse impacts of global climate change on society. In 2014, China was the top contributor of CO_2 emissions contributing 30 per cent of total global emissions (Figure 4.8). The other significant contributors included USA, European Union, Japan, India and Russian Federation. The two emerging economies, India and China, together accounted for 37 per cent of the total global emissions.

It is pertinent to mention that data in Figure 4.8 includes CO_2 emissions from fossil fuel combustion and other industrial processes such as cement manufacturing and gas flaring. These sources altogether account for a larger share of total global CO_2 emissions. Reducing the impact of climate change is both a critical as well as crucial policy goal of all nations to achieve sustainable development. In line with the Paris Agreement all nations have pledged to lessen CO_2 emissions so that increase in global average temperature can be put within limits. The goal to limit global temperature implicitly needs a shift towards a low-carbon energy sector, which currently accounts for two-thirds of global emissions. In order to provide reductions in CO_2 emissions by 2050, renewable energy sources accompanied with energy efficiency gains can provide nearly 90 per cent reductions. Renewable energy sources accompanied with energy efficiency gains can provide nearly 90 per cent reductions in CO_2 emissions by 2050.

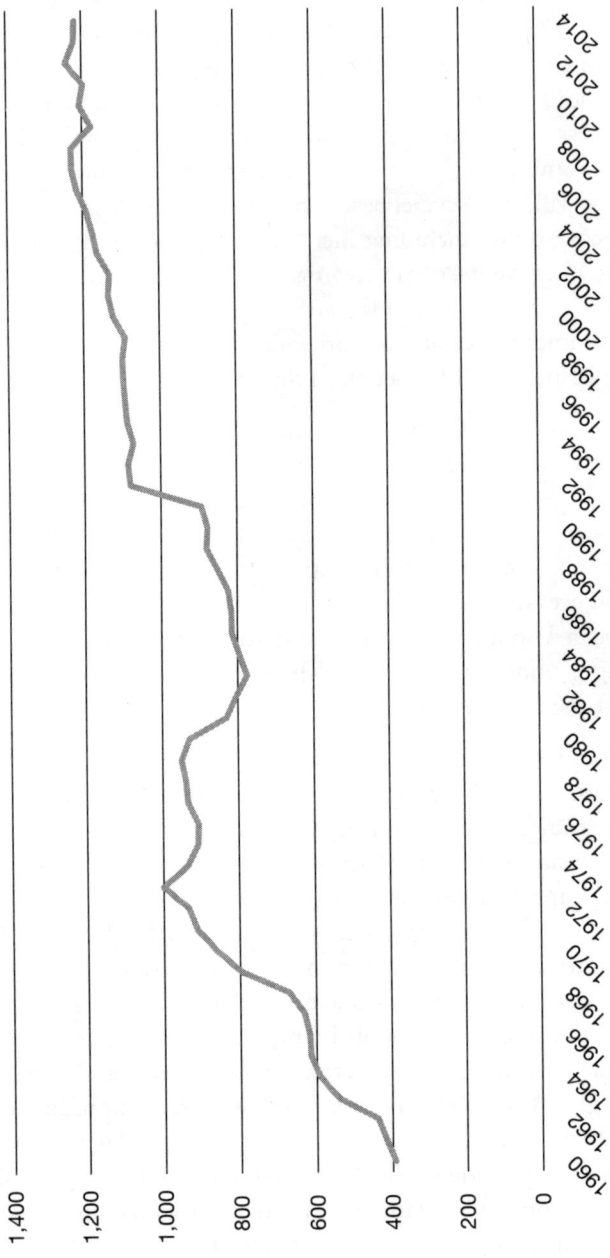

Figure 4.7 Global CO$_2$ Emissions (1960–2014; Mt)

Source: World Bank (2019).

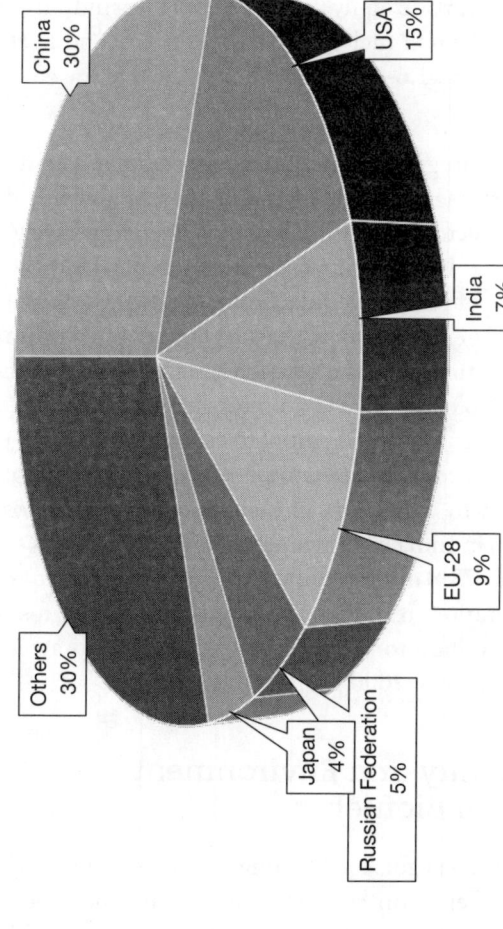

Figure 4.8 Emissions by Country

Source: World Bank (2019).

Bioenergy use in the modern times is an opportunity to lessen CO_2 emissions contributing to anthropogenic climate change by offsetting the use of non-renewables. Staples, 2017 quantified the possible reductions in global GHG from the bioenergy use so as to offset electricity derived from fossil fuel in 2050. Findings from the study indicated that bioenergy use could help in avoiding 9–68 per cent or 4.9–38.7 Gt Carbon dioxide equivalent (CO_2e). The study also finds that counterbalancing fossil fuel-generated electricity and heat with bioenergy is found to be 1.6–3.9 times more effective for emissions mitigation.

Renewable energy in general and bioenergy can play a significant role in extenuating the serious impact of climate change while decarbonizing the energy sector. Biofuels as a source of energy have greater potential to reduce GHG emissions. To better understand the possible effect of the use of renewables like biomass energy, International Renewable Energy Agency (IRENA) has developed a tool estimating the GHG emissions that are avoided each year as a consequence of renewable energy deployment in a country known as the Avoided Emission Calculator. It has the potential to estimate the GHG emissions avoided due to a country's renewable electricity generation in a given year compared to various fossil fuel generation scenarios. For instance, renewables in India have avoided 180.1 million tonnes CO_2e in 2016 compared to 73.8 million tonnes CO_2e in 2000. Also renewable electricity generation in India in 2016 has replaced the fossil fuel emissions by 181.8 million tonnes CO_2e. Total emissions avoided in India from bioenergy since 2000 is given in Figure 4.9.

Economic Viability and Environment Sustainability of Biofuels

The major policy drivers for establishing sustainable bio-economy are to reduce dependence on resources that cannot be renewed as well as to adapt and mitigate global climate change. The objective of dependence on bioenergy as an alternate energy resource is to enhance further economic growth accompanied by job creation and improving nation's balance of trade. Other objectives that are equally

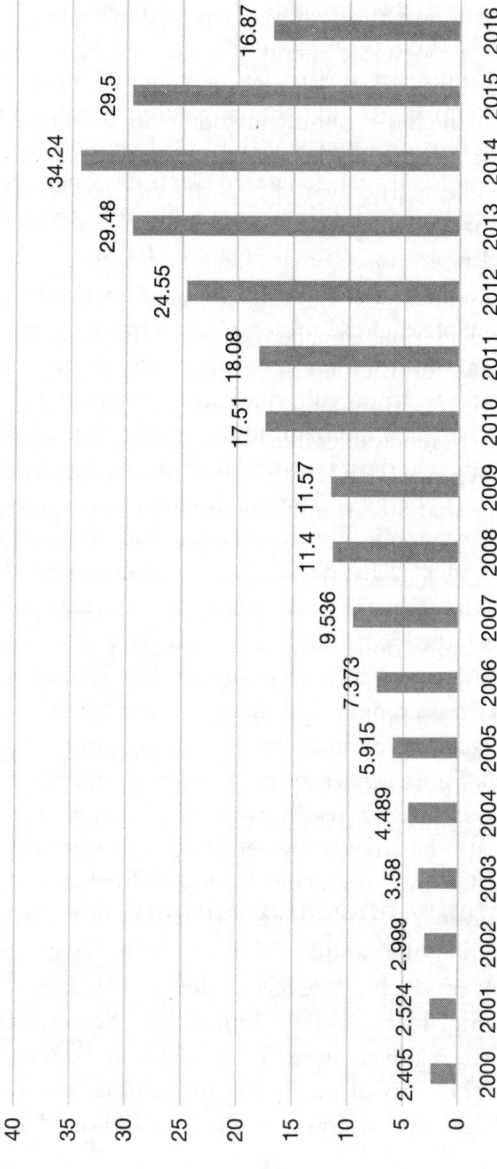

Figure 4.9 Avoided Emissions CO_2e (Bioenergy; Mt)

Source: IRENA (2019).

important towards this transition are to ensure food security, and proper and sustainable management of natural resources. There has been a huge global support through major policy initiatives for the production and use of renewable energy sources relating particularly to climate change and bioenergy (Elobeid et al., 2013). These initiatives towards sustainable bio-economy include among others United States Environmental Protection Agency's Renewable Fuel Standard (RFS2), American Clean Energy and Security Act (2009), Brazil's National Climate Change Policy (2009), Renewable Fuels Regulations in Canada (2006), Energy and Climate Change Package, European Union (2009) and National Policy on Biofuels, India (GOI, 2018). The underlying principles behind these policy initiatives range from minimum reliance on imported fuels, reducing fuel prices, enhancing economic growth and improving rural economy to adapting and mitigating climate change. The main intention of this analysis is to analyse the constraints that limit biofuels from becoming an efficient or sustainable alternate energy resource. An important feature of an energy resource to be economically viable is that it must be competitive both as a crop and as a fuel (Khanna, 2008). Therefore, energy derived from biofuels needs to successfully compete with the energy produced from fossil fuels given the identified policy initiative across the globe. Producers of feedstock for biofuels will only produce if the economic return earned from these crops is equivalent or more than the returns earned from profitable conventional crops. The opportunity cost of producing feedstock for energy crops is the returns undergone from conventional crops. Economic feasibility in the cost of production of these crops will also be affected by geographical variations across different locations. Cost of producing feedstock for bioenergy will vary substantially given the underlying differences in the yields as well as costs of land. For example, Khanna (2008) estimated the cost and quantity of producing biofuels in the case of Illinois under the high cost scenario. Her estimates found that the costs of corn stover production are relatively lower in northern and central parts of Illinois whereas the costs of producing miscanthus are relatively lower in south-western and southern regions of Illinois than other parts of the state.

Biofuels as an alternate energy source are justified if they reduce market failures caused by environmental externalities. Biofuels provide a range of environmental benefits depending upon different feedstocks across biofuels. For example, feedstocks like switchgrass may provide a better habitat for wildlife and others like miscanthus have greater potential to mitigate GHG emissions. Feedstocks that can enhance biodiversity and other ecological benefits are Indian grass and Big Bluestem. Khanna (2008) estimated the mitigation of GHG emission of biofuels in Illinois and found that corn and corn stover have the potential to reduce gas emissions by 37 per cent and 94 per cent, respectively, in comparison to energy equivalent gasoline (Khanna, 2008). Therefore, given the advancement in energy technologies, biofuels can be rewarding because of their potential for environmental services, which will also help in internalizing environmental externalities and promotion of sustainable mix of feedstocks. GHG, through aligning energy policy and climate policy (e.g., the inverse relation between tax credits and carbon footprint), can provide incentives to produce low carbon feedstocks. Moreover, policy incentives across the nations could be created to encourage feedstocks that can enhance biodiversity and improve ecosystem services.

In the attainment of sustainability in the energy sector and overall development of an economy bioenergy can play a critical and significant role. However, it requires innovations responding effectively to socio-economic as well as environmental and ecological deliberations. Therefore, in order to enhance efficient use of natural resources through the deployment of biofuel energy, there is a requirement of integrated assessment of production chains. Moreover, proper management of land, water and biodiversity need a landscape approach enhancing sustained production and productivity of bioenergy, food, feed, feedstocks and timber.

According to Nogueira et al. (2015), five key insights that need to be considered for promoting sustainable development via bioenergy use should include:

1. Improved data and efficient analysis: This asks for bioenergy research and development so as to generate improved data for

efficient analysis so that it provides a base for suitable public policies and governance systems

2. Assessing, monitoring and evaluation: Estimation of socio-
   economic as well as environmental cost and benefit of bioenergy
   structures ask for improved assessment, monitoring and evaluation

3. Institutional and human resource capacity: For the improvement
   in governance, generation of knowledge and service extension in
   bioenergy systems require institutional as well as improved resource
   measurement and capacity both in public and private sectors

4. Development and promotion of innovative financing schemes:
   It is equally important to enable and empower societies to take
   advantage from small scale bioenergy projects

5. Communication tools: All bioenergy stakeholders in tandem with
   civil society participation for developing integrated bioenergy
   investments and operations require advanced communication skills
   and tools.

Bioenergy Benefits and Sustainable Development Goals

Sustainable development is development meeting the basic human
needs such as food, clothing, energy and shelter of the current generation within the sustainable and equitable carrying limits of natural systems. Presently, achievement of sustainable development goals require
modern, efficient and well-designed bioenergy systems and structures
that enable an effective conversion towards sustainable and renewable
energy systems. Bioenergy can contribute towards sustainable development; however, its distribution as well as deployment needs to be
well planned and should be carefully planned. Various environmental
and social risks are involved asking for appropriate safeguards which
need to be put in place and effectively implemented. Despite these
risks, bioenergy use contains benefits that can help in operationalizing
sustainable development and contribute vehemently to various policy
objectives. These are listed as below.

1. **Diverse and secure energy supplies:** Agriculture, forest prod-
   ucts/residuals and urban wastes in various countries can be prime

sources of producing bioenergy. Production of energy from biomass at local level will reduce dependence on imported fossil fuels benefiting countries in the form of saving their finances. Bioenergy as an alternative energy resource increases a nation or region's energy capability and security.

2. **Easy and equitable energy access:** Across the world more than a billion have no access to electricity and the access of an additional 1 billion is unreliable. Therefore, to achieve universal access to modern energy services by 2030, bioenergy can play a significant role particularly in developing countries such as India and China. Additionally, expertise and technology associated with modern bioenergy can help in improving the living conditions for more than two and half billion people that are solely dependent upon biomass and traditional fuels for cooking and heating.

3. **Rural development:** One of the significant goals of bioenergy development is to enhance the living conditions of rural people. Agriculture is the mainstay of about 74 per cent of world's poor for sustenance. Bioenergy production can enhance agricultural growth for rural development. Bioenergy development in rural areas can contribute towards transitioning from traditional biomass use to modern use. This transition will reduce the time required for the collection of water and firewood so people can use this time in generating incomes from other sectors.

4. **Employment:** Bioenergy development can create employment opportunities particularly in developing countries. Job opportunities can be found as well as created throughout the bioenergy value chain. Bioenergy can act as a driver of industrial development creating more skilled labour force overtime with increase in scale as well as sophistication.

5. **Health benefits:** Bioenergy in its modern form replaces traditional inefficient biomass combustion reducing indoor pollution along with consequent health impacts.

6. **Food security:** Bioenergy production can guarantee food security if investment spending improves agricultural productivity as well as availability of food grains. It will also improve family incomes enhancing purchasing power to purchase food. Food accessibility will reduce due to higher prices but new infrastructure and

technological developments can support development of bioenergy sector improving accessibility to markets in many industries. Further, over all improvements can be enhanced through increased access to bioenergy enabling crop drying, cooking as well as drinking water decontamination.

7. **GHG emission reduction:** Bioenergy use has the advantage of limiting the GHG emissions. Use of biomass for energy can be a substitute to reduce excessive utilization of fossil fuels specifically coal.

8. **Climate change adaptation:** Bioenergy as a secure and renewable energy source has the capability of reducing the emission of GHG particularly CO_2. Since bioenergy production is directly dependent upon rainfall and climatic conditions, it involves improved and adapted germplasm enhancing resilience to climate change.

9. **Biodiversity and land cover:** Bioenergy structure ought to be promoted in places or areas that are environmentally and ecologically subtle. Bioenergy systems should consider adequate measures so that natural landscape areas must be preserved thereby reducing the impacts on biodiversity.

10. **Deforestation:** Bioenergy production evades cutting of trees if done in a sustainable way by promoting increasing availability of woody biomass. This can be done through proper management of forest resources as well as through plantation of more trees. Sustainability in bioenergy production can be maintained by replacing natural forest firewood, which is considered as the main source of deforestation in the present times. However, developments in productive feedstocks have lessened pressures on first generation biofuels (particularly forestry).

Sustainable energy is considered crucial for the attainment of sustainable development. Various studies have pointed out that bioenergy can play a significant role in achieving sustainable energy mix in the future (GEA, 2012; Greenpeace, 2008). Bioenergy has both traditional as well as modern use. It accounts for more than 10 per cent of total primary energy mix globally. However, its sustainable use in transportation and other sectors of the economy depends on the needs and conditions prevalent in particular areas and regions.

Its intensive deployment and the socio-economic as well as environmental benefits can be maximized by making scientific and technological advancements, innovations in business models and public policies in conjunction with continuous enhancement and extension services grounded on learning from experience concerning all these aspects.

Bioenergy Production and Policy in India

India as an emerging economy is also one of the fastest growing economies in the world. Its development goals focus mainly on economic growth, equity and enhancement of human welfare. For the socio-economic development of an economy, energy is considered as a critical input. In India energy security, economic growth and environmental protection are the key national energy policy drivers. India's population has reached 1.3 billion in 2019, so the demand for energy resources will grow exponentially. Improved human well-being and energy demand rise together asking for alternate energy resources that are economically viable and environmentally justifiable. However, in India's energy basket non-renewable fossil fuels are playing and will continue to play a dominant role. But these resources need to be used sensibly since they are limited and polluting. Renewable energy resources, on the other hand, are indigenous, non-polluting and non-exhaustible, and their use should be encouraged in every possible manner. India's dependence on petroleum-based fuels makes energy security more vulnerable. India's total final energy consumption by source in 2016 was dominated by oil products amounting to more than 31 per cent followed by coal and natural gas which accounted to 17 per cent and 6 per cent, respectively. India is still a net importer of energy products and its energy imports have increased by more than 53 per cent from 2010 to 2016 (Figure 4.10).

Therefore, these resources need to be supplemented and substituted by alternative renewable energy resources. Energy derived from biofuels enables energy security while addressing concerns about suppression of CO_2 emissions. In India, the transportation sector has been

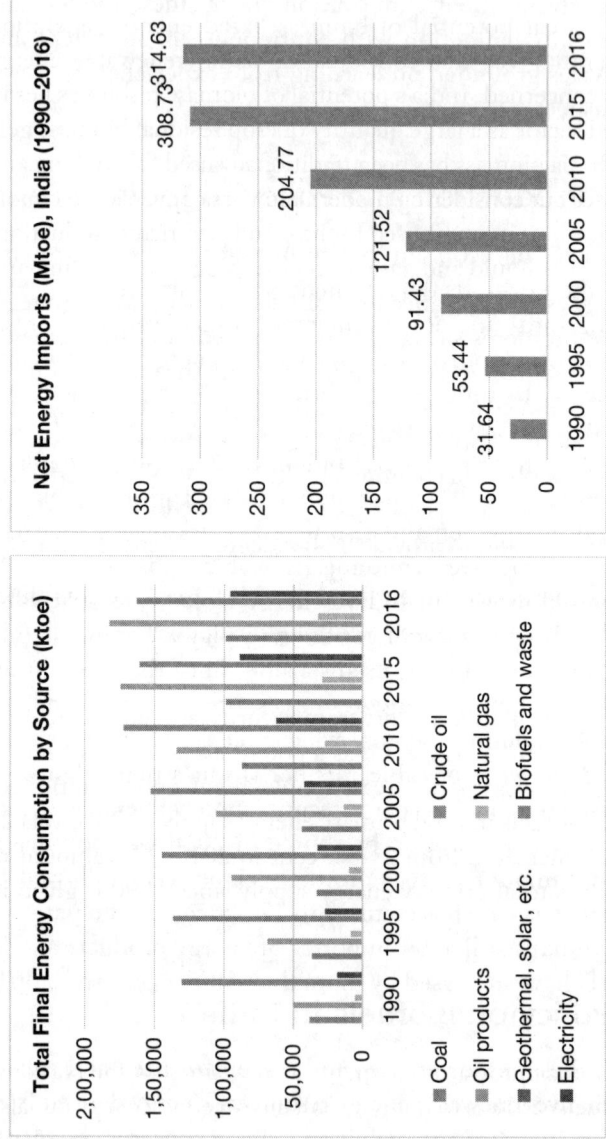

Figure 4.10 *Total Final Consumption and Net Imports of Energy Sources in India*
Source: IEA (2019).

identified as the main polluting sector and bioenergy use is therefore compelling to reduce harmful gas emissions to curb air pollution.

India has a great potential of biomass-based energy generation and it is currently given due consideration as far renewable energy programme is concerned. India's potential of biomass resources lies in the agricultural sector as a large quantity of crop residual biomass gets generated. In India biomass has been traditionally used for cooking and heating purposes but considering modern biomass conversion technologies and innovations it can be used for heat and electricity production, in transportation as liquid and gaseous fuel, as biogas for cooking and so on. Bioenergy as an alternative to fossil fuels is encouraged strategically because it promotes sustainable development and supplements the conventional sources of energy while meeting the energy requirements of vast Indian population particularly in rural areas. Biofuels have the potential to satisfy the increasing energy demands driven by high economic growth in an environmentally benign and cost-effective manner. They are also encouraged particularly to reduce dependence on fossil fuel imports and to provide higher degrees of energy security.

Globally bioenergy accounted for about 11 per cent of total final energy consumption and 1.85 per cent of global power generation in 2016 (Figure 4.11).

In developing economies, apart from security and environmental considerations, bioenergy is viewed as a potential means to stimulate development in rural areas to create employment opportunities. In India, share of biofuels in total primary energy supply in 2016 was 22 per cent, which increased from 21 per cent in 2015. The amount of biofuels in India's total primary energy supply since 1990 is given in Figure 4.12

National Policy on Biofuels in India

The Indian approach towards bioenergy as contained in the National Policy on Biofuels, 2018 is to not only enhance energy security but also to maintain food security. Therefore, the policy document's emphasis is not on traditional food feedstocks but solely on non-food feedstocks

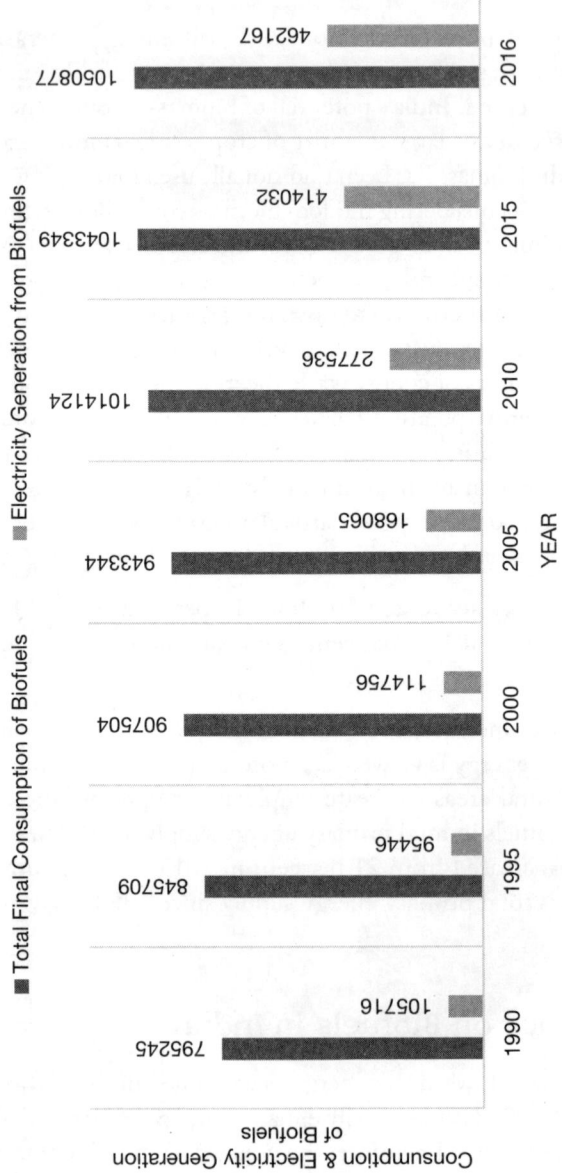

Figure 4.11 Total Final Consumption of and Electricity Generation from Biofuels

Source: IRENA (2019).

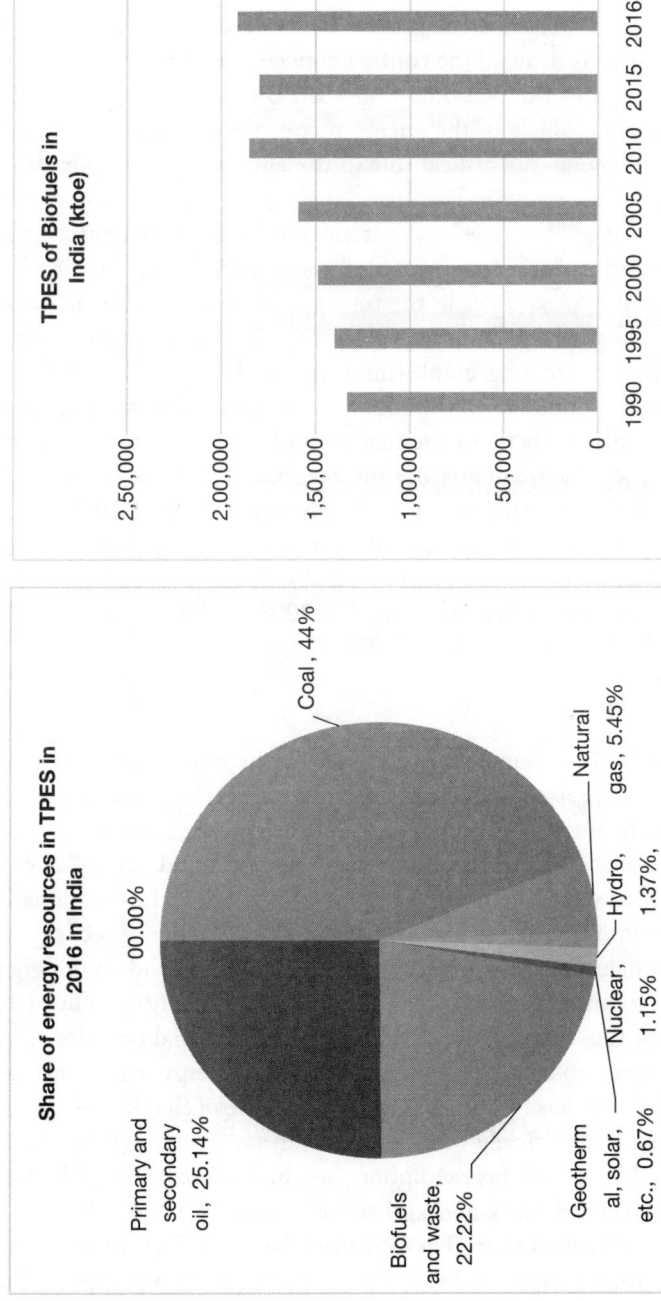

Figure 4.12 *Share of Energy Resources in TPES and Total Primary Supply of Bioenergy in India*
Source: IEA (2019).

which are to be raised on degraded lands or wastelands. In other words, the goal is to avoid the conflict between fuel and food security. The prime aim of the National Policy on Biofuels is to give central importance to biofuels in the energy mix of the country. Therefore, it envisions bioenergy's critical role in the energy and transportation sectors of the economy in the upcoming decades. The vision of the Policy is to augment development as well as advancement of the cultivation, production and use of biofuels so that biofuels can supplement/substitute petro fuels in the transportation sector. Bioenergy is expected to assume a major role in ensuring energy security, mitigating climate change, creating employment opportunities and promoting sustainable development in the country. To ensure minimum level of biofuels readily available in the market and to meet rising demands at any time are the main goals of the National Policy on Biofuels. A proposed and indicative target of 20 per cent blending of biofuels has already been put in agenda both for bio-diesel and bio-ethanol. Bio-ethanol's blending level was made obligatory that lead up to the indicative target effective from October 2008.

Conclusion

Bioenergy has been a major achievement in the sense that it has enabled nations to strengthen national energy security by substituting significant quantities of imported fossil fuel products with biofuels. Given this success, governments across the world and particularly in the developed world are now promoting biofuels as an internationally traded commodity. To achieve the objectives of energy security as well as climate change mitigation, bioenergy sector had to undergo important technological and organizational transformations. The main objective of this chapter was to highlight the potential benefits of an alternate renewable energy source called as bioenergy. Bioenergy, as discussed above, has by and large grown because of fluctuating global oil prices and specifically onus goes to various government policies such as feed-in-tariffs, tax exemptions and biofuel mandates. This has led to connected energy and agricultural markets while influencing food and feed prices as well as land-use changes which in turn lead to apprehensions from food security and environmental outlook. The benefits of developing a bio-economy are seen with much optimism since substantial trade-offs and risks also exist. Bioenergy is promising in ensuring environmental sustainability and climate security in modern energy systems. Policy makers worldwide should use suitable assessment practices to influence the deployment of sustainable bioenergy. Proper assessment of environmental impacts should take the cognizance of different characteristics of various bioenergy cropping systems, positive as well as negative. It is proposed that bioenergy production can be sustainable only if it is based and supported by good governance, reliable scientific evidence, strong institutions, voluntary certification and proper management policies supporting sustainable use of resources and benefits biological diversity. It is through these strategies that bioenergy can help in realizing its potential in mitigating the extraordinary environmental and climate change that threaten the future of humankind.

Governments and policy makers around the world must enhance cooperation to encourage sustainability of bioenergy systems/structures in the context of rising global temperatures and their potential devastating impacts on humankind. The positive as well as negative impacts of bioenergy systems need robust assessments both at local and global level. It will help in the selection of new bioenergy croplands through strategic environmental impact assessments. Coordinative efforts among state governments, institutions at global level, nongovernmental organizations and private players need to be enhanced to achieve bioenergy goals, objectives and planning procedures. Therefore, it is important to identify the interconnectedness that exists between sectors such as forestry and agricultural policies so that bioenergy production and supply could be harmonized. Land organized for bioenergy should be avoided or minimized through encouraging bioenergy crops that have positive characteristics with respect to water use, soil impacts and biological diversity; the share of bioenergy derived from wastes and residuals should increase; the production of bioenergy should be integrated with systems of crop production and landscape planning; crop land productivity particularly in developing countries should be enhanced so that more land can be freed for bioenergy crops and deployment of waste, marginal, degraded and waste lands for bioenergy production. There is also a need to promote cross-sector data and gathering of information so that innovative designs and continuous monitoring systems of bioenergy can be informed. Socio-economic and environmental assessment integration should be promoted by adopting landscape approach of natural resources so that productivity of bioenergy, food, feedstocks, timber, environmental and ecological services such as hydrology, biological diversity, carbon and economic value can be enhanced which can serve as a benchmark for innovation framework. Bioenergy policies should also reflect short-term and long-term benefits, and costs to avoid or minimize social and environmental impacts while offering safer investment conditions. Development of financing schemes and business models must enable communities to gain from bioenergy projects especially from small-scale projects. Lastly, in a developing country like India apart from other considerations there is a need to conduct extensive research to clarify the impact of bioenergy production on rural and urban food security as well as understanding the catalytic role of bioenergy in promoting economic and agricultural development.

References

Elobeid, A., Carriquiry, M., Secchi, S., & Yu, T. (2013). Economics of bioenergy. *Economics Research International, 1,* 1–3.

Food and Agriculture Organization of the United Nations. (2008). *Biofuels: Prospects, risks and opportunities—The state of food and agriculture.* Rome: Author.

Global Energy Assessment (GEA). (2012). *Toward a sustainable future.* Cambridge: Cambridge University Press & Laxenburg: International Institute for Applied Systems Analysis.

GOI. (2018). *National policy on biofuels.* New Delhi: Ministry of New & Renewable Energy, 1–18.

Greenpeace. (2008). *Greenpeace policy on bioenergy* (Richert, W. Ed.). Amsterdam: Author.

Hochman, G. (2014). Economic policy analysis of advanced biofuels. *Choices, 29* (1), 1–2.

IEA. (2012). World Energy Outlook. http://www.worldenergyoutlook.org/publications/weo-2012/ - accessed March 2019

IEA. (2018). *World energy outlook 2018.* Paris: International Energy Agency.

IEA. (2019). *Renewable energy employment.* Retrieved from https://www.iea.org/statistics/renewables/

IRENA. (2019). *Renewable energy employment by country.* Retrieved from https://www.irena.org/Statistics/View-Data-by-Topic/Benefits/Renewable-Energy-Employment-by-Country

Kessler, E. (2012). Biofuels, climate change, and human population. In D. Pimental (Ed.), *Global economic and environmental aspects of biofuels.* Boca Raton, FL: CRC Press.

Khanna, M. (2008). Cellulosic biofuels: Are they economically viable and environmentally sustainable? *Choices, 23* (3), 16–21.

Khanna, M., Scheffran, J., & Zilberman, D. (Eds.). (2010). Bioenergy economics and policy: introduction and overview. *Handbook of bioenergy economics and policy.* New York, NY: Springer.

Msangi, S., Ewing, M., & Rosegrant, M. (2010). Biofuels and agricultural growth: challenges for developing agricultural economies and opportunities for investment. In Madhu Khanna, Jürgen Scheffran & David Zilberman (Eds.), *Handbook of bioenergy economics and policy.* New York, NY: Springer.

Msangi, S., Sulser, T., Rosegrant, M., & Valmonte-Santos, R. (2007). Global scenarios for biofuels: Impacts and implications. *Farm Policy Journal, 4* (2): 1–18.

Nogueira, L. A. H., Leal, M. R. L. V., Fernandes, E., Chum, H. L., Díaz-Chavez, R., Endres, J., ... van der Wielen, L. (2015). Sustainable development and innovation. In *Bioenergy & sustainability: Bridging the gaps.* Retrieved from http://rembio.org.mx/wp-content/uploads/2014/10/bioenergy_sustainability_scope-report.pdf

Pimentel, D. (Ed.). (2012). Biofuels cause malnutrition in the world. In *Global economic and environmental aspects of biofuels.* Boca Raton, FL: CRC Press.

REN21. (2013). *Renewables 2013 global status report* (p. 178). Paris: REN21 Secretariat.

Taheripour, F., & Tyner, E. W. (2008). Ethanol policy analysis-what have we learned so far? *Choices, 23* (3), 6–11

UNEP. (2009). *Towards sustainable production and use of resources: Assessing biofuels.* Paris: Author.

UNEP GRID Arendal. (2011). *Impacts of conventional biofuel production on agricultural prices.* Retrieved from http://www.grida.no/publications/vg/biofuels/- accessed March 2019.

Van Meijl, H., Smeets, E., & Zilberman, D. (2015). Bioenergy economics and policies. In G. M. Souza, R. L. Victoria, C. A. Joly & L. M. Verdade (eds.), *Bioenergy & sustainability: Bridging the gaps.* Retrieved from http://rembio.org.mx/wp-content/uploads/2014/10/bioenergy_sustainability_scope-report.pdf

Williams, G. L., Dahiya, A., & Porter, P. (2015). Introduction to bioenergy. In A. Dahiya (Ed.), *Bioenergy: Biomass to biofuels.* London: Academic Press.

CHAPTER 5

Energy Governance in India
A Conundrum of Competing Claims

Debasis Poddar

Introduction

In the wake of reasonable apprehension for catastrophic climate change across the world, followed by the national commitments of the Republic of India to the United Nations Framework Convention on Climate Change (UNFCCC) Secretariat, a climate watchdog on behalf of the United Nations (UN), stocktaking of relevant legislative instruments to bring in progress vis-à-vis climate discipline in India appears imperative. In the wake of 2020 in particular, several commitments were set to get complete by the deadline of 2020 with numeric rhetoric of its own.

Albeit too many statutes are incidentally connected to discipline climate by circuitous routes, there are but few—too few—connected to discipline climate with unambiguous legislative intent, for example, the Energy Conservation Act of 2001 and the Electricity Act of 2003. While the latter is primarily engaged in the market economic discourse, except piecemeal emphasis upon the generation of energy from renewable sources, there is want of substantive provisions to grapple with climate change. The forthcoming effort, therefore, revolves around the former to decipher the governmentality behind the purpose of the statute apparent in its nomenclature itself. Whether and how far the statute serves the legislative intent (energy conservation) constitutes the moot point raised by the author. Also, the author strives to testify the premise with reasoning of his own to fix climate diplomacy played out by India to carry forward its parochial energy agenda ahead.

To initiate review of the given statutory regime for energy conservation, that is, the Energy Conservation Act of 2001, besides other legislative instruments, let us explore the history of energy governance in India. Way back since the Stockholm Conference of 1972, India emerged as a responsible stakeholder in global environmental governance to turn the table on the then bipolar politics. A newer genre, environmental politics, thereby got initiated to supplement ideological politics. In its initial years, therefore, concern was concentrated upon rudimentary issues, for example quality of soil, water and air, and compassion for flora and fauna, endangered species in particular. Since all these were connected to the development discourse in a way or other, environmental politics did suit India to get the voice of the then Non-aligned Movement (NAM) heard across the world, thereby spearheading its own agenda.

However, from the 1980s onwards,[1] India has been stuck to its own politics. On one side, an emerging economy, India got distanced from the NAM realpolitik. On the other, in course of 'tryst with destiny' toward energy sovereignty, Nehruvian India went ridden with the struggle between two priority areas of concern: economy and environment: none was lesser than other anyway. Thus, energy and environment were juxtaposed, with the immediate consequence that India got trapped—along with China—on the receiving end. Also, initiated with naïve issues, the ozone debate flagged off the

---

[1] Vide the Vienna Convention for the Protection of the Ozone Layer, 1985. Also, the Montreal Protocol on the Substances that Deplete the Ozone Layer, 1987.

void between energy and environment as if they were binary opposites of one another. Thereafter, 1992 onwards, the UNFCCC regime[2] initiated its course to discipline climate sinners including India. As a responsible stakeholder, India initiated reforms in its environmental governance through several statutes. While the connectivity between energy and environment was proved beyond reasonable doubt, India was left with no other option but to continue the reforms through introduction of the Energy Conservation Act, 2001, thereby carrying forward the legacy of docility. Indeed, not documented, the legislative intent may get substantiated by the circumstantial evidence vis-à-vis chronology of international instruments, followed by statutory compliance—albeit arguably. For instance, basic legislations followed the Stockholm Declaration of 1972,[3] a comprehensive statute and another on public insurance liability were enacted to reflect knee-jerk effect of the mass disaster after leakage at commercial premises of the Union Carbide Corporation in Bhopal.[4] Likewise, statutes upon energy conservation and biodiversity were enacted as a result of commitments made by India in the forum of Rio, 1992.[5] Taken together, this may reasonably get derived that the energy law in India has had its genesis in the contemporary polemics across the world. As per the text of the statute, conservation and efficiency were taken interchangeably. While the title of the statute spells energy conservation, provisions therein establish institutional apparatus of the Bureau to ascertain energy efficiency accordingly.

Epistemic Limits in Energy Jurisprudence

In the hitherto political economy across the world, India appears to be no exception to this end, energy governance is stuck to discursive limits of its own. Two dominant genres govern global energy economy to minimize the given conflict between energy and environment, that is,

---

[2] Vide the United Nations Framework Convention on Climate Change of 1992, read with the Kyoto Protocol, 1997.

[3] The Water (Prevention and Control of Pollution) Act, 1974 and The Air (Prevention and Control of Pollution) Act, 1981.

[4] The Environment (Protection) Act, 1986.

The Public Liability Insurance Act, 1991.

[5] The Energy Conservation Act, 2001, and The Biological Diversity Act, 2002.

conservation and efficiency. They are most often than not conceptualized interchangeably while there are borderlines between these two otherwise different genres, albeit with several occasions of functional overlap inter se.[6] So far as nomenclature is concerned, 'conservation' refers to optimization of demand with supply by restraint in consumption out of utilitarian consideration to maximize pleasure vis-à-vis availability of energy and minimize pain vis-à-vis unavailability of energy. On the contrary, energy efficiency is a product of poles apart discourse—to continue the consumption pattern with technology which is efficient enough to reduce the incidental environmental cost out of energy consumption. To quote from the wisdom of a veteran, Andrew Rudin (quoted in Herring, 2006), 'While energy efficiency tells us what to buy, energy conservation tells us how to behave.' Indeed, another side of the same coin of utilitarianism, energy efficiency need not call for restraint, something disliked by the hedonist West. The underlying fallacy lies here: (a) Despite the given (read aggressive) consumption pattern getting proven antithetical to sustainability, energy conservation calls for the restraint upon the same as a strategy to slow down the catastrophic climate change. (b) Energy efficiency appears a step ahead and does not call for restraint. To the advocates of energy efficiency, consumption ought to get neutral to environment and the same may get done by better efficiency in technology, nothing more and nothing else. To get candid, none of these genres calls for restraint upon the behavioural pattern, that is, upon the given (read aggressive) consumption pattern, on the basis of principles.

---

[6] 'Energy efficiency' and 'energy conservation' are terms which are often used interchangeably, but which mean different things.

· · · · · · · · ·

It was in the wake of the 1973 oil crisis that most countries first became interested in the scope for reducing energy consumption as a means of lessening dependence upon imported oil. The term 'energy conservation' thus came to be used to encompass a wide range of actions such as restricting electricity supply to consumers at certain times, rationing petrol supplies, encouraging people to insulate buildings, alter thermostats, switch off lights and setting minimum efficiency standards for appliances.

Until the 1980s, the term 'energy conservation' was widely used. However, during the 1980s, most of the English-speaking countries—United Kingdom, United States, Canada and Australia—tended to switch to the term 'energy efficiency'(Owen, 2000).

Both conservation and efficiency are meant to ascertain the continuity of productivity. So far as productivity is concerned, capitalism and socialism have had synergy since both these genres have been concerned about the state of affairs during the early industrial era. Therefore, resort to socialism cannot settle the energy-environment debate; despite the same getting systemic syndrome for capitalist energy economy. Apart from production relations, there is little difference between classical capitalism and classical socialism since both are two sides of the same coin. After all, both Adam Smith and Karl Marx are children of their given time and space, they thereby preach the utilitarian model of interest to spearhead respective politics of their own.[7, 8] In the name of reform, otherwise *bona fide* concern for conservation and efficiency-get the given production pattern and the consequent uncertainty perpetuated. Neither Smith nor Marx raised the most rudimentary questions vis-à-vis environmental cost of production; something beyond the foresight of time and space they lived. The discursive concern for environment is a characteristic of the post-industrial society, something that went uncontested by either genre—conservation and efficiency. At bottom, both are troubleshooters to make production unproblematic. They never contest consumption since the same ought to turn production problematic. Same is also the case of the organogram of the UN institutional apparatus; both the UNFCCC and the International Labour Organization (ILO) serve the same purpose. Despite the diversified domains, both

[7] It is not from the benevolence of the butcher, the brewer, or the baker, that we expect our dinner, but from their regard to their own interest. We address ourselves, not to their humanity but to their self-love, and never talk to them of our own necessities but of their advantages. Nobody but a beggar depends chiefly upon the benevolence of his fellow citizens. (Smith, 1981)

[8] The bourgeoisie keeps more and more doing away with the scattered state of the population, of the means of production, and of property. It has agglomerated population, centralized the means of production, and has concentrated property in a few hands. The necessary consequence of this was political centralization. Independent, or but loosely connected provinces, with separate interests, laws, governments, and systems of taxation, became lumped together into one nation, with one government, one code of laws, one national class-interest, one frontier, and one customs-tariff. (Marx & Engels, 1848)

spearhead reforms with the status quo approach to avert radical forces and subvert the system, be it climate change or class struggle. Likewise, energy conservation and energy efficiency are ridden with piecemeal approach, with no intent to cure the given crisis from within. Indeed, irony of fact, while the ILO was established immediately after the USSR took off, the UNFCCC was established immediately after the USSR broke down. The anti-establishment legacy thereby turns to nature once again, the way ancient tribesmen initiated their ordeal to cope with nature. To quote Eliot (1934),

> The cycles of heaven in twenty centuries
> Bring us farther from God and nearer to the Dust.

Not without reason that in the age of energy efficiency through recourse to technology, recourse to religion is back, along with prejudices involved therein since human agency fell short of getting good energy governance, and thereby returned to the ancient antiquity; where the civilization once initiated its ordeal to cope with natural order. In ancient times, faith in the Almighty was handy to cope with nature. Indeed, modernity introduced reason to replace faith, but reason succumbed to vested interests. Consequently, reason fell short of getting nature neutralized while vested interests wreaked havoc on nature. While renewable energy is required, atomic energy is getting advocated and the UNFCCC observes silence since the UN cannot afford to call a spade a spade with its headquarters at New York. What appears missing is virtue, after Montesquieu (1748),[9] something essential for reasoning not to get corrupt by vested interests. In final count, *salus populi suprema lex*: Public interest is the supreme law of the land.

In the absence of virtue, reasoning behind public policymaking was vitiated and turned reason to another evil force in the same way religion was reduced to mundane rites and rituals, and thereby turned to

---

[9] Virtue in a republic is a most simple thing; it is a love of the republic; it is a sensation, and not a consequence of acquired knowledge; a sensation that may be felt by the meanest as well as by the highest person in the state. When the common people adopt good maxims, they adhere to them steadier than those we call gentlemen. It is very rare that corruption commences with the former: nay, they frequently derive from their imperfect light a stronger attachment to the established laws and customs.

bigotry followed by myriad evils. Reasoning behind the energy regime suffers from want of virtue and here is the fallacy. After the sunset of left-wing politics, the way right-wing politics is back and across the contemporary world there is resurrection of religion to replace reason devoid of virtue.

Class Characteristics of the Energy Regime

The energy regime, in India and elsewhere alike, has had class characteristics of its own and the same suffers from bias in favour of the gentry reining the contemporary society across the world. Thus, in the course of energy governance, domains where the global poor operate are subjected to disproportionate discipline. But, the domains where the global elite operate earn indulgence of the people in power. Irrespective of the political character of the regime concerned, global environmental regime follows class characteristics of its own, the same way global economic regime by and large follows the capitalist legacy. In India, the given environmental governance speaks for class character on its own. For instance, under Section 51 of the Wildlife (Protection) Act of 1972 (http://nbaindia.org/uploaded/Biodiversityindia/ Legal/15.%20Wildlife%20(Protection)%20Act,%201972.pdf) pecuniary cap of the penalties for poachers engaged in illegal trade amounts to 25,000 rupees, something de minimis compared to market value of their illegal target products. The pecuniary cap of penalties to punish tribesmen for illegal access to forest produces under Section 7 of the Scheduled Tribes and Other Forest Dwellers (Recognition of Forest Rights) Act of 2006 (https://tribal.nic.in/FRA/data/FRARulesBook. pdf) amounts to 1,000 rupees, something deterrent enough compared to economic standards of the poor tribesmen dependent upon forest produces. Also, even within the wildlife protection regime, poachers themselves are not predators. These poor men act for monsters to earn petty amounts to maintain themselves. If poachers are caught, the monsters withdraw patronage and hire others for the crime, while the statecraft turns savage and demonstrates punitive deterrence upon these small players. Despite the illegal trade in endangered species getting condemned and poachers being caught, the trade appears on its rise due to want of prudence in the given wildlife jurisprudence. In contrast, due to want of prudence in forest rights jurisprudence, left-wing extremism appears on its rise in the forestry to regiment traditional forest dwellers against the state. Consequently, with the rise in wildlife savagery on one side and left-wing regimentation on the other, forestry emerges as a 'no-go zone' for wildlife administration.

So far as energy governance is concerned, an effort is on to get the focus of the regime diversified towards the multilateral approach and thereby generate comprehensive coverage to sustain carrying capacity of planet Earth. Indeed, prima facie impressive enough, there is but scepticism that the same is run by realpolitik of the occidental hemisphere to shift focus of news headlines elsewhere, thereby tricking global energy governance. In the post-bipolar world, 'the Merchants of Venice', merchants incorporated (under regulatory regime for statutory registration as companies) in particular, set the energy regime to suit their mercantile agenda. Thus, the global elites put the climate to peril. In turn, the myriad evils push the global poor to pandemonium.

In global energy governance, for instance, the developed hemisphere commits the sin while the developing hemisphere pays the price despite lesser contribution to emission. Several small island states are set to get inundated to the seas[10]; also, developing states across the tropics are likely to get hit by erratic weather syndrome in time ahead.[11] Thus, in the community of nation states, mighty states commit the climate sin to the detriment of commoners across the world. Similar is the case for national energy regime in India. While the given electricity regime primarily provides for commercial legal framework, the energy regime primarily provides for institutional framework through establishment of the Bureau of Energy Efficiency

[10] It has long been recognized that greenhouse gas emissions from small islands are negligible in relation to global emissions, but that the threats of climate change and sea level rise to small islands are very real. Indeed, it has been suggested that the very existence of some atoll nations is threatened by rising sea levels associated with global warming. (Nurse et al., 2014)

[11] Major monsoon systems are associated with the seasonal movement of convergence zones over land, leading to profound seasonal changes in local hydrological cycles. Section 14.2 assesses current understanding of monsoonal behaviour in the present and future climate, how monsoon characteristics are influenced by the large-scale tropical modes of variability and their potential changes and how the monsoons in turn affect regional extremes. (Christensen et al., 2013)

(BEE) with its functional domains getting specified. The same saga vis-à-vis bias stands reflected in the statutory regime.

The Energy Conservation Act of 2001 was meant to establish the BEE and the same initiated its operation on 1 March 2002. An advisory agency, the BEE has had three regulatory functions, independent, yet interconnected, to attain energy efficiency:

1. Standards and labelling of electrical appliances
2. Energy conservation codification for buildings
3. Energy conservation normativity for industries

The technical nitty-gritty apart, all three variants mentioned above speak for themselves. After the launch of National Action Plan on Climate Change (NAPCC) of 2008, the BEE operated as its nodal agency to spearhead the National Mission on Energy Efficiency. Thus, coexistence of two genres—conservation and efficiency—in the same statutory regime may get read as an effort to attain synergy, albeit arguably. In practice, however, the BEE is reduced to a state-sponsored think tank with its given statutory mandate to recommend to the central Government,[12] thereby hinting whether and how far recommendations will be entertained is left to Government if the corollary implication from Ajay Mathur—former director of the BEE—stands as it is (Kandhari & Umashankar, 2015). What went missing, yet deserve cognizance, are 18 other provisions in Section 13 of the Act whereby the legislative intent went clear and unambiguous upon the BEE to build an ecosystem vis-à-vis energy efficiency, something yet to transcend the threshold of utility. Besides, market-driven policymaking of the BEE—as articulated by Mathur—ought to offer a speed-breaker to energy efficiency while climate change appears as a global emergency.[13] Consequently, the wish list of the

---

[12] Vide Sections 13(2) (a), (b) and (c) of the Energy Conservation Act of 2001.
[13] How much of this (statutory) mandate has it (BEE) carried out?

We bring new appliances for standards and labelling on voluntary basis and advertise about the labels. If the consumer finds them useful, meaning, if the consumer starts buying those products, we make the programme mandatory. (Kandhari & Umashankar, 2015)

BEE takes an aspirant take-off—as drawn by the Director Abhay Bakre[14]—with chronic lethargy since its establishment, something that hardly suits to think tanks running the energy regime. The BEE has had the potential to emerge as an energy watchdog to bring in reform well within the given statutory corpus. Subject to political will, the BEE appears blessed with powers to accelerate the energy regime. For instance, it may move to the apex court with prayer for guidelines to spearhead energy justice through residual clause under Section 13(2) (e) of the Act—the way non-governmental think tanks push their cause of action to the court. With judicial trapping, guidelines ought to earn better legal sanctity for the community. Also, it may set reasonable standards for appliances, buildings and industries on its own and insist stakeholders in the market—both sides alike—to act upon the given standards, thereby accelerate energy efficiency. Besides, logistically prudent measures are required to get the entrepreneurship of those designated under the Act sustainable enough. All these are suggestive, with the given inventory getting inclusive.

The BEE is whistling upon standards of appliances and buildings, rather than industries, thereby earning discredit of slumbering upon big players. The ground reality, however, deserves the technical agency to act in the opposite manner since with its given intensity and frequency, industrial emission constitutes the Achilles' heel for energy governance across the world. While clarion call is issued by the UNFCCC for global climate action,[15] such inaction appears

[14]What are BEE's top priorities over the next two to three years?

Firstly, to accelerate the implementation of building energy efficiency programmes across the country. We would also fast-track industrial energy efficiency improvement by establishing robust infrastructure to support energy efficiency financing. Another priority is to improve the enforcement mechanism for ensuring compliance with set energy efficiency norms and standards. Further, we will focus on expanding energy efficiency improvements in the transportation sector, including the promotion of electric vehicles. (Power Line, 2017)

[15] For details, refer to full programme of the Global Climate Action Events at COP24. Retrieved from https://unfccc.int/climate-action/events/global-climate-action-events-at-cop24-full-programme>

unbecoming of the BEE as an energy watchdog. Taking cue from a literary classic, 'To BEE or not to BEE, that is the question.' Also, the same appears inimical to India with aspirations to usurp the global leadership.[16] Despite its inconvenience, therefore, India is left with no other option but to respect international environmental obligations, climate obligations in particular. The energy governance driven by the BEE, more so while the same is a nodal agency for the NAPCC, has had potential to offer cutting edge to draw the roadmap of India as a messiah in time ahead. International aspirations apart, respect for multilateral environmental agreements—where India is a party—is imperative after its own Directive Principle of State Policy.[17] Interestingly enough, energy-aspirant India kept no stone unturned to find fault lines in these agreements and thereby escaped object and purpose of the global climate regime.

For instance, as part of market-driven mechanism, there is a provision for international emissions trade in favour of state parties to the UNFCCC, something contentious enough and thereby earned criticism due to its potential to subvert the regime from within.[18] India has adopted the same to its advantage. Subsequently, under

[16] Climate change poses particularly difficult challenges for India. On the one hand, India does not want any constraints on its development prospects. On the other, it also wants to be seen as an emerging global power. While the former may be best served by its current position, the latter will, however, require it to take leadership role on key global issues—climate change being a critical one. (Kapur, Khosla, & Mehta, 2009)

[17] For details, refer to Article 51(c) under Part IV of the Constitution of India, 1950.

[18] Article 17 of the Kyoto Protocol to the United Nations Framework Convention on Climate (Retrieved from https://unfccc.int/sites/default/files/kpeng.pdf) Change states:

The Conference of the Parties shall define the relevant principles, modalities, rules and guidelines, in particular for verification, reporting and accountabili/ty for emissions trading. The Parties included in Annex B may participate in emissions trading for the purposes of fulfilling their commitments under Article 3. Any such trading shall be supplemental to domestic actions for the purpose of meeting quantified emission limitation and reduction commitments under that Article.

the disguise of reform in the given energy regime, India followed the clause to hoodwink object and purpose of the national energy conservation regime.[19] At bottom, through resort to such market economic tricks, sustainable climate is put to jeopardy. The default object and purpose behind capping lies in conservation through restraint in emissions of the greenhouse gas (GHG) substance. Thus, rationale lies in the restraint of national consumption pattern for each state party. Emissions trade dilutes the very rationale of restraint through the shift of consumption elsewhere, something not at all in tandem with object and purpose of the climate regime. The impugned provision of the Kyoto Protocol has had vices to get construed ultra vires to the UNFCCC of 1992. India has introduced the same in its internal legal regime while (a) India is not party to the same; (b) the Kyoto commitment is nearing the given deadline. Indeed, India went incredible through resort to lapse of the multilateral environmental agreement while not getting bound by those doable under the same. Apart from the query, whether and how far such clandestine social engineering facilitates emerging economy, the same ought to defeat the agenda of global leadership for India.

Another lapse in the national energy conservation regime lies in remedial provisions under the Act, after the amendment in particular. Accordingly, the earlier penalty amount for excessive energy consumption stands multiplied manifold to shoot through the roof

---

[19] After section 14 of the principal Act, the following sections shall be inserted, namely:

14A. (*1*) The Central Government may issue the energy savings certificate to the designated consumer whose energy consumption is less than the prescribed norms and standards in accordance with the procedure as may be prescribed.

(*2*) The designated consumer whose energy consumption is more than the prescribed norms and standards shall be entitled to purchase the energy savings certificate to comply with the prescribed norms and standards.14B. The Central Government may, in consultation with the Bureau, prescribe the value of per metric ton of oil equivalent of energy consumed for the purposes of this Act.'

(The Energy Conservation (Amendment) Act, 2010; Section 7)

for defaulters.[20] The rationale behind the same appears prima facie reasonable enough that the escalation of penalty amounts is meant to invoke deterrence against defaulters. A minute reading of the statutory regime, but, raises scepticism about such otherwise unproblematic jurisprudence since the institutional apparatus that is, Appellate Tribunal for Energy Conservation under the Act, for disposal of the cases is yet to be constituted till date, sporadic conversation apart.[21] Thus, in the absence of institutional presence, there is no conviction followed by penalties to fix the crisis of excessive consumption. With ritual presence of the BEE in advisory role on one side and absence of the tribunal for disposal of cases on the other, the given system is reduced to naught.

Besides, even if the institutional apparatus is constituted, deterrent amount of the penalty for excessive consumption ought to provoke corrupt practices to hoodwink the system, something public administration of India cannot afford with its transparency scoreboard one among the worst in the world. Low-risk business ought to indulge in wrongs. Same is the case wherever the bribery is institutionalized and India is no exception to this end. Thus, at the very threshold of institutional proceeding, the matter is likely to get settled to mutual

[20] The Energy Conservation (Amendment) Act, 2010, Section 8 provides:

In section 26 of the principal Act,-

a) in sub-section (1),-
    i)   the words, brackets and letter 'or clause (n)' shall be omitted;
    ii) for the words 'ten thousand rupees', the words 'ten lakh rupees' shall be substituted;
    iii) for the words 'one thousand rupees', the words 'ten thousand rupees' shall be substituted;
b) after sub-section (*l*), the following sub-section shall be inserted, namely:

'(1A) If any person fails to comply with the provisions of clause (n) of section 14, he shall be liable to a penalty which shall not exceed ten lakh rupees and, in the case of continuing failure, with an additional penalty which shall not be less than the price of every metric ton of oil equivalent of energy, prescribed under this Act, that is in excess of the prescribed norms.'

[21] The Energy Conservation Act, 2001, Section 30 states, The Central Government shall, by notification, establish an Appellate Tribunal to be known as the Appellate Tribunal for Energy Conservation to hear appeals against the orders of the adjudicating officer or the Central Government or the State Government or any other authority under this Act.

satisfaction of both sides, for example, sinners and sentinels alike, with the patronage of deterrent amount of the penalty. The amount appears enough to create the ecosystem for low-risk business, thereby indulge in corrupt practices. Whether or how far tribunal may be fortified is a point apart and beyond purview of this effort.

Political Economy of the Renewable Energy

A trend appears in the offing to advance the *arguendo* for renewable energy as panacea of hitherto climate crises. Accordingly, after the trend, renewable energy has emerged as messiah of the world in the wake of apprehension for climate change to such extent that the shift to renewable energy is elevated to icon of integrity for the UNFCCC regime. Regrettably, despite ocular opulence, the given position suffers from epistemic fallacy on several counts: (a) the fiction of renewable energy is hardly corroborated by science. Rather, the rising reliance upon renewable energy has had manifold cost upon the larger development discourse to the travesty of sustainability; something most often than not went unnoticed in the whirlpool of hitherto climate debate since the same suited to the intent of vested interest of the West as default forerunner in the marathon race of the civilization. (b) So also is the case of contemporary political economy vis-à-vis renewable energy since the same is ridden with hidden consequences. Taken together, renewable energy has had hurdles of its own to supplant the resource out of fossil fuel. While fossil fuel ought to get subjected to phase out without doubt, a moot point may get raised: Whether and how far replacement is devoid of the void and how to avoid the same in time ahead to gallop for affordable and clean energy, after the given UN-set agenda.[22]

To get candid, renewable energy appears loaded enough with the renewed apprehension vis-à-vis environmental disaster. Besides, the contemporary renewable energy advocacy is charged with the real-politik to get hitherto economic agenda of the West perpetuated. In the given energy discourse, therefore, renewable energy falls short of

---

[22] Vide Sustainable Development Goal 7. Retrieved from https://sustainabledevelopment.un.org/sdg7.

getting justice upheld throughout the world. The caveat hereby raised is not meant to get the fossil fuel economy fortified but to flag-off the lapse in the renewable energy economy in practice for comparative study of competing—sometimes conflicting—claims in these two genres inter se, thereby carve out a creative energy jurisprudence for sustainable development of the civilization. At bottom, this effort is meant to get the energy debate disillusioned about the sacrosanctity of either resource anyway.

With the given purpose of ecological economy,[23] while states engage public exchequer in a quest for sustainable energy economy,[24] the epistemic premise for renewable energy economy ought to stand tenable enough and thereby prove better than fossil fuel economy in cost–benefit analysis between them. Here lies a fallacy in major renewables as green resources. For instance, the so-called green energy is stuck to 'rare earth effect', something acknowledged at large. These solar panels and wind turbine materials contain rarest minerals and excavation of these minerals requires extraction of contaminated mine wreckage en masse in disproportionate quantity to get sustainability messed up (Driessen, 2011).[25] The given statement needs little articulation since the veteran readership is well versed in hard facts uncontested

---

[23] ... if the operation of the subsystem, the economy, is not compatible with the behavior of the larger system—the earth's ecosystem—both will eventually suffer. The larger the economy becomes relative to the ecosystem, and the more it presses against the earth's natural limits, the more destructive this incompatibility will be.

An environmentally sustainable economy—an eco-economy—requires that the principles of ecology establish the framework for the formulation of economic policy and that economists and ecologists work together to fashion the new economy. (Brown, 2001)

[24] This transition is now building its own momentum, driven by an intense excitement from the realization that we are tapping energy sources that can last as long as the earth itself. Oil wells go dry and coal seams run out, but for the first time since the Industrial Revolution began we are investing in energy sources that can last forever. (Brown, 2009)

[25] For details, refer to Klinger (2017).

in the public domain. Even otherwise, cost–benefit analyses apart, there lies jurisprudent reasoning against the proposed paradigm shift—from the fuel to the renewable—in hurry, with worry for sustainability getting doomed. Thus, plenty of questions may and do arise upon the intellectual integrity of intergenerational equity which thereby gets renewable energy advocacy silenced due to want of answers to the same.[26] In the anxiety of equity of generations ahead, whether and how far equity of those present in real life and in real time may get compromised pose a moot point contentious enough to get subjected to public debate. Rather than getting consumption justified, the author intends to expose otherwise unproblematic mythology behind environmental buzzwords and the governmentality involved therein to get the global public behaviour customized (read disciplined) the way those in power wish. With clandestine scientific reasoning, by courtesy precautionary principle, legal recourse is reversed. The law follows the fact by default. For instance, the legal recourse acts upon offences and wrongs committed, and not reverse. Here, under the disguise of prevention, the so-called precautionary principle but drives the law to cure something yet to arrive at in public life. Thus, the law is put to the quixotic rush to engage unreal struggle against the

---

[26] Mankind advanced at a snail's pace for thousands of years. As the modern fossil-fuel industrial era found its footing, progress picked up at an increasingly breathtaking pace. Today, change is exponential. As we moved from flint to copper, to bronze, iron, steel and beyond, we didn't do so because mankind had exhausted Earth's supplies of flint, copper, tin and so on. We did it because we innovated–invented something better, more efficient or practical. Each advance required different raw materials.

Who today can foresee what technologies future generations will have 25, 50 or 200 years from now? What raw materials they will need? How we are supposed to ensure that those families meet their needs?

Why then would we even think of empowering government to regulate today's activities today based on the wholly unpredictable technologies, lifestyles, needs, and resource demands of distant generations? Why would we ignore or compromise the needs of current generations, to meet those totally unpredictable future needs-including the needs of today's most impoverished, energy-deprived, malnourished people, who desperately want to improve their lives? (Driessen, 2017)

non-existent and the public receives system-sponsored scientific (!) sermon to suffer from energy starvation forever; thereby, the state apparatus copes with the environmental problem non-existent and serves the people non-existent. These rites and rituals are but in practice at the cost of access to energy—a basic human right—for those innumerable commoners who exist and suffer in real life and in real time. At bottom, what appears missing is falsifiability as one among epistemic markers of science. Also, official patronage for emissions trade well within the given climate regime[27] (Klinger, 2017) corroborates the inbuilt scepticism hereby raised: upon intellectual integrity in the given energy governance. Taken together, contradiction in otherwise unproblematic *arguendo* for the renewable energy advocacy went apparent with a curtain call for the reverse side of the 'inconvenient truth'—by courtesy, Al Gore.[28] The author hereby swears, with affidavit in good faith, that

[27] The term (rare earths) is extended to incorporate other elements as technology and politics change. although the name is hardly an accurate descriptor for this suite of soft, ductile metals, it continues to function as a politically expedient term in the ongoing quest to acquire these resources, whether the intention is to avoid or impose the hazards associated with their extraction in specific places. For more details, refer to Klinger (2017).

[28] The notion that we are running out of energy (and metal) resources also reflects an abysmal grasp of basic mineral economic principles. 'Proven reserves' is not a static number. It reflects what we can expect to extract from known deposits at a particular commodity price and with existing technology. As more deposits are discovered, prices increase, and technologies improve, proven reserve numbers also rise, often dramatically.

... ...

Moreover, societal needs and scientific breakthroughs constantly change the kinds and amounts of energy, metallic and non-metallic resources we need.

... ...

Third and most important, for Northern Hemisphere NGOs and policy makers to tell Third World nations that they must rely on wind and solar power-and forego hydroelectric or fossil fuel projects-is to deprive the world's poorest citizens of reliable, affordable energy. It condemns billions of people to continued poverty and misery.

(Driessen, 2003)

this effort is not meant to get the given hedonistic consumption pattern under the disguise of eco-scepticism endorsed sans reasonable heed to the life-sustaining climate. With due concern for environment, an unpopular perspective went sounded to decipher the realpolitik behind eco-economy. Even without scepticism to global climate change ahead, as apprehended by the IPCC, the global public has had cynicism upon the given scepticism and the crux of its communique, albeit with innuendo, lies in sermons for the global poor continue their sacrifice (read suicide)- the way they have endured so far- and, now onward, to serve the cause of climate, thereby paying the price for the sinister development enterprise indulged in by the gentry.

The assumption advanced, albeit appears prejudiced by polemics—and at times politics—of the global south may get substantiated by the recent Indo–US solar panel case where the struggle between free trade and protection of infant industries constituted the case.[29] Both the panel and the appellate body under the WTO dispute settlement mechanism upheld the former despite the given fact that the latter was meant to mainstream the trend of home-grown solar energy by public procurement system, not in the open market.[30,31] With their institutional commitment toward free trade, what went missing was fair trade towards good governance in the open market economy.

Last yet not least, a corollary inference may get drawn to expose the green imperialism in disguise, while the same appears on its rise. The WTO's position demonstrates insignia of the trend: that the West ought to usurp the producer (the supplier at its least) to get the rest of the world reduced to the consumer, a conventional cliché vis-à-vis orchestrated demand–supply cycle by default served in the niche of international trade. The position resembles green diplomacy of the developed hemisphere to get imperial trade extended through export of the green technology either way: through finished product or, at least, raw materials, as the case may be. Thus, what went once

[29] For details, refer to Jayagovind (2016).
[30] For details, refer to WTO, 2016 (24 February).
[31] For details, refer to WTO, 2016 (16 September).

initiated by the Occident with Industrial Revolution and consequent export of goods to rest of the continents continues till date
through export of goods (and services) including raw materials for
the production of green energy, something initiated to get the effect
of Industrial Revolution neutralized for public good. In final count,
the Occident has had the last laugh with renewable energy economy
(read eco-economy) while rest of the world is left out to receiving
end of the economy. Thus, in either case, the developed hemisphere
gains from the economy, be the same fossil fuel or renewable.

Conclusion

To get major points of concern—rather than conclusion—summarized,
the following heads may reflect the given thought hereby articulated:
(a) conservation and efficiency ought to arrive at synergy to get energy
jurisprudence sustainable enough across the world; (b) India ought to
tie the knot between its international energy diplomacy on one side
and its national energy policy on the other; and (c) renewable energy
deserves due attention to get priority as it is green energy by default;
more so while India has had the privilege of its geographical position-
ing well within the tropics with bountiful blessings of nature. Thus,
India has had the potential to attain total energy security through the
use of hydro-electrical energy, solar energy, wind energy, tidal energy,
geothermal energy, bioenergy and so on. Taken together, sustainable
resources with multilateral approach appear appropriate to boost the
energy governance in India. Also, the energy regime ought not to get
vitiated by want of virtues towards public good. While getting into
deliverables of the renewables, care and caution appear imperative not
to fall into the pitfalls around.

Besides, in the given chessboard of ecological economics (eco-
economics), India ought to strike a functional balance between
competing claims since they indulge in conflict with no satisfac-
tory solution in sight—for instance, class struggle between the
elites and the commoners, between the urban and the peri-urban,
between the factory and the farm, between the ideology and the
technology, and between the access and the success. By courtesy,

its commitment to its own people and to all peoples across the world alike, India ought to promote economic justice for its people along with environmental justice for the world. Taken together, here lies a contemporary tryst with destiny of the Republic to get functional balance between intergenerational equity and intra-generational equity optimized, thereby corresponding to justice for all its stakeholders.

References

Baron de Montesquieu, C. D. S. (1748). *The spirit of laws*, Book V, Chapter II. Retrieved from https://oll.libertyfund.org/titles/montesquieu-complete-works-vol-1-the-spirit-of-laws

Brown, L. R. (2001). *Eco-economy: Building an economy for the earth* (p. 4). New York, NY: W. W. Norton. Retrieved from http://library.uniteddiversity.coop/Money_and_Economics/Eco-Economy.pdf

Brown, L. R. (2009). *Plan B 4.0: Mobilizing to save civilization* (pp. 141–142). New York, NY: W. W. Norton. Retrieved from http://www.earth-policy.org/images/uploads/book_files/pb4book.pdf

Christensen, J. H., Kumar, K. K., Aldrian, E., An, S., Cavalcanti, I. F. A., Castro M. de., Dong, W., ... Zhou, T. (2013). Climate phenomena and their relevance for future regional climate change. In T. F. Stocker, D. Qin, G. K. Plattner, M. Tignor, S. K. Allen, J. Boschung, A. Nauels, Y. Xia, V. Bex & P. M. Midgley (Eds.), *Climate change 2013: The physical science basis* (Contribution of Working Group I to the Fifth Assessment Report of the Intergovernmental Panel on Climate Change). Cambridge: Cambridge University Press. Retrieved from https://www.ipcc.ch/site/assets/uploads/2018/02/WG1AR5_Chapter14_FINAL.pdf

Driessen, P. (2003). Eco-imperialism: Green power-black death. In *Renewable energy mirages*. London: Merlin Press. Retrieved from http://www.hacer.org/pdf/Driessen01.pdf

Driessen, P. (2011). The 'sustainable future' is not sustainable. *Energy and Environment*, *22*(6), 758.

Driessen, P. (2017). *The hidden agendas of sustainability illusions* (Guest essay in *Watts Up With That*). Retrieved from https://wattsupwiththat.com/2017/02/09/the-hidden-agendas-of-sustainability-illusions/

Herring, H. (2006). Energy efficiency: A critical view. *Energy*, *31*, 15. Retrieved from http://www.fraw.org.uk/library/economics/herring_2006.pdf

Jayagovind, A. (2016). Missing the wood for the trees: A critique of the WTO ruling in India: Solar cells and modules. *Indian Journal of International Law*, *56*(2), 201–220. Retrieved from https://link.springer.com/article/10.1007%2Fs40901–017–0048–5

Kandhari, R, & Umashankar, S. (2015, 4 July). *Energy conservation is a moving target* (Interview with Ajay Mathur). Retrieved from https://www.downtoearth.org. in/interviews/energy/energy-conservation-is-a-moving-target-33617

Kapur, D., Khosla, R., & Mehta, P. B. (2009, 1 August). Climate change: India's options. *Economic and Political Weekly*, *44*(31), 41.

Klinger, J. M. (2017). *Rare Earth frontiers: From terrestrial subsoils to lunar land-scapes*. Ithaca, NY: Cornell University Press. Retrieved from https://www.jstor. org/stable/pdf/10.7591/j.ctt1w0dd6d.6.pdf?refreqid<hig><hig>=</hig></hig >excelsior%3Aefe70d512316211fe02dfdc3a496683a

Marx, K., & Engels, F. (1848). *The manifesto of the communist party* (p.17). Moscow: Progress Publishers. Retrieved from https://www.marxists.org/ archive/marx/works/download/pdf/Manifesto.pdf

Nurse, L. A., McLean, R. F., Agard, J., Briguglio, L. P., Duvat-Magnan, V., Pelesikoti, N., Tompkns, E., & Webb, A. (2014). Small islands. In V. R. Barros, C. B. Field, D. J. Dokken, M. D. Mastrandrea, K. J. Mach, T. E. Bilir, M. Chatterjee, K. L. Ebi, Y. O. Estrada, R. C. Genova, B. Girma, E. S. Kissel, A. N. Levy, S. MacCracken, P. R. Mastrandrea & L. L. WhiteClimate (Eds.), *Climate Change 2014: Impacts, adaptation, and vulnerability* (Part B: Regional Aspects. Contribution of Working Group II to the Fifth Assessment Report of the Intergovernmental Panel on Climate Change; pp. 1613–1654). Cambridge: Cambridge University Press.

Owen, G. (2000). Energy efficiency and energy conservation: Policies, pro-grammes and their effectiveness. *Energy and Environment*, *11*(5), 553.

Power Line. (2017, November). *BEE has successfully scaled several milestones*. Retrieved from https://powerline.net.in/2017/11/04/interview-with-abhay-bakre/

Smith, A. (1981). *An inquiry into the nature and causes of the wealth of nations* (pp. 26–2). Indianapolis, IN: Liberty Fund. (Reprint from *An inquiry into the nature and causes of the wealth of nations*, 1979. New York, NY: Oxford University Press.) Retrieved from http://files.libertyfund.org/files/220/0141–02_Bk.pdf

WTO. (2016, 16 September). *India-certain measures relating to solar cells and solar modules: Report of the WTO Appellate* Body. Retrieved from https://www.wto. org/english/tratop_e/dispu_e/456abr_e.pdf

WTO. (2016, 24 February). *India-certain measures relating to solar cells and solar modules: Report of the WTO panel*. Retrieved from https://www.wto.org/ english/tratop_e/dispu_e/456r_e.pdf

CHAPTER 6

Waste-Based Power Generation Supply Chain
A Case Study

Md Hafiz Iqbal

Introduction

Waste is part of every urban society and the natural environment. Mismanagement of waste creates negative impacts in urban areas all over the world except in a few high-income countries. The increased population and the rapid economic growth accelerate waste generation. Generally, the greater quantities of waste, its characteristics and composition create more complexity in the city. When a society becomes more industrialized and urbanized, its surrounding communities become more congested through the mismanagement of waste. Waste from households, industrial sector, trade and commerce, official building, institution and small business, bulky waste, yard and garden waste, street sweepings, the contents of litter containers and market cleansing waste contaminate air, water and soil of our society by continuing dumping and burying of waste (Stessel, 2012). Solid waste in landfills is from mixed streams and not sorted, allowing for chemicals and harmful metals to mix with organic degradable materials. Heavy metals, pathogens and other hazardous substances can also contaminate the environment. Most disposal sites not only release untreated and potentially toxic leachate directly into the waterways or soil but also harmful greenhouse gases (GHGs) such as methane and carbon dioxide (Dethier, 2017).

The environmental degradation in a city is exposed through the deposited waste in a landfill which is contaminated by toxicological properties, degradation of soil by direct waste contact and pollution of air by burning waste (Singh, Singh, Araujo, Ibrahim, & Sulaiman, 2011). It generally trends that city households are habituated to deposit or dump their waste indiscriminately by the street side or roadside, or throw it in the drain or sewerage. Pabna city is no exception to this.

Solid waste management in Pabna city is facing serious challenges. In particular, the practice of landfilling is unsustainable and no longer an adequate solution because of its negative impacts on society and the environment. Waste-based power generation is the potential solution to get rid of this unexpected situation. It provides long-term sustainable waste management, reduces GHG emissions from waste, enhances income generation capacity, promotes the feed-in tariff[1] system and is a new source of renewable energy for Pabna city.

To implement the waste-based power generation project in Pabna city, a new waste collection strategy is needed for the proposed power plant. The game theory helps us to make waste collection strategy in terms of co-opetition[2] strategy. A large number of studies give emphasis on conceptualize the effectiveness of biomass[3] feedstock

---

[1] The feed-in tariff is generally associated with renewable energy and creates rapid growth in sources. It helps households to generate their own electricity. Households can sell their excess electricity collectively to the government on a contract basis. Germany, Japan, Spain and France have successfully implemented feed-in tariff in their society.

[2] Combination of co-operation and competition makes a co-opetition strategy.

[3] Biomass is organic matter, matter from any living organism. It ensures environmental benefits and energy security.

supply system with the approach of the game theory, econometric modelling and cost–benefit analysis (Sun, Lin, & Qian, 2013; Wen & Zhang, 2015). Zhang, Luo and Tan (2017) successfully applied the game theory in their study of the biomass supply system and its management technique. A large number of studies of energy economics have asserted co-opetition strategy. For example, co-opetition is a good market-driven strategy for better management of waste-based energy or green energy (Carfi & Romeo, 2015). This strategy is the main strategy to reach a desirable outcome compared to other strategies (e.g., competition and co-operation) of the game theory. The players gain more benefits under this game strategy (Brandenburger & Nalebuff, 1996). It is suitable for renewable energy and supply chain management (Wang, Long, & Sun, 2014; Zhang et al., 2017).

An effective strategy or plan is essential for setting up an affordable and renewable energy plant and implementing an air pollution-free settlement project. On this ground, several strategies of the game theory can work as a principal catalyst to meet Goals 7 and 11 of the Sustainable Development Goals (SDGs). Goal 7 covers affordable and clean energy, and Goal 11 covers sustainable cities and communities. The above statements provide a background to the origin of thoughts and motivation to carry out this research.

The study provides an overview of waste-based power generation supply chain of Pabna city through different strategies of the game theory. Data from 392 households are collected using a random sampling technique. Nash equilibrium[4] Monte Carlo simulation and sensitivity analysis are used to analyse the data. In general, this study is significant in a number of ways. It provides management techniques of waste-based power generation. This study aims at contributing in a number of ways to the body of knowledge which might lead to the relevant policy in the field of green growth, waste-based power generation and low-carbon society. More specifically, the findings from the study may be valuable to institutions, future researchers, policymakers and individuals who may want to have a nuanced understanding of

---

[4] Nash equilibrium is a situation in which economic actors interacting with each other for every choice by applying their best strategy (Mankiw, 2008).

how to handle waste-based power generation supply chain. They can also use this document as a reference.

The purpose of this paper is to test the effectiveness of a co-opetition organic waste supply strategy for the waste-based power plant in Pabna city where the broker, household and mohalla (area) methods work as key factors. Under this strategy, the waste collection from the broker method and the mohalla committee (MC; salaried committee either by municipality, city office or *Paurashava*[5]) method co-exist. MC is a concerned body that monitors waste collection and management, and influences households to maintain the supply chain of waste. More specifically, this committee is responsible to co-operate with households for waste collection and delivery of organic waste to the plant, improve waste mismanagement and provide public welfare. Solid waste has many forms. It includes household garbage, rubbish, sanitation residue, packaging material, plastic, bottles, cans, scrap iron and other trash. Such kinds of waste are generally collected from households, gardens, parks, commercial or institutional entities such as schools and businesses (Chua, Endang, & Leong, 2011). Wastewater, all forms of waste from the industrial sector, toxic/hazardous waste, medical waste, construction and demolition waste, and disaster waste are not counted in this study.

With this in mind, the study is structured as follows: After the introduction, theoretical motivation is mentioned with particular emphasis on the concept of the game theory, Monte Carlo simulation and sensitivity analysis. The materials and methods are presented. Next, results and discussion are highlighted. Finally, the study area and methods of data collection are described in materials and methods section. Next, results and discussion are highlighted. Finally, key findings are presented in the concluding part of the study.

Theoretical Motivation

Theory helps us to develop an idea of any particular issue in the field of research. The game theory of microeconomics, Monte Carlo

---

[5] Paurashava is Bangla world which means Municipality.

simulation technique, and financial internal rate of return (FIRR) and economic internal rate of return (EIRR) under the sensitivity analysis will help to conduct this research and provide the scientific ground. The following sections will explain briefly about the game theory, Monte Carlo simulation and sensitivity analysis.

The Game Theory

The game theory is an effective theoretical approach for analysing the best strategy and outcome in energy economics (Berry, Hobbs, Meroney, O'Neill, & Stewart, 1999). In addition, it is also suitable for parlour games, political negotiations, producer behaviour under the duopoly market structure, consumer behaviour, aggression, cooperation, hunting, optimization of water resource and collection (Madani, 2010; Porter, 1991). There are three strategic options or building blocks, that is, competition, co-opetition and co-operation of this theoretical approach. The next sections will briefly explain these fascinating building blocks of the game theory.

Competition

Strategic interaction has the option to involve many players and strategies, but this study will only limit to the MC or area committee game with a large number of strategies. Households, brokers and owners or operators of the energy generation plant are the key actors of this strategy. Their interactions can make the equilibrium condition for waste collection and management. Households are assumed as a single-game player, player f and its payoff function[6] is shown in equation (1) with the two committee members' payoff as equation (2).

$$\pi_f(a) = aq_a \qquad (1)$$

where a represents the unit profit of the household'from per day's organic waste; q_a is the total organic waste purchased by brokers, subject to $q_a = q_1 + q_2$.

---

[6] Payoff function in the game theory is a mathematical formation describing the award given to a particular actor or player or consumer as the part of outcome of a specific game.

$$\pi_i(q_i) = (p_2 - p_1 - c_1 d)q_i, \quad i = 1, 2 \tag{2}$$

When we deal with more than one game player, equation (1) will be turned into equation (2) where q_i denotes the organic waste purchased by broker i; p_2 is the procurement price for the plants; P_1 is the procurement price for brokers, subject to $p_1 = a + b\sqrt{q_1 + q_2}$; C_1 is the unit cost related to transportation; d is the distance of transportation; b is treated as a coefficient of organic waste collection cost subject to $b = 2\sqrt{2c_1}/3\sqrt{\pi y}$ and y is the unit of collected organic waste.

Co-opetation

Under this strategy it is possible to maintain the organic waste supply chain to generate energy. Broker and mohalla methods are the main building blocks under this strategy. Households also play an important role to implement the strategy because they are a co-operating concern with MC for providing waste; they make decisions as one played with the payoff function like equation (3).

$$\pi_{f+2}(a, q_2) = aq_1 + (p_2 - b\sqrt{q_2} - c_1 d)q_2 \tag{3}$$

The brokers' payoff function holds the same characteristics as equation (2) with i=1. Under this circumstance, we can calculate the equilibrium condition as equation (4).

$$a^e = \frac{p_2 - c_1 d}{3}; q_1^E = \frac{12(p_2 - c_1 d)}{27b^2}; q_2^E = \frac{4(p_2 - c_1 d)^2}{6b^2} \tag{4}$$

Cooperation

Under this strategy, only the MC methods are mostly activated. Its payoff function and the equilibrium condition are shown in equations (5) and (6).

$$\pi_{f+2}(q_0) = (p_2 - c_1 d - b\sqrt{q_a})q_a \tag{5}$$

$$q_a^e = \frac{4(p_2 - c_1 d)^2}{9b^2} \tag{6}$$

The payoff function of all the strategies of the organic waste-based power plant yields an identical scenario as expressed in equation (7).

$$\pi_p(q_w) = p_e(q_o + q_w) - p_2 q_a - p_w q_w - c_p \tag{7}$$

Where q_w is the organic waste that the energy plant would like to purchase; $p_e = (p_e - c_0)\tau$ is the approach of feed-in tariff concern to the organic waste-based electricity and responsible for providing excess electricity to the national grid in terms of contract price in certain years; c_0 is the unit operating cost of the energy plant of the conversion of organic waste to electricity (τ); p_w is the price of the organic waste subject to $p_w = \alpha + \beta q_w (\alpha, \beta > 0)$; c_p is the annual fixed cost (FC) of the energy plant.

All equilibrium conditions of different strategies are obtained by partial differentiation of profit in terms of strategy and setting them equal to zero. This practice is known as the first-order condition for

Table 6.1 *Parameter Assumptions*

Parameter (Unit)	Distribution Parameters	Parameter (Unit)	Distribution Parameters
α, β	**Constant: 137, 0.302**	P_2(Tk/ton)	Mean = 201, SD = 17
p_e(Tk/kWh)	**Constant: 0.45**	Q_m(hundred ton)	Constant: 117
c_0(Tk/kWh)	**Constant: 0.17**	c_1(Tk/kWh × km)	Mean = 3.3, SD = 1.9
c_p(million TK)	**Constant: 7**	y_r(ton/km²)	Constant: 21.75
γ(kWh/ton)	**Constant: 557**	d(km)	Max: 21, Min: 0

Source: Author's calculation using data from survey, 2018.

Note. Tk. stands for taka (Bangladeshi currency) and its rate of exchange US$1: BDT82.27 at 2 May 2018.

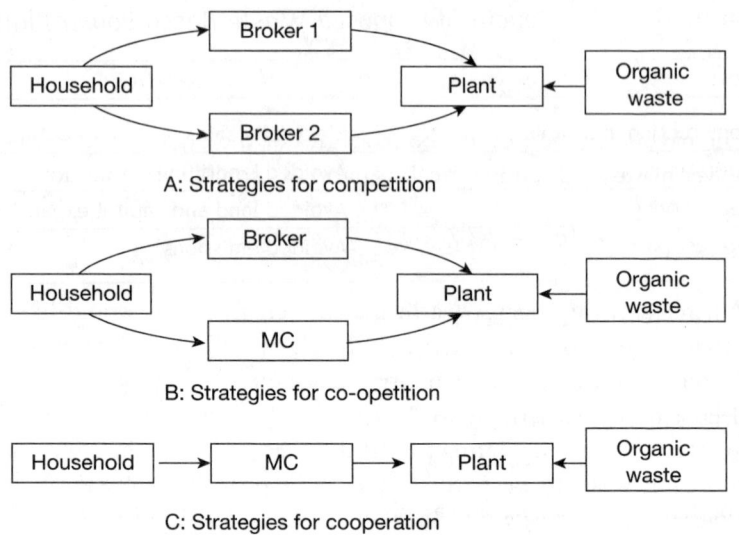

A: Strategies for competition

B: Strategies for co-opetition

C: Strategies for cooperation

Figure 6.1 *Supply Chain Architectures with Different Strategies*

Source: Zhang et al. (2017).

optimization. The proposed strategies of the game theory are shown in Figure 6.1.

Under these strategies, farmers prefer unit profit and brokers prefer to purchase organic waste. The equilibrium condition is calculated by the approach of Nash equilibrium and the prisoners' dilemma[7]under the oligopoly market structure which is given as equation (8).

$$a^E = \frac{p_2 - c_1 d}{2}; \quad q_1^E = q_2^E = \frac{32(p_2 - c_1 d)^2}{225b^2} \tag{8}$$

Here, E denotes the level equilibrium for the corresponding variable.

---

[7] Prisoners' dilemma in a particular "game" between two captured persons that presents why cooperation is difficult to maintain even when it is mutually beneficial (Mankiw, 2008).

Table 6.2 Cost-Benefit of Proposed Waste-Based Power Plant

Cost	Benefit
Construction and capital	Electricity sales
Operational costs	Avoided landfilling
Debt service	Avoided land and capital expansion
Interest paid	Avoided emissions

Source: Prepared by the author, 2018.

Monte Carlo Simulation

It helps us to identify the required physical level of organic waste for producing energy in a power plant. The principal objective of the simulation is to identify the daily physical average level of organic waste from the households for an energy plant. The parameters hold the different characteristics under the simulation process which are shown in Table 6.1. Data are collected from the households and the Pabna Municipality Office. The expected amount of organic waste from households and its price are collected from the households of Pabna Municipality area, and the total amount of organic waste collected daily and the distance of the waste collection area from the proposed power plant are collected from the Pabna Municipality Office.

Sensitivity Analysis

The sensitivity (cost–benefit) is taken into account for both financial and environmental considerations. Financial costs include both equipment and operation costs. On the other hand, environmental costs are the valuation of net emissions from the energy plant under the different strategy of the game theory. Financial benefits cover revenue collection and sales of electricity. In addition, environmental benefits cover the net emission reduction from energy plant for each strategy of the game theory. The costs and benefits of organic waste under different strategies are shown in Table 6.2.

Materials and Methods

Study Area

Like other cities of Bangladesh, solid waste collection of Pabna Municipality or City Office is not controlled by any specific waste management law and regulation. The local government of this municipality and other development partners took many initiatives for proper waste management in this city. These initiatives are definitely laudable, but several weaknesses in the implementation process for waste management exist. Low political commitment, mismanagement practice of waste, ignorance of city dwellers about waste management and lack of awareness are responsible for making this situation worse. As a consequence, mismanaged and uncollected wastes are dumped by the roadside or in drains of the city. Such practice contributes to unexpected flooding, and breeding of insect and rodent vectors. It is responsible for spreading of diseases. In addition, such practice also creates serious environmental problems by the uncontrolled release of methane from waste and is a source of welfare losses in the city.

Pabna city is located in the north-western region of Bangladesh. The main Pabna city is bounded by the Government Edward College in the north, the Ichamati river in the east, Pabna Mental Hospital in the west and central bus terminal in the south. It is approximately 223 km away from Dhaka, the capital city of Bangladesh. High population growth, rapid urbanization and domestic migration from other regions into Pabna city contribute to waste generation. Figure 6.2 shows the map of Pabna city.

Data Description

This study employed qualitative analysis to determine potential demand for waste-based energy plant, low-carbon society and waste issues. Findings from the qualitative analysis are further applied to policy considerations. The qualitative data were obtained by applying the instruments of key informant interview, focus group discussion (FGD) and semi-structured interview questions.

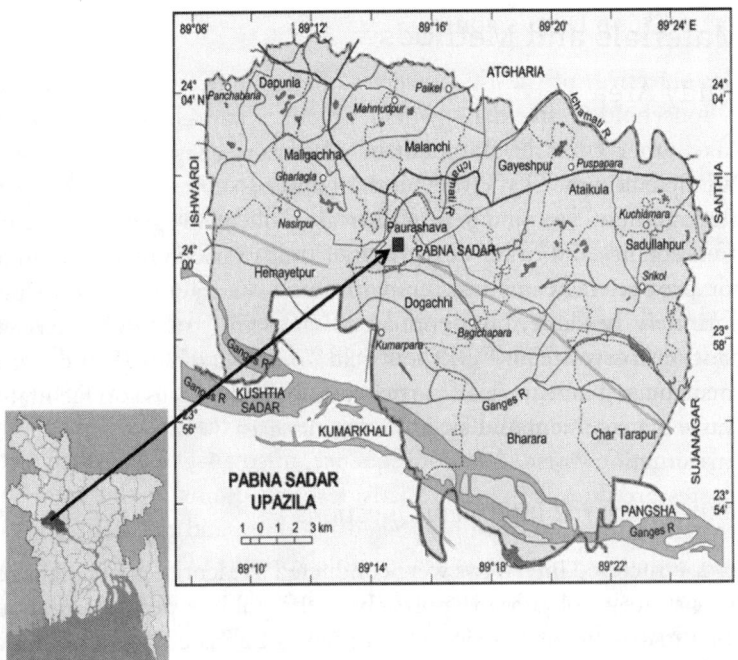

Figure 6.2 *Study Area (Pabna City)*

Source: Prepared by the author based on Google Map, 2019; adapted from Bangladesh Bureau of Statistics 2011.

Note: This figure is not to scale. It does not represent any authentic national or international boundaries and is used for illustrative purposes only.

Key Informant Information

The study conducted a series of interviews with local and national officials and experts from May to June 2017 to better understand the waste collection process, management strategy, price mechanism for generated electricity, policy and other priorities. Individuals interviewed included national expert of organic waste-based energy, bilateral donors, development partners, officials of the Ministry of Energy, experts of Bangladesh's waste and climate change working group, and local government officials working in Pabna Municipality. Interview topics included the evolution of waste management policy, budgeting, finance for waste services, and inter-agency cooperation and coordination for waste management.

Focus Group Discussion

The objectives of the FGD were to better understand the nuances of household waste management practices and challenges, and to contribute to the development of a relevant questionnaire survey. Participants in the FGD were heads of different communities, brokers, salaried committee members of the waste collection agency and heads of households. The focus group participants provided first-hand individual experiences and practices with waste management that helped to inform the design and content of the semi-structured interview questions survey. The FGD was held on 23 March 2018 and lasted three hours. There were 12 participants and one discussion facilitator who was a representative from Pabna city area.

Semi-structured Interview Questions

Semi-structured interviews were conducted to identify waste management strategy, obtain an approach of the public's perception about waste management practice and service in Pabna city, and potential new waste management programmes. The target respondents were adult household members, community leaders, brokers, waste pickers and business owners or managers in Pabna city. Respondents were randomly selected from throughout the city. The interviews were carried out in April 2018 through random sampling where the final sample size was 392.

Results and Discussion

Based on the estimated result, we can say that co-opetition strategy maintains the highest equilibrium level of organic waste with respect to quantity and price for power generation and ensure the highest profit $\pi_{pw}^E = (p_e - \alpha)q_{qw}^E - \beta(q_w^E)^2$, followed by the proposed strategies of the game theory. Table 6.3 shows the details of the equilibrium positions of different strategies of waste-based power generation.

Simulation results also support that the co-opetation strategy is the best strategy for organic waste-based power generation compared to those of other strategies (see Table 6.4 for more details).

Table 6.3 Equilibrium Positions of Different Strategies of Waste-Based Power Generation

Strategy	Equilibrium Amount of Organic Waste	Equilibrium Level of Profit
Competition	$0.1984\,\dfrac{(p_2-c_1d)}{b^2}$	$0.0080\,\dfrac{(p_2-c_1d)^3}{b^2}+0.0917\,\dfrac{(p_2-c_1d)^2(p_e-p_2)}{b^2}+\pi_{pw}^E-c_p$
Co-opetition	$0.5136\,\dfrac{(p_2-c_1d)}{b^2}$	$0.3916\,\dfrac{(p_2-c_1d)^3}{b^2}+0.5073\,\dfrac{(p_2-c_1d)^2(p_e-p_2)}{b^2}+\pi_{pw}^E-c_p$
Cooperation	$0.4143\,\dfrac{(p_2-c_1d)}{b^2}$	$0.2892\,\dfrac{(p_2-c_1d)^3}{b^2}+0.1407\,\dfrac{(p_2-c_1d)^2(p_e-p_2)}{b^2}+\pi_{pw}^E-c_p$

Source: Author's calculation using data from survey, 2018.

Table 6.4 Simulation Results

Strategy	Amount of Organic Waste/ton	Total Profit/ Million Tk	Plant Profit/ Million Tk
Competition	80	16.70	11.37
Co-opetition	120	51.02	32.49
Cooperation	92	37.96	26.71

Source: Author's calculation using data from survey, 2018.

From Table 6.4, we see that the estimated amount of organic waste under competition strategy is 80 tons daily, and 120 and 92 tons daily when we have co-opetation and cooperation strategies. Thus, it is clear that the co-opetation strategy is the best strategy to collect organic waste for power generation in the Pabna city. Similarly, the highest yearly total profit of households and brokers, and total profit of plant are estimated at 51.02 million and 32.49 million taka under the co-opetation strategy which is also greater than the other two strategies.

It is also possible to evaluate these strategies for waste-based power generation in terms of sensitivity analysis: FIRR and EIRR. Table 6.5 shows sensitivity analysis under different strategies for waste-based power generation. Highest FIRR and EIRR are estimated under

Table 6.5 *Sensitivity Analysis of Proposed Waste-Based Power Generation*

Strategy	FIRR (%)	EIRR (%)
Competition	0.89	0.82
Co-opetation	1.38	1.63
Cooperation	1.07	0.17

Source: Author's calculation using data from survey, 2018.

the strategy of co-opetation and it is 1.38 per cent and 1.63 per cent respectively.

Conclusion

Organic waste is the potential source of energy generation in Bangladesh but it faces few implementation challenges. For example, Bangladesh has no waste collection strategy from households. Therefore, it requires an effective waste collection strategy for power plant. Based on the estimated results, we propose co-opetition strategy for waste-based energy or power plant. Households, brokers and MC are the main building blocks of the co-opetition strategy. Results show that co-opetition strategy ensures maximum amount of organic waste, maintains the supply chain and brings the highest profits for the households, brokers and energy plant.

The findings of the study generate cutting-edge and effective knowledge in the energy sector which are essential for a healthy city and low-carbon society. It is expected that other urban areas or cities will generate more organic waste-based electricity and promote green growth from the findings of this study.

Due to the time limitation, deficit budget and other logistic supports, this study is not free from certain lacunas. Pabna city is the study area of this study. It is not possible to include all cities of Bangladesh and interview large number of respondents and thus, it reduces the merits of the research. Thus, this study recommends further study to overcome such shortcomings and get good findings to develop a waste-based energy policy.

References

Bangladesh Bureau of Statistics. (2011). *Population and housing census 2011.* Dhaka: Ministry of Planning.

Berry, C. A., Hobbs, B. F., Meroney, W. A., O'Neill, R. P., & Stewart W. R., Jr. (1999). Understanding how market power can arise in network competition: a game theoretic approach. *Utilities Policy, 8* (3), 139–158.

Brandenburger, A. M., & Nalebuff, B. (1996). *Co-opetition.* New York, NY: Daubleday Dell Publishing Group.

Carfi, D., & Romeo, A. (2015). Improving welfare in Congo: Italian National Hydrocarbons Authority strategies and its possible coopetitive alliances with green energy producers. *Journal of Applied Economic Sciences, 10* (4), 34.

Chua, K. H., Endang, J. M. S., & Leong, Y. P. (2011). Sustainable municipal solid waste management and GHG abatement in Malaysia. *ST–4: Green & Energy Management, 4* (2), 1–8.

Dethier, J.-J. (2017). Trash, cities, and politics: Urban environmental problems in Indonesia. *Indonesia, 103,* 73–90.

Madani, K. (2010). Game theory and water resources. *Journal of Hydrology, 381* (3–4), 225–238.

Mankiw, N. G. (2008). Principles of microeconomics. Mason, MI: South-Western Cangage Learning.

Porter, M. E. (1991). Towards a dynamic theory of strategy. *Strategic management journal, 12* (S2), 95–117.

Singh, R. P., Singh, P., Araujo, A. S., Ibrahim, M. H., & Sulaiman, O. (2011). Management of urban solid waste: Vermicomposting a sustainable option. *Resources, Conservation and Recycling, 55* (7), 719–729.

Stessel, R. I. (2012). *Recycling and resource recovery engineering: principles of waste processing.* New York, NY: Springer.

Sun, J., Lin, J., & Qian, Y. (2013). Game-theoretic analysis of competitive agri-biomass supply chain. *Journal of Cleaner Production, 43,* 174–181.

Wang, D. Z., Long, M. X., & Sun, Y. (2014). Evolutionary game analysis of co-opetation relationship between regional logistics nodes. *Journal of Applied Research and Technology, 12* (2), 251–260.

Wen, W., & Zhang, Q. (2015). A design of straw acquisition mode for China's straw power plant based on supply chain coordination. *Renewable Energy, 76,* 369–374.

Zhang, X., Luo, K., & Tan, Q. (2017). A game theory analysis of China's agri-biomass-based power generation supply chain: a co-opetition strategy. *Energy Procedia, 105,* 168–173.

CHAPTER 7

Rural Household Decision-Making about Water Consumption

Karthick Radhakrishnan,
Aparna Radhakrishnan and Niti Saxena

Introduction

Water is a renewable resource. However, the availability of clean freshwater is gradually decreasing (Al-Khatib, Kamal, Taha, Al Hamad, & Jaber, 2003; Harris, Jalloh, & Kooy, 2012) while its demand is progressively increasing due to progressive urbanization, rapid population growth (Lee, Park, & Jeong, 2012) and factors like climate change that have caused enormous stress on water resources in low and middle-income country. Water scarcity is a rampant problem across the globe. It is tough to transport water from water-abundant areas to water-scarce regions. As Nash (2010) explains, 18 per cent of the world's population lacks access to safe drinking water. According to a UN estimate, by the year 2025, around two thirds of the world's population will face acute water shortage (Aureli & Brelet, 2004).

Rural household water consumption is under-researched compared to urban residential water demand in spite of a large difference in urban and rural household water consumption patterns (Domene, & Saurí, 2006; Sivakumar et al., 2010).

Households with no access to safe drinking water adopt different measures (e.g., bottled water) to access safe drinking water without confronting a financial burden. Households are willing to pay for an improved water supply system provided by the public sector, and this willingness to pay is significantly determined by awareness (Jalan, Somanathan, & Chaudhuri, 2009; Khan, Brouwer, & Yang, 2014), levels of education (Kwak, Yoo, & Kim, 2014), social capital (Nauges & Strand, 2007; Polyzou, Jones, Evangelinos, & Halvadakis, 2011) and household income (Genius et al., 2008). Several studies have been conducted to understand residential water consumption which clearly have shown that water use varies significantly across households (Beal & Stewart, 2011; Heinrich, 2007; Lee et al., 2012; Loh & Coghlan, 2003; Mayer et al., 1999; Roberts, 2005; Sivakumaran & Aramaki, 2010; Willis, Stewart, Panuwatwanich, Capati, & Giurco, 2009).

More importantly, capturing the variability of household water consumption for predicting water demand is essential to carry an efficient and effective supply–demand balance assessment. Coultas, Maheepala and Mirza (2011), Maheepala, Coultas, Neumann, and Sharma (2013) and Mitchell, Siriwardene, Duncan and Rahilly (2008) have shown the importance of capturing the variability of household water use to quantify the yield from a cluster of rainwater tanks to inform supply and demand assessment at precinct and city scales. Thus, the importance of understanding the variability of household water demand is imperative to planning interventions for improving equitable and sustained water access.

Rural household water consumption is under-researched and often neglected in the provision of clean drinking water compared to its urban counterparts despite significant differences among the two (Domene & Saurí, 2006; Nash, 2010; Sivakumar et al., 2010; World Health Organization, 1992). Making provisions to improve access to clean drinking water in rural areas does not address the problems as the solutions should align with the existing social norms. The present study addresses this research gap through investigation of the social aspects of water access and estimating the factors influencing select households' decisions on opting for different water supply sources for use in select villages of Nuh. The study is further disaggregated into three sections, namely, methodology that outlines the study location, tools used; results and discussion detailing key findings emanating from analysis of data; and conclusion.

Methodology

Study Location

The study has been carried out in Nuh district, which is among the 22 districts of Haryana, popularly known as Mewat. It is located in the northern part of Haryana and lies between 27^0 38', 28^0 20' north latitude and 76^0 51', 77^0 20' east longitude with an area of 1,507 square kilometres (582 sq. m), and has a total population of 1,089,406. The district is inhabited by Meo Muslims. Nuh is bounded by Gurugram district in the north, Rewari district in the west, and Faridabad and Palwal districts in the east. The district has five blocks that have 431 villages in total. Agriculture is the predominant occupation in the district, which is mostly rain-fed except in small pockets with canal irrigation (http://nuh.gov.in). Agriculture productivity in Nuh is low in comparison to the other districts in the state. Animal husbandry, particularly diary, is the secondary source of income. Families that live closer to the hilly ranges of the Aravallis also rear sheep and goats. Milk yield is not so low. However, due to high indebtedness, most of the farmers are forced to sell the milk to the lenders at lower than average price, which drastically reduces their income from milk. The normal average annual rainfall of the district is 594 mm spread over 31 days (CGWB, 2012) with arid air most of the year, and the annual rainfall varies between 336 and 440 millimetres (CGWB, 2012).

More than 90 per cent of the district population is engaged in agriculture and allied activities, and more than 50 per cent of the population earns less than ₹5,000 month. The district suffers from acute portable water scarcity due to the tough terrain and lack of water

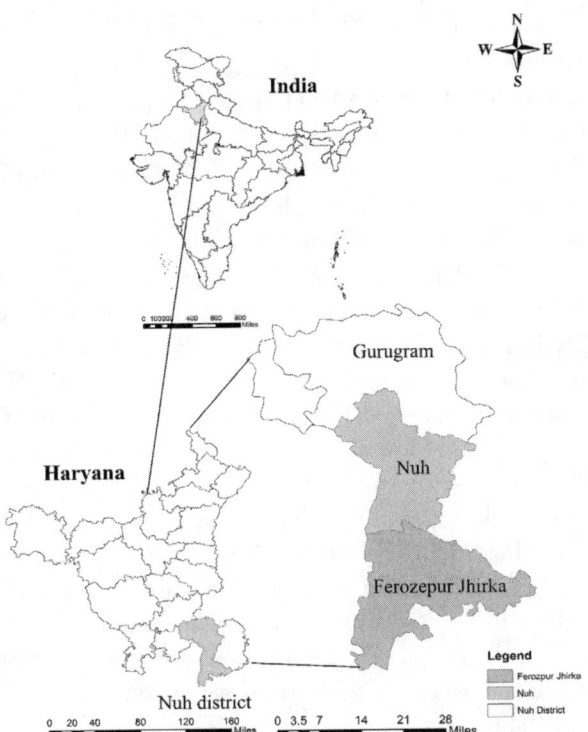

Figure 7.1 Map of Study Location

Source: Authors own computation using Qgis.

recharge in the aquifers, which has resulted in 78 per cent of the area suffering from problems like severe salinity and 22 per cent of the area is under freshwater zone (CGWB, 2012). However recently, the district witnessed as a case point fluoride contamination. Water scarcity has a direct impact on the drudgery that women and young girls have to fetch water. Every day they must walk about 3–4 kilometres, walking a minimum of an hour each trip. On average, a household that can't afford to buy water from tankers has to make five such trips to collect water to meet daily domestic requirements (Sharma, Satyavada, & Chowdhury, 2014). The district has different sources of water for drinking and agricultural purposes. Around 23,348 pump sets and 76 bore wells exist (Government of Haryana, 2011).

Tools for Data Collection and Sample Selection

Nuh district was purposely selected because 55 per cent of its ground-water is saline (CGWB, 2012). Household data was collected from six villages (Kaheri, Madhi, Rajaka, Bajidpur, Farkarpurkhori and Khedi) located in two blocks (Nagina and Punana) from June to November 2018. They were randomly selected based on different sources of drinking water within the village. A structured question-naire was used for data collection, which was pre-tested and modified before the initiation of the actual survey. Surveyors involved in the data collection were familiar with the social and cultural practices in the area. Data was collected in Ferozepur Jhirka and Nuh block of Nuh district in Haryana; 178 households were selected for inter-views in six villages. Households were selected on the basis of the stratified random sampling method. Out of 178 households, 172 samples were taken for the analysis. The data collected was peri-odically examined in order to minimize and correct the errors. Data pertaining to household socio-economic information such as age, gender, education, occupation, drinking-water-related details such as time taken, the frequency of collection, number of members that collect water and access to the various water sources were collected as a part of the project.

Tools for Analysis

To examine the choice of a water source over another and analyse the determinants of household water consumption from various sources, the multinomial logit model was used (Jalan et al., 2009; Rauf, Bakhsh, Hassan, Nadeem, & Kamran, 2015). The dependent variable of the multinomial logit model is natural category not ordered in nature.

The model used in this study can be written in the following general form.

$$P_n(Y_i = 1) = F(X_{i1}, X_{i2}, X_{i3}, \ldots \ldots X_{iM})$$

Here, Y_i is the dependent variable where $Y_i = 1$ for adoption and $Y_i = 0$ for non-adoption, and X_i are the explanatory variables.

Logistic function which is central to the logit model can be represented as follows:

$$P_n(Y_i = 1) = P_n = \frac{1}{1 + e^{-W_i}}, i = 1, 2, \ldots \ldots, N$$

Here, $W_i = b_0 + \sum_{j=0}^{M} b_j x_{ij}$ is a linear combination of the independent variables and a set of coefficients which are to be estimated.

$$Y_{in} = \beta_0 + \beta_1 x_1 + \beta_2 x_2 + \ldots \ldots \ldots + \beta_n x_n \qquad (1)$$

Where, Y_{in} is source of water, x_1 to x_n includes general information, water consumption parameters, willingness to pay for water, decision to procure water and access to water. The marginal effects x_k for the factor determining different water source, the equation is as follows:

$$\frac{\partial \Pr(y = 1)}{\partial x_k} = \frac{e^{x\beta}}{(1 + e^{x\beta})^2} \frac{\partial(x\beta)}{\partial x_k}$$

$$= \frac{e^{x\beta}}{(1 + e^{x\beta})^2} \beta_k$$

$$= \delta(x\beta)(1 - \delta(x\beta))\beta_k$$

$$= \Pr(y = 1) \times \Pr(y = 0) \times \beta_k \qquad (2)$$

Here, $\Pr(y = 1)$ is the probability of using the public source for drinking purposes, private source and other source. Equation (2) gives the coefficient of marginal effect.

Results and Discussion

The results section consists of two subsections (a) household perception of drinking water and (b) parameter estimation of the multinomial logit model. The descriptive statistics of the variables used in the regression analysis are shown in Table 7.1. The survey was conducted among the households of six villages in Nuh district in

Table 7.1 *Descriptive Statistics of Variables Used in Regression Analysis*

Variable	Description	Mean	Std. Dev
Source of Water			
Public	If household is using public source, then 1; otherwise 0	0.37	0.48
Private	If household is using private source, then 1; otherwise 0	0.50	0.50
Other sources	If household is using another source, then 1; otherwise 0	0.13	0.33
General Information			
Male	If respondent is male, then 1; otherwise 0	0.59	0.49
Female	If respondent is female then 1; otherwise 0	0.41	0.49
Family size	Total number of family members	7.91	3.79
Water Consumption Parameter			
Water supply source	If sources are located inside household, then 1; otherwise 0	0.51	0.50
Total people fetch water	Number of household members involved in fetching water	1.76	0.84
Frequency of water collection	Number of times household members involved in fetching water	1.82	0.56
Distance covered	Distance covered in Meters	169	233
Time consumed	Time consumed in minutes	19	13
Total water expenses	Total expenses in INR	3613	10,233
Willingness to Pay for Water			
WTP for drinking water	Willingness to pay for drinking water in INR	230	176
WTP for farming water	Willingness to pay for farming water in INR	510	477

Variable	Description	Mean	Std. Dev
Decision to Get Water			
Sweet water	If sweet water, then 1; otherwise 0	0.17	0.38
Water availability	If water is available, then 1; otherwise 0	0.27	0.45
Nearby location	If water is available at nearby location then 1; otherwise 0	0.24	0.43
Access to Water			
Drinking	If water access to drink, then 1; otherwise 0	1.00	0.00
Bathing	If water access to bathe, then 1; otherwise 0	0.48	0.50
Washing	If water access to wash, then 1; otherwise 0	0.12	0.33
Livestock	If water access to livestock, then 1; otherwise 0	0.63	0.48
Cleaning	If water access to clean, then 1; otherwise 0	0.20	0.40
Cooking	If water access to cook, then 1; otherwise 0	0.96	0.20

Source: Primary Survey, 2017

which 59 per cent of respondents were male and 41 per cent were female. Interestingly, the population of Nuh has increased drastically with respect to growth transiting from −12.80 (1911) to 38.65 (2011) (Census India), which clearly implies that the average family size of a household is eight. The district has different sources of water. In the study villages, there were three sources of water namely: (a) public source (water supplied by the village panchayat or district authority), (b) private source (water supplied by private vendors like tank water suppliers) and (c) other sources (like borewells, which are extensively used for irrigation but sometimes also utilized for drinking purposes). The survey was administered in such a way that it covered respondents using public water sources (37%), private sources (50%) and other sources (13%). More importantly, Nuh faces profound water scarcity with 51 per cent of sampled households having water supply inside (government supply) the household being fetched by an average of two people from the household. The average time spent by a household member to collect water from the sources was 20 minutes covering an average distance of 170 meters.

Table 7.1 depicts that the average willingness to pay for farming (₹510) is more than drinking water (₹230) in Nuh. This implies that people are more willing to pay for irrigation to the borewell owners located in proximity to their farmlands to irrigate fields. However, drinking water is usually collected from these borewells at a specific period of the day without any monetary exchange. The socio-religions ethics of the region are such that they prevent people from selling water meant to be used for drinking as well as for irrigation. Bartering with crops is permitted and very common in villages. The study proposes villages are getting access to sweet water as well as saline water from the villages in which 17 per cent of respondents collect the water only if it is sweet water, 27 per cent of the respondents collect water only if water is available within the village and 24 per cent of the respondents make that decision only if the water available is nearby to their house. One hundred per cent of the respondents get access to water for only drinking purposes, 48 per cent of clean water access is only for bathing purposes, 63 per cent for livestock, 96 per cent get the clean water access to use for cooking purposes in the house.

A total of 172 sampled households were represented by six villages across the two blocks in the most underdeveloped district of India. The dependent variable used in the regression model is categorical in nature: the households in the village using the public sources, private sources and other sources of drinking water (Table 7.2). The other water source is used as the base outcome in the dependent variable. The independent variable includes general information, water consumption, willingness to pay for drinking water, decision to get water and the different purposes of water. The description of the independent variable used in the regression was explained in Table 7.1. The probability of household using public water source is 43 per cent, private water source is 51 per cent and other sources is 0.56 per cent for drinking. The marginal effect of

Table 7.2 Results of Marginal Effects of the Multinomial Logit Model

Variables	Public Water Source Pr(0.432)		Private Source Pr(0.513)		Other Source* Pr(0.056)	
	dy/dx	Std. Err.	dy/dx	Std. Err.	dy/dx	Std. Err.
General Information						
Gender	−0.008	0.134	−0.059	0.137	0.067	0.043
Family size	0.003	0.022	0.015	0.022	−0.018**	0.009
Water Consumption Parameter						
Water supply source	−0.379***	0.148	0.466***	0.145	−0.087	0.061
Total people fetch water	0.033	0.095	−0.035	0.096	0.002	0.030
Frequency of water collection	−0.222*	0.125	0.292**	0.127	−0.070	0.044
Distance covered	0.001**	0.000	0.000	0.000	−0.001**	0.000
Time consumed	−0.013*	0.007	0.008	0.007	0.005*	0.003
Total water expenses	0.000	0.000	0.000	0.000	0.000	0.000
Willingness to Pay for Water						
WTP for drinking water	−0.001	0.001	0.001	0.001	0.000	0.000
WTP for farming activity	−0.0001	0.0002	0.0001	0.0002	−0.00001	0.0001
Decision to Get Water						
Sweet water	−0.153	0.189	0.117	0.203	0.036	0.066
Water availability	0.455***	0.169	−0.542***	0.140	0.088	0.086
Nearby location	−0.122	0.192	−0.037	0.210	0.160	0.116
Access to Water						
Drinking	0.221	0.158	−0.200	0.165	−0.021	0.048
Bathing	−0.285	0.194	0.335*	0.201	−0.050	0.042
Washing	0.570***	0.161	−0.449**	0.213	−0.120	0.120
Livestock	0.636***	0.124	−0.581***	0.123	−0.055	0.038
Cooking	−0.284	0.465	0.526***	0.093	−0.242	0.459

Note: *, ** and *** represent 90%, 95% and 99% level of significance, respectively.
Source: Primary Survey, 2017.

the multinomial logit model is presented in Table 7.2. The gender (especially women) plays a significant role in collecting drinking water from the appropriate source. Comparing with private water sources, the public (−0.379) and private water sources (−0.087) were negatively affecting the overall consumption of water in Nuh district. This is because borewell owners allow people to take water for drinking purposes. Thus, their accessibility to water is not difficult when compared with a public and private source. The family size of the household positively impacts the accessibility of drinking water. If the household has more members in the family, they have easy access to water with the help of other members. More importantly, family size negatively impacts other sources. The nuclear family having more access water just because they require minimum water quantity which is available for them without any hurdle.

Household water demand and consumption directly depend on the number of members in the family and the availability of clean water. The decision to collect water from a specific source is based on the availability of water from the source, distance and time taken to procure water. Comparing a public and private source in terms of water supply, the public source (−0.379) is negatively affecting and private source (0.466) is positively significant. Households collecting drinking water from public sources (−0.222) are negatively significant with the frequency of collection, whereas the private source is positively significant. More importantly, collecting water from public sources increases the time and reduces the number of tanks of water to be collected, whereas, even though households pay for drinking water from private sources, it increases the number of tons of water for household consumption. Comparing with other decisions to select the source in the semi-arid region, a household is making a decision based on the availability of water rather than time and distance from the source to the house. Comparing with water access to cleaning, bathing is negatively impacting public sources and is positively impacting private sources. Households are not willing to use private sources for bathing, washing and livestock. They prefer to use public sources. Interestingly, people do not prefer using water from a public source for cooking; rather, they are willing to pay for a private source, which is statistically significant.

Conclusion

Availability of clean water can have serious and direct implications on human and societal well-being. In recent decades, Nuh district has faced a massive water scarcity problem. Households face significant challenges to collecting water from different sources for cooking and other activities in the region. The results reveal that households in the villages make the decision based on the availability, distance and the frequency of procuring water from a source. In this regard, the present study attempted to determine the factors influencing the decision made by the households in Nuh district. Overall, the economic status for all households in the region to collect water makes it difficult to afford water from a personal source. The less affluent cannot afford it and largely rely on a donation from the rich or on physical effort. One of the major findings is that women are the key decision-makers with regard to managing the needs of water for the household. They are more vulnerable to collecting water from different sources in the villages that are more than a kilometre away. One of the main highlights of the findings is that, besides water being a major element of survival, women are indispensable entities in the region. While this may be true for other regions as well, the paradox which exists in Nuh is unique. Even though women are the ones who look after the entire water management of a household, from procuring to using water sources, they have a grim presence in the decision-making scenario in other areas. The water requirements are high in most families, as the average family size is large. As a consequence, households that do not have access to water within the village must traverse kilometres together to procure water. To reduce the burden on one woman in the household, girls accompany their mothers and sisters to fetch water. Therefore, females in the region remain in the vicious cycle of not being able to attend their school (since they must fetch water instead) and hence, receive no education.

Acknowledgments

The authors would like to thank the field enumerators for collecting the data from Nuh district and also thank the team of Sehgal Foundation for funding this study.

References

Al-Khatib, I., Kamal, S., Taha, B., Al Hamad, J., & Jaber, H. (2003). Water-health relationships in developing countries: A case study in Tulkarem district in Palestine. *International Journal of Environmental Health Research*, *13*, 199–206.

Aureli, A., & Brelet, C. (2004). *Water and ethics, women and water: An ethical issue.* Paris: United Nations Educational, Scientific and Cultural Organization.

Beal, C., & Stewart, R. A. (2011). *South East Queensland residential end-use study: final report* (p. 47). Queensland: Urban Water Security Research Alliance.

Central Groundwater Board (CGWB). (2012). *District profile: Mewat.* Government of India (GoI). Retrieved from www.cgwb.gov.in/district_profile/haryana/mewat.pdf.

Coultas, E. H., Maheepala, S., & Mirza, F. (2011). Towards the quantification of water quantity and quality impacts of rainwater tanks in South East Queensland. *Proceedings of MODSIM 2011, International Congress on Modeling and Simulation.*

Domene, E., & Saurí, D. (2006). Urbanisation and water consumption: Influencing factors in the metropolitan region of Barcelona. *Urban Studies*, *43*(9), 1605–1623. doi: 10.1080/00420980600749969

Genius, M., Hatzaki, E., Kouromichelaki, E. M., Kouvakis, G., Nikiforaki, S., & Tsagarakis, K. P. (2008). Evaluating consumers' willingness to pay for improved potable water quality and quantity. *Water resources management*, *22*(12), 1825.

Government of Haryana. (2011). *Agriculture contingency plan of Mewat: District profile.* Haryana: Author.

Harris, D., Jalloh, G., & Kooy, M. (2012). *Political economy of the urban water pricing regime in Freetown, Sierra Leone* (ODI Working Paper 348). London: Overseas Development Institute. Retrieved from http://www.odi.org.uk/resources/docs/7668.pdf

Heinrich, M. (2007). *Water end use and efficiency project (WEEP): Final report* (BRANZ study report 159). Judgeford: Branz.

Jalan, J., Somanathan, E., & Chaudhuri, S. (2009). Awareness and the demand for environmental quality: Survey evidence on drinking water in urban India. *Environment and Development Economics*, *14*(6), 665.

Khan, N. I., Brouwer, R., & Yang, H. (2014). Household's willingness to pay for arsenic safe drinking water in Bangladesh. *Journal of environmental management*, *143*(1), 151.

Kwak, S. Y., Yoo, S. H., & Kim, C. S. (2013). Measuring the willingness to pay for tap water quality improvements: Results of a contingent valuation survey in Pusan. *Water*, *5*(4), 1638.

Lee, D. J., Park, N. S., & Jeong, W. (2012). End-use analysis of household water by metering: The case study in Korea. *Water and Environment Journal*, *26*(4), 455–464.

Loh, M., & Coghlan, P. (2003). *Domestic water use study.* Western Australia: Water Corporation. Retrieved from http://www.water.wa.gov.au/PublicationStore/first/42338.pdf.

Maheepala, S., Coultas, E., Neumann, L., & Sharma, A. (2013). *Quantification of regional scale water quantity and quality implications of rainwater tanks in South East Queensland* (Technical report no. 104). Queensland: Urban Water Security Research Alliance.

Mayer, P. W., DeOreo, W. B., Opitz, E. M., Kiefer, J. C., Davis, W. Y., Dziegielewski, B., & Nelson, J. O. (1999). *Residential end-uses of water.* Denver, CO: American Water Works Research Foundation.

Mitchell, V.G., Siriwardene, N., Duncan, H., & Rahilly, M. (2008). Impact of temporal and spatial lumping on rainwater tank system modelling. *Conference Proceedings of Water Down Under,* 15–17 April 2008, Adelaide, South Australia.

Nash, K. (2010). *Women and water rights: Rivers of regeneration.* Regis Center for Art, University of Minnesota. Minneapolis. Retrieved from www.womenandwater.net.

Nauges, C., & Strand, J. (2007). Estimation of non-tap water demand in Central American cities. *Resource and Energy Economics, 29*(3), 165.

Polyzou, E., Jones, N., Evangelinos, K. I., & Halvadakis, C. P. (2011). Willingness to pay for drinking water quality improvement and the influence of social capital. *The Journal of Socio-Economics, 40*(1), 74.

Rauf, S., Bakhsh, K., Hassan, S., Nadeem, A. M., & Kamran, M. A. (2015). Determinants of a household's choice of drinking water source in Punjab, Pakistan. *Polish Journal of Environmental Studies, 24*(6), 2751–2754. doi: 10.15244/pjoes/59256

Roberts, P. (2005). *Residential end-use measurement study.* Melbourne: Yarra Valley Water.

Sharma, L. M., Satyavada, A., & Chowdhury, A. (2014). Water quality and human health in Mewat. In Anjal Prakash, Saravanan V. S., & Jayati Chourey (Eds.), *Interlacing water and human health: Case studies from south Asia, water in south Asia* (Vol. 3). New Delhi: SAGE Publications.

Sivakumaran, S., & Aramaki, T. (2010). Estimation of household water end use in Trincomalee, Sri Lanka. *Water international, 35*(1), 94–99.

Willis, R., Stewart, R. A., Panuwatwanich, K., Capati, B., & Giurco, D. (2009). Gold Coast domestic water end use study. *Water, 36*(6), 79–85.

CHAPTER 8

Coal Mining
Development of Eco Parks

Afkar Ahmad and
Aounkar Anand

Introduction

India is the second largest producer of coal after China. There are two ways in which coal mining is done. The first being OC mining and the second is underground mining. Coal production is very important as most of the industries are directly linked to coal and produce various other substances. As mining is a temporary use of land, this land can be reused for the other purposes too. However, with coal mining there are various factors that harm the environment and are considered bad for the ecosystem. This chapter deals with the hazards of coal mining to the ecosystem and how the new concept of development of eco parks can help in controlling pollution. The chapter firstly deals with the pollution caused by or the hazards of coal mining. The chapter utilizes empirical data from the Coal India Limited (CIL) and its subsidiary (BCCL).

Air Pollution

The main sources of air pollution are movement of overburden (OB)/ coal by road, transfer points at crushers and loading/unloading operations in coal handling plants (CHP) besides drilling (Sharma, 2019). These operations generate suspended particulate matter (PM_{10}) and respirable particulate matter ($PM_{2.5}$). Some fugitive gaseous emissions such as carbon dioxide, carbon monoxide, sulphur dioxide (SO_2) and oxides of nitrogen are also caused by automotive, generators and blasting operations.

Shortcomings in Implementation of Air Pollution Control Measures

For mitigating air pollution, generation of dust is to be controlled at the source with necessary measures during drilling, loading, unloading, CHP transfer points and so on (Ward, 2019). Further, dust generation is to be minimized along coal/waste transportation roads and green belts are to be created around the source of dust. CIL prescribed (March 2014) guidelines for adherence so that air pollution can be mitigated. Audit visited (27 June 2018, 10 July 2018 and 17 July 2018) three mines and observed the shortcomings, as detailed further:

S. No.	Parameter	Mines where Parameters Violated
1.	Wetting of top surface of coal loaded trucks by sprinklers/ mist sprays	Kuya, DBOCP
2.	Use of mechanical brooming/ industrial cleaner	Kuya, DBOCP
3.	Wet drilling	Kuya, DBOCP
4.	Drills fitted with dust extractor	DBOCP
5.	Mechanically covered truck transportation	Kuya, DBOCP
6.	Use of fixed sprinkler for dust suppression at railway siding	Kuya
7.	Avenue plantation	Moonidih, Kuya (partially plantation done)

No reason for violation of the above parameters was found on record. BCCL continued mining activities without initiating remedial action.

Environmental clearance (EC) relating to clusters of mines of BCCL stipulated to conduct a source apportionment study and mineralogical composition study for Jharia Coalfield (JCF) to ascertain sources and extent of air pollution due to mining activities so that appropriate mitigating measures could be taken. It was observed that BCCL did not conduct these studies and hence the source and extent of pollutants generated due to mining activities could not be ascertained. This could undermine the mitigation plan for effective control of pollutants.

Deficiencies in Air Monitoring

The Central Pollution Control Board (CPCB) had notified National Ambient Air Quality Standards (NAAQS) in November 2009 with 12 identified pollutants and prescribed their maximum permissible limits in air (MINEO Consortium, 2000). It include five gaseous pollutants namely sulphur dioxide (SO_2), nitrogen dioxide (NO_2), ozone (O_3), carbon monoxide (CO) and ammonia (NH_3); two dust related parameters (PM_{10} and $PM_{2.5}$); three metals (lead, nickel and arsenic); and two organic pollutants (benzene and BaP-particulate). While granting EC to coal projects, the Ministry of Environment, Forest and Climate Change (MoEF&CC) stipulated that the prescribed limit of above pollutants should be monitored regularly and necessary mitigation measures be taken to restrict the pollutants up to their prescribed limits to avoid their adverse impact (International Institute for Environment and Development, 2002).

Further, NAAQS, 2009 extended discretion to industries, wherein, PM_{10} and $PM_{2.5}$ could be monitored either on an annual basis or on a 24 hours basis (Agarwal and Narain, 1991). In the case of monitoring on annual basis, annual arithmetic mean of minimum 104 measurements in a year at a particular site taken twice a week at uniform intervals was to be considered, while in the case of monitoring on 24 hours basis, the prescribed norms were to be complied with 98 per cent of the time in a year. However, the values could not exceed the limits on two consecutive days of monitoring.

Audit observed that although these norms came into effect from November 2009, BCCL started complying with them from September 2015 only. Moreover, ambient air quality was monitored on fortnightly basis which was required to be done twice a week at uniform intervals to complete 104 observations in a year as per NAAQS, 2009. NAAQS prescribed the maximum permissible level of PM_{10} and $PM_{2.5}$ concentration in industrial, residential, rural and other areas. Audit observed that the presence of PM_{10} and $PM_{2.5}$ in air exceeded the levels prescribed in NAAQS in two mines namely Dahibari–Basantimata OCP (DBOCP) and Moonidih UG during 2013–2014 to 2017–2018 as detailed further:

Pollutants	Maximum Permitted Level (µg/cum)	Range of Actual Levels Recorded (µg/cum)	No. of Occasions the Reading Exceeded the Specified Standards in the Mines DBOCP	Moonidih UG
PM_{10}	100	101 to 660.06	31	13
$PM_{2.5}$	60	60.5496 to 480	26	8

Source: CMPDIL monitoring report and data furnished by BCCL.

It was further observed that no action was initiated to analyse the reasons for the pollution in excess of prescribed limits for remedial action.

Non-installation of Continuous Ambient Air Quality Monitoring Station

As per the Consent to Establish (CTE) certificate issued (August, 2014) to Madhuban Washery and East Bassuriya OCP by the Jharkhand State Pollution Control Board (JSPCB), BCCL was required to install continuous ambient air quality monitoring station for online monitoring of ambient air quality with its connectivity to JSPCB server. However, BCCL had not complied with these directives so far.

Water Pollution

The major source of water pollution in coal mines is the suspended solids in the drainage system of mine water and storm water (Wathern,

1988). Effluent from washeries and coal preparation plants generally contain fine coal particles, suspended solids, washery medium, reagents and sometimes oil and grease. In heavy earth moving machineries (HEMM) and light vehicles workshops, the workshop floors mix oil and oily matters into water along with dirt that is being washed. Besides this the sewage from residential complexes contaminates water with mainly organic matter.

Shortcomings in Implementation of Water Pollution Mitigation Measures

Non-installation of effluent treatment plant: Water generated during the course of coal mining is contaminated and needs to be treated so that it can be recycled. EC stipulated for installation for effluent treatment plant (ETP) at Kuya, DBOCP and Moonidih mines.

It is observed that BCCL did not install ETPs at the workshops and CHPs of the above mentioned mines. Absence of ETP not only violated the stipulations contained in EC but also continuously exposed the ground water to contamination.

Non-installation of sewage treatment plant (STP): As per the decision (July 2015) of the Committee of Jharkhand Legislative Assembly on environment and pollution control, BCCL had to install sewage treatment plant (STP) at residential colonies of the BCCL to treat the waste water of residential colonies. Accordingly, four STPs were required to be installed in residential areas of Koyla Nagar, Jagjiwan Nagar, Karmik Nagar and Harina Bagan.

It is however observed that no STP has been installed in the above residential colonies till date exposing the soil and underground water to contamination (Ghose, 2004).

Deficiencies in Monitoring of Ground Water Level

As per the specific condition of EC, regular monitoring has to be done in respect of ground water level and quality by establishing a network of existing wells and construction of new piezometers. Further, monitoring for quantity of ground water should be carried out four times in a year.

As per Central Mine Planning and Design Institute's (CMPDI) report (21 March 2018) It was observed that ground water level in mines located under administrative block of Baghmara in Cluster V, administrative block of Dhanbad in Cluster VI and XI, and administrative block of Jharia in Cluster X showed a declining trend during 2013–2014 to 2016–2017.

However, BCCL did not install piezometers for monitoring ground water level and its quality, violating EC condition.

As per Central Ground Water Authority (CGWA) guidelines (16 November 2015), industries/infrastructure/mining projects in Dhanbad are required to obtain no objection certificate (NoC) to use ground water. However, again it was observed that BCCL continued using ground water for its mining operation without obtaining NoC from CGWA.

Treatment of Mine Water

EC condition stipulates that mine water must be treated before it is discharged into natural water course. The quality of water discharged is to be monitored at the outlet points and proper records are to be maintained (Singh, 2005).

It is observed that BCCL had discharged 328 million litres of mine water per day into natural water course during 2017–2018. Whereas BCCL mine water treatment plant had the capacity to treat 81.17 million litres of mine water per day. Thus, in absence of required water treatment capacity, 246.83 million litres per day (75.25%) of mine water was discharged into the natural water course without any treatment. It was also examined and observed from the reports of CMPDI regarding quality of water discharged at the outlet points in DBOCP during 2014–2015 to 2015–2016 that presence of total suspended solid (TSS) in the water was in the range of 138–142 mg/L against the permissible limit of 100 mg/L. BCCL did not initiate any action to increase the capacity of mine water treatment plant.

EC condition stipulated that discharged mine water must be gainfully utilized for industrial and domestic purpose. Audit observed that during 2017–2018, 46 per cent of mine water of BCCL was discharged into natural water course without utilization. As per the Memorandum of Understanding (MoU) (October 2017) entered between CIL and Government of Jharkhand, BCCL was required to supply approximately 30 million gallons surplus mine water per day to Government of Jharkhand. However, no further development has taken place for supply of surplus mine water to Government of Jharkhand till date.

Land Management

Mining involves government forest land and non-forest land, and tenancy or private land for its development as well as operational activities. During exploration, land degradation due to change in land use takes place. An external dump is created to accommodate OB removed to extract coal and it is continued till internal dumping or backfilling commences.

The process of land management includes topsoil management, technical reclamation of external OB dump, internal dump/backfilled area, management of void left after completion of extraction and plantation, that is, biological reclamation of technically reclaimed dumps. (Biswas and Agarwal, 1992).

Improper Management of Topsoil

Topsoil is the upper and outer most layer of soil, usually the top 5 centimetres (cm) to 20 cm. It has the highest concentration of organic matter and microorganisms wherein most of the earth's biological soil activity occurs. It takes approximately 1,000 years for one inch of topsoil deposit to be formed. This soil requires to be removed for OC mining of coal. Given the time taken to generate and the importance of topsoil, MoEF&CC stipulated that topsoil be stacked at earmarked specific sites with adequate measures to preserve and be used as top layer for reclamation of mined-out areas. A record of topsoil indicating the area of stacking along with the date was to be maintained and topsoil was to be stacked in such a way so as to facilitate its issue on first-come-first-go basis. Regulation 108 of Coal Mines Regulation 2017 also stipulated that topsoil be stacked in a separate place.

It was observed that records of topsoil indicating the quantity and areas of stacking were not maintained in Kuya and Dahibari–Basantimata mines, which is indicative of ineffective management of top soil.

Improper OB Management

Overburden is required to be managed properly to prevent pollution of air, water, land and sliding of land during rainy season. Guidelines for Preparation of Mine Closure Plan 2009 stipulate that measures are to be implemented for reclamation and rehabilitation of mined-out land. Reclamation of the mined-out land is carried out through backfilling of OB. Audit observed that as on 31 March 2018 despite availability of fully mined-out land, BCCL dumped OB in the partially mined-out areas as detailed further:

Mines	Mined-out Area Available (ha)	Total Backfilled in Mined-out Area (ha)	Mined-out Area Available for Backfilling (ha)	Backfilling in Partially Mined-out Area (ha) in Place of Mined-out Area
Sijua Area (Mudidih and Kankanee Mines)	122.44	76.26	46.18	20.72
Kusunda Area (Godhur and Kusunda Mines)	108.5	97.4	11.1	33

OB backfilled in the partially mined-out areas is again required to be shifted before extraction of coal lying under the partially mined-out areas. Thus, backfilling of OB in partially mined-out area in place of totally mined-out area would result in unnecessary re-handling of OB causing additional cost of re-handling of OB and delay in reclamation of mined-out areas.

Specific condition of EC of the Cluster XVI (a group of mines) stipulated that no OB was to be dumped near water bodies and rivers, and a safety barrier of a minimum 60 meter width was to be maintained along the water/nalas to avoid the contamination the water/nalas.

We saw that in DBOCP, OB was dumped along the banks of Khudia River without maintaining the minimum distance, and hence it spilled continuously into the river. Further, garland drainage and embankment of suitable dimension with stone pitching were not provided to prevent spillage of OB into the river, thereby resulting in contamination of the river water.

Deficiencies in Plantation Surrounding the Coal Mines of BCCL

Biological reclamation by way of broadcast seeding of grass seeds and plantation/afforestation is to be undertaken for stabilization of OB dumps against erosion or minimization of soil erosion and best utilization of land. Tree plantation is to be taken up on external OB dumps and backfilled/internal dump areas including terraced slope, vacant land and avenue plantation as a mitigation measure. Tree plantation is one of the cost effective remedial measures to mitigate air and noise pollution. As per CIL Environmental Guidelines, it was decided to develop heterogeneous mix of forest with local species so that the survival rate remained high and evergreen. These species of trees were to have combined properties like medicinal, timber-yielding and fruit-bearing. However, it was observed that though BCCL is meeting the year-wise target of biological reclamation, no records were produced showing the species of trees used for plantation in each area. Further, no mechanism to monitor and ensure survival of the existing plantation was found on record.

Closed Mines

Mineral deposits being exhaustible, once the process of economical extraction of mine is complete, there is a need for its closure (Bagchi and Gupta, 1990). Planning for mine closure is necessary and is to be done systematically so as to ensure safety, post-closure monitoring, control of safety hazards, decommissioning of infrastructures, closure of entries to the mine, management of final voids, reclamation of forest/vegetation and financial aspects involving closure costs.

Mineral Conservation and Development Rules, 1988 (MCDR), stipulate that the owner of mine shall not abandon a mine without prior permission in writing and without obtaining a certificate from the regional controller of mines or the officer authorized by the state government in this behalf to the effect that protective reclamation and rehabilitation work have been carried out in accordance with the final mine closure plan. For financial assurance of mine closure expenses, BCCL was to open an escrow account with a scheduled bank with the Coal Controller Organization (CCO) and deposit money at prescribed rates. Up to 80 per cent of the total amount deposited including interest accrued in the escrow account or the expenditure incurred towards progressive mine closure in the past five years, whichever is less, could be claimed from CCO by BCCL for reimbursement of expenditure on mine closure activities.

Production above Environmental Norms

The Environmental Clearance (EC) and the Forest Clearance (FC) issued by MoEF&CC permits the maximum quantum of coal to be extracted from the mines after compliance of various measures specified in this regard.

Penalty due to Excess Production of Coal Violating EC

The production of coal beyond the quantity specified in EC attracts penalty at the rate of 100 per cent of the price of the illegally or unlawfully mined mineral under Section 21(5) of the MMDR Act, 1957.

Operation of Mines/Washeries without EC, CTE and CTO

Environmental Impact Assessment (EIA) notification 2006 of MoEF&CC stipulates that every project has to get EC to control the adverse impact of coal mining. Further, Water (Prevention and Control of Pollution) Act, 1974 and Section 31A of Air (Prevention and Control of Pollution) Act, 1981 require that every project should obtain CTE for establishment of a new unit or expansion/modernization of any existing unit from SPCB. After obtaining CTE, the project requires to obtain Consent to Operate (CTO) before commencing commercial production for a specific period, which needs to be renewed periodically.

Change in Mining Technology

General condition of EC provides the details of mining technology to be used for coal extraction (Saxena et al. 2000). In case a project proponent (PP) intends to use a different mining technology other than what is stated in EC, then PP must obtain a modified EC from MoEF&CC. Scrutiny of ECs obtained for Basantimata underground mines, Dobari underground mines, Gopalichak underground mines and Gaslitand underground mines revealed that management were required to use bord and pillar method for mining of coal. Audit however observed that these mines were operated as OC mines using dumper and shovel combination. Change in mining technology without taking prior permission from MoEF&CC tantamount to violation of the General EC conditions.

Jharia Mine Fire

Mining areas in JCF within the leasehold land of BCCL are faced with problems of fire and subsidence due to the century-old history of mining in this coalfield. Fire in JCF was first reported in 1916. Issues relating to pervasive mine fire include health and well-being of the persons living around the fire areas in terms of air and water pollution, subsidence, threat to infrastructures such railway lines, roads, buildings and rivers have been major concerns from time to time (WHO, 1946). To deal with the problems of fire, subsidence and rehabilitation, CMPDIL prepared (March 1999) Jharia Master Plan (JMP) which was approved (April 1999) by BCCL Board. The JMP was revised in 2004, 2006 and 2008 and finally it was approved by the Government of India in 2009 wherein a time frame of 10 years was allowed for dealing with the fire.

As per JMP, 67 places under JCF are under fire which requires mitigation measure for its extinguishment and for controlling the adverse environmental impact due to fire. JMP recommended conventional method as well as other method for controlling or extinguishing the fire. Conventional methods included total excavation of fire, isolation by trenching, blind flushing, surface sealing, isolation by underground stopping, quenching and cooling, cooling by water curtain, flooding and natural burnout. Other methods included inert gas injection, chemical treatment, burnout control, modified bulk filling (water/slurry and pneumatic) and underground coal gasification.

However, the following deficiencies/shortfalls are present in the implementation of JMP.

Delays in Implementation of Fire Dealing Activities

In the JMP to deal with fire, 67 fire places under JCF were grouped into 45 fire projects. A timeline of 10 years was earmarked to extinguish fire in these 45 fire projects. Audit observed that even after completion of nine years from approval of JMP, fire dealing activities could be started only in 25 fire projects. In other 20 fire projects, no firefighting activities had been undertaken so far. Delay in implementation of JMP not only resulted in spreading of fire around the JCF but also endangered the lives of the people residing in and around the fire area. Also, it has had an adverse impact on environment.

Rehabilitation of Affected Population from Endangered Areas

JMP recommended rehabilitation of affected families by constructing 79,159 quarters which included 25,000 quarters for families of BCCL employees and 54,159 quarters for outsiders. These houses were to be constructed in identified non-coal bearing places within a period of 10 years. Construction of quarters for the BCCL employees was to be carried out by BCCL and the same for the outsiders was to be carried out by the Jharia Rehabilitation and Development Authority (JRDA).

As per the data, only 6,668 quarters for families of BCCL employees and 4,352 quarters for outsiders were constructed till date (August 2018). Further, only 3,361 families of BCCL employees and 2,122 families of outsiders had been shifted into the newly constructed quarters in non-coal bearing area as detailed further:

Target for Quarter Construction (in Numbers)							
Quarters Target		Quarters Built		Shortfall		Shortfall in (%)	
BCCL	Outsiders	BCCL	Outsiders	BCCL	Outsiders	BCCL	Outsiders
25,000	54,159	6,668	4,352	18,332	49,807	73.32	91.96

Quarter Built and Occupied (in Numbers)							
Quarters Built		Quarters Occupied		Shortfall		Shortfall in (%)	
BCCL	Outsiders	BCCL	Outsiders	BCCL	Outsiders	BCCL	Outsiders
6,668	4,352	3,361	2,122	3,307	2,230	49.60	51.24

Non-shifting of the families from fire-affected areas exposed the inhabitants to the risk of subsidence and other environmental hazards.

Diversion of Stretch of National Highway 32 between Putki and Godhur

JMP recommended diversion of stretch of National Highway 32 between Putki and Godhur, passing over coal bearing fire-affected area. In November 2009, BCCL and Government of Jharkhand decided that the fire-affected stretch would be handed over to BCCL on lease basis to excavate coal from the entire fire-affected area. After excavation of coal, the stretch was required to be handed over to Government of Jharkhand. To deal with NH traffic passing through this stretch In the meantime, it was decided to develop an alternate route at par with NH standards as a short-term measure. BCCL was required to bear the cost of developing the alternate route. The proposal was concurred in July 2010 and accordingly BCCL deposited (February 2012) Rs. 198.5 million with the JRDA, Dhanbad.

Non-assessment of Quantum of Underground Fire

In JCF fire exists on surface as well as below the ground. BCCL assessed expansion of mine fire on the surface from time to time through the National Remote Sensing Centre (NRSC), Hyderabad. In 2014, the NRSC reported that the quantum of surface fire covered an area of 2.18 sq. km which expanded to 3.28 sq. km in 2018 due to opening of underground fire by excavation method.

As the surface fire further expanded over 1.10 sq. km in last four years, likelihood of further spreading of the existing underground fire cannot be ruled out. No records were produced regarding initiatives taken by BCCL for assessment of the quantum of underground fire.

Hazardous Substance Management

The hazardous substance management includes management and handling of hazardous wastes, bio-medical wastes, batteries and e-waste. Hazardous wastes in coal mines include used/spent oil and wastes/residue containing oil arising out of the process of industrial operation using mineral/synthetic oil as lubricant in hydraulic systems or other applications, chemical sludge from waste water treatment, and oil and grease skimming residue resulting from the process of purification of air, water and waste water. E-waste is waste generated out of damaged electrical/electronic products (Bose and Singh, 1989). Hazardous Wastes (Management, Handling and Transboundary Movement) Rule, 2008, was applicable to the company till March 2016. In April 2016, Hazardous and other Wastes (Management and Transboundary Movement) Rules, 2016 (Rules), were issued in supersession of 2008 Rules. These Rules defined hazardous waste as any waste which by reason of characteristics such as physical, chemical, biological, reactive, toxic, flammable, explosive or corrosive, causes danger or is likely to cause danger to health or environment, whether alone or in contact with other wastes or substances. Handling, gen-eration, collection, storage, packaging and transportation of used oil required authorization from the JSPCB, in accordance with Clauses 5 and 6 of the above Rules.

Deficiencies in Management of Hazardous Waste

In accordance with the Rules, authorization was to be obtained for handling the hazardous waste. Kuya mines and Bhojudih Coal

Washery handled the hazardous waste without obtaining the authorization from the JSPCB. DBOCP, Putki Balihari and Moonidih UG mines handled the hazardous waste without obtaining authorization from JSPCB till July 2017. Hazardous waste collected, received, treated, transported, stock and disposed of by BCCL in the above mentioned mines and washeries during 2013–2017 (July 2017) is detailed further:

S. No.	Mine/ Washery	Burnt Oil (in kl)	Used Cotton Waste (in kg)	Lead Acid Automobile Batteries (in nos)	Lead Acid Cap Lamp Batteries (in nos)	Metal Scrap (in kg)
1.	Kuya[1]	21.355	1,211	39	-	29,950
2.	PB Project	1,460	-	-	-	-
3.	Moonidih	1.8	60	NA	NA	NA
4.	Bhojudih Washery	655	-	43	NA	Estimated 80 Ton

Note: For the period of 2013-2018.

Handling of waste without proper authorization is a pointer to deficient monitoring.

Under clause 23 of Hazardous and other Wastes (Management and Transboundary Movement) Rules, 2016, BCCL was to obtain insurance cover as contemplated under Section 4 of the Public Liability Insurance Act, 1991, as a safeguard against liability for damages caused to the environment to third party due to improper handling and management of hazardous and other wastes.

Corporate Social Responsibility

Mining of coal has adverse impact on the ecosystem and biodiversity in and around the areas where the mines are in operation. Therefore, projects should be designed on the principle of sustainable development with due consideration for environment, conservation, safety, quality and aspirations of the community around it. Expenditure on corporate social responsibility (CSR) is required for activities relating to protect and safeguard environment, and to maintain ecological balance.

Shortfall in CSR expenses

In accordance with specific condition of EC granted by the MoEF&CC, five rupees per tonne of coal produced was to be earmarked for activities under CSR. The amount was to be spent for community development under CSR activities.

There was a shortfall in CSR expenses actually incurred by BCCL by Rs. 38.24 crores as compared to the amount mandated by the MoEF&CC during the year 2014–2015 to 2017–2018 as detailed further

Year	CSR Expenditure to Be Incurred as Mandated by the MOEFandCC (in Crore)	Actual CSR Expenses (in Crore)	(+) Excess (–) Shortfall (2) – (3)	Percentage of (4) to (2)
1	2	3	4	5
2014–2015	17.26	14.33	(–) 2.93	16.98
2015–2016	17.93	3.26	(–) 14.67	81.82
2016–2017	18.52	11.45	(–) 7.07	38.18
2017–2018	16.31	2.74	(–) 13.57	83.20
Total	70.02	31.78	(–) 38.24	54.61

No reasons were found on record for shortfall in actual expenses.

Conclusion

You can't start with imbalance and end with peace, be that in your own body, in an ecosystem or between a government and its people. What we need to strive for is not perfection, but balance

—Ani DiFranco

Sustainable development aims at the creation of sustainable improvements of the quality of life for all people and this should be the principle goal of development policy. As far as the development of eco parks to safeguard the ecosystem is concerned, firm steps are required to be taken to bridge the gap between regulations and its proper implementation. Although in this regard, there have been successful examples of mining land being reclaimed and restored into sustainable structures like eco parks. Development of eco-restoration site at Gokul Park, Lodna Area has become a major tourist attraction. Jhunkundar closed OC mine has been converted into a beautiful lake which is acting as rain water harvesting structure and helping in recharging the ground water level. Pisciculture by local villages is done here. The site has been restored to a natural ecosystem. MoEF&CC through its EC conditions directed companies to have well-laid down system of reporting of non-compliances/violations of environmental norms to ensure proper checks and balances.[1]

References

Agarwal, A., & Narain, S. (1991, October). Global warming in an unequal world. *International Sustainable Development*, 1, 98–104.

Bagchi, A., & Gupta, R. N. (1990) *Surface blasting and its impact on environment*. Workshop on Environmental Management of Mining Operations, Varanasi, pp. 262–279.

Biswas, A. K., & Agarwal, S. B. C. (1992). *Environmental impact assessment for developing countries* (p. 249). Oxford: Butterworth Heinemann.

Bose, A. K., & Singh, B. (1989). environmental problem in coal mining areas, impact assessment and management strategies-case study in India. In L. J. Brasser & W.C. Mulder (Eds.), Man *and his* Ecosystem, *Proceedings of the 8th World Clean Air Congress* (Vol. 4, p. 243). Amsterdam: Elsevier.

Ghose, K. M. (2004), *Effect of opencast mining on soil fertility*. Dhanbad: Centre for Mining Environment.

International Institute for Environment and Development (2002). Local communities and mines. In *Breaking New Ground: Mining, Minerals and Sustainable Development*. Retrieved from https://pubs.iied.org/pdfs/9084IIED.pdf

MINEO Consortium. (2000). *Review of potential environmental and social impact of mining*. Retrieved from http://www2.brgm.fr/mineo/UserNeed/IMPACTS.pdf

Sharma, P. D. (2019, March). *Coal mining and pollution*. Knol.

---

[1] During 2013–14, against CSR expenditure of Rs. 16.31 crores as mandated by MoEF&CC, BCCL actually spent an amount of Rs. 20.00 crores.

Saxena N. C., Singh, G., & Ghosh, R. (2000). *Environment management in mining areas.* Dhanbad: Centre of mining environment, I.S.M.

Singh, G. (2005). *Water sustainability through augmentation of underground pumped out water for portable purpose from coalmines of eastern India*: Dhanbad: Indian School of Mines.

Ward, K., Jr. (2019, 17 March). Important new study details mountaintop removal coal mining's huge carbon footprint. *Coal Tattoo.* Retrieved from http://blogs. wvgazettemail.com/coaltattoo/2010/03/17/important-new-study-details-mountaintop-removal-coal-minings-huge-carbon-footprint/

Wathern, P. (Ed.). (1988). *An introductory guide to EIA.* In *Environmental impacts assessments* (2nd ed., pp. 3–28) London: Unwin Hyman.

World Health Organization. (1946). Preamble to the Constitution of the World Health Organization. In *Official Records of the World Health Organization* (No. 2, p. 100). Geneva: World Health Organization.

CHAPTER 9

Environmental Externality to Human Health near the Coal Mining Area

Tapaswini Nayak and
Indrani Roy Chowdhury

Introduction

Mining in Odisha has an ancient origin and the mining industry occupies a special position in the state's economy. Specifically, the development of coal mining is undoubtedly a milestone in the field of industrial development of the state. Among minerals, coal—'the black diamond'—is considered as one of the crucial natural resources, which have immense possibility of contributing to the growth and development of not only the state's economy but also of the nation. Coal mining activities have different types of environmental, social and economic influences at international, national and regional levels. On the one side, opening of a new mining site creates job facilities for the unemployed people directly and through its different types of constructive activities indirectly. Mining activities also generate large amount of tax revenue for the state government and earns foreign exchange. Mining-related activities provide different kinds of businesses to local people, and basic facilities such as roads, schools and primary hospitals to remote areas. At the same time, displacement, deforestation and fertile land loss, and air and water pollution problems have been major issues for the nearest residing communities. Starting from mining to combustion, combustion to waste disposal, each and every process with coal sceptically affects public health and the local environment (Hota & Mishra, 2010; Mishra 2012; Singh et al., 2010). More production of coal increases the load of release of toxic chemicals into the air, which influences the PM_{10} level in the atmosphere (Pope, 1995; Pope, Bates, & Raizenne, 2007).

Mining-related activities, particularly near opencast coal mines create irreparable losses to the local environment, which have long-term future impacts. The intervening processes of extractions release many toxic pollutants such as Respiratory Suspended Particulate Matter (RSPM), carbon dioxide and sulphur dioxide (SO_2) which devastate the ambient air quality over time (WHO, 2002). Longer exposures to these pollutants have critical health effects on human beings residing near the coal field. World Health Organization (WHO) argues that the quality of environment has been playing a vital role to determine good health, and the standard of health and quality of life is considered as a key parameter to attain sustainable development (WHO, 2002). Thus, the prime aim of this chapter is to find out the health impacts of air pollution due to the mining extraction-related activities. Chapter is decorated as follows: Second section represents the review of literature, third section presents the overview of study field, fourth section tells the methodology that argues about how the human health and exposure to air pollution are correlated to each other, fifth section depicts about primary survey design and data sources, sixth section describes the econometric regression model, seventh section discusses the regression results and finally eighth section presents the main findings.

Review of Literature

'Quality of health' is considered as the fundamental ingredient to measure the efficiency and productivity of economic development. Being healthy is not only being entirely free from diseases physically but is also connected with quality of environment which is conducive to mental health (WHO, 2005). In lower-middle income countries, health problems have been rising mainly because of malnutrition, environmental degradation (due to urbanization, industrialization, natural resource exploitation and ecological imbalance), unfavourable occupational environment and indoor pollution (Banerjee, 2001; Ostro, 1994). It is very evident that the quality of health and well-being of a community is inseparably linked with the surrounding environmental quality (Kamjan, 2010). The exploitation of natural resources like minerals has several environmental, economic and social consequences for the local communities in the mining belt. Among all minerals, mining of coal and its activities are unhealthier as they lead to more negative health externalities in comparison to their positive values to the local communities. Income and employment creation, infrastructure development, foreign exchange earnings and so on are the benefits which can be extracted from coal mining industries in the short-term while the negative externalities such as health hazards due to environmental degradation, displacement, forest and biodiversity loss are borne over a long period of time which can't be compensated properly over time (Mishra, 2009; Singh et al., 2010). The quality of life of the local communities in the coal field area and the environmental status near the coal mining area are very bad (Murthy & Patra, 2006). It is evident that each stage of mining, starting from extraction to transportation and processing to combustion, generates different types of problems for human health and local environment. These losses are external cost for the coal industry, which we know as the externalities of mining extraction activities (Epstein et al., 2011; Finkelman et al., 1999). However, undoubtedly it can be said that coal mining areas are characterized by greater socio-economic disadvantages, riskier health behaviours and environmental pollution associated with reduced health-related quality of life (HRQOL; Julling & Hendryx, 2010). There are various environmental challenges the coal mining industry is facing such as the problem of greenhouse gases and acid rain, which indirectly leads to the climate change problem. Another problem the coal mining industry is facing is coal mining-induced displacement and resettlement that create main risks to societal sustainability (Singh, 2007; Goswami et al., 2010).

In case of Odisha, coal mining activities and the problem of environmental pollution is very alarming and serious so it needs to be properly highlighted. The Odisha State Pollution Central Board (OSPCB) has explained that all areas near the opencast coal belt in the state are the most hazardous zones for health and have the worst living conditions for human beings. The concentration of suspended particulate matter (SPM) and respiratory particulate matter (RPM) is much higher than the prescribed regulatory standard by the pollution control board (Hota & Mishra, 2010). The Angul–Talcher region in Odisha is counted as one of the most polluted industrial regions when opencast coal mining activities are concerned. Water pollution problems arise in this region mainly due to acid mine drainage, heavy metal contamination, chemical pollution, erosion and sedimentation. The condition of groundwater is miserable too. Potable water is transported to this area by different sources and livestock and local community suffer from various epidemic diseases such as acute respiratory infection, bloody dysentery, malaria and skin diseases (Das, 1995; Hota & Mishra, 2010; Reza et al., 2009). Mining and its allied industrial activities in opencast coal belt are harmful to land use pattern. There has been a reduction in forest area cover (from 696.04 km to 503.2 km) and agricultural land (from 758.43 km to 520.96 km) due to mining and industrial activities in the region from 1978 to 2007 (Hota & Mishra, 2010). This mining region has undergone rampant fluctuations from its 'culture of ecology' to 'culture of pollution'. The cause is that coal extraction has not only devastated the livelihood of small farmers to access the agronomy but has also affected their accessibility to common property resources (CPRs) (Garada, 2013). The current literature is mostly confined to estimating the morbidity and health impact costs of water pollution in the mining region, quality of life and forest loss and so on. While some other studies exist on the health impact of air pollution in the iron mining region of Odisha (Saha, Pattanayak, Sills, & Singha, 2011) and health impact of occupational hazards (i.e., direct impact) on mining (Sarkar et al., 2004), we found there are very few studies (Hota & Mishra, 2010; Mishra, 2012; Singh et al., 2010) in India on the health impact of air pollution induced by opencast coal mining. Given that coal is the most polluting natural resource and its dust is more contaminant and hazardous in nature in comparison to other minerals, the health outcomes of exposure to it are supposed to be very critical and demand serious policy intervention. There is no empirical study on health and air pollution (i.e., environmental health or indirect health impact) in opencast coal belt particularly in Mahanadi Coal Field Limited (MCL) region in Angul–Talcher area, Odisha. Thus, the study attempts to explore the linkage between the environment (air pollution) and human health near the coal belt of Odisha.

Overview of Study Area

Odisha is blessed with abundant mineral resources, which include coal, iron ore, chromite, bauxite, graphite, copper and lead. The state has been occupying a vital place in mineral resources reserves in India. Within the state, coal occupied a greater share, that is, 88 per cent among all the mineral deposits apart from iron ore and bauxite. A total of 51 per cent of coal is extracted from MCL coal field (situated in Angul-Talcher) region and the rest from Jharsuguda, Sundargarh and Sambalpur districts (Economic Survey, Odisha 2012–2013). Our study was located in MCL coal field area in Angul district. Even though this district is blessed with rich natural resources, it is considered as the hottest place in India from a pollution point of view, where the maximum temperature goes up to 50°C during summer. The PM_{10} is pretty high than the prescribed level by OSPCB all year around.

Besides air pollution, the river Brahmani passing through this area also gets polluted through coal mining and other industrial activities (State of Environment Report, Odisha 2011–2012). Due to the critical pollution level, many epidemic diseases are highly prevalent which hamper the health and well-being of common people near the mining area.

Table 9.1 Ambient Air Quality of the Study Region 2015–2016

Month	Station 1 (MCL) Average		Station 2 (TTPS) Average		Station 3 (NALCO Nagar, Angul) Average		Station 4 (Industrial Estate, Angul) Average	
	RSPM (PM_{10})	$PM_{2.5}$	RSPM (PM_{10})	$PM_{2.5}$	RSPM (PM_{10})	$PM_{2.5}$	RSPM (PM_{10})	$PM_{2.5}$
January	171	130	154	122	137	98	137	94
February	186	99	165	115	117	80	108	80
March	161	87	136	76	129	65	118	74
April	177	105	91	53	108	57	92	51
May	149	93	123	79	97	80	95	50
June	140	87	71	44	78	38	84	47
July	126	72	56	34	80	47	88	53
August	100	57	61	34	79	39	65	49
September	87	39	70	51	100	49	96	57
October	133	48	95	75	91	52	98	54
November	135	75	126	68	105	57	105	54
December	134	79	164	86	107	54	105	56
Average annual	140	81	111.08	69.75	102	57	99.25	60

Source: State Pollution Control Board, Odisha.

Epidemic diseases and infections such as gastroenteritis, acute respiratory infection, bloody dysentery, malaria, blindness, leprosy, tuberculosis and skin diseases are major public health problems of this area. The prevalence of malaria is very high even throughout all the season. The other ailments such as joint pain, dysentery, skin diseases are highly prevalent among children due to use of polluted water and exposure to polluted air. Waterborne diseases are very common in this region (32.88%). A large section of population (53.15%) suffers from malaria and acute respiratory infection (Community Health Fellowship Programme [CHF], 2009).

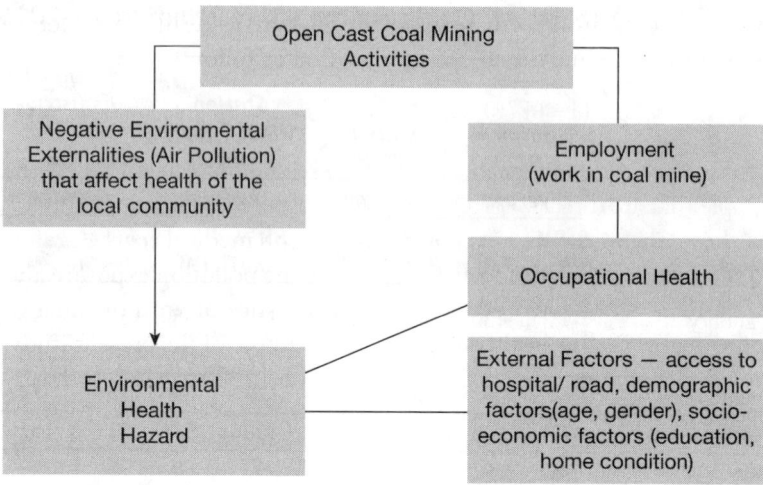

Figure 9.1 *Conceptual Framework: Mining Activities and Environmental Health*

Source: Subhrendu K. Pattanayak et al. (2006).

Methodology

Following Ostro (1994), Alberini et al. (1997), Gupta (2006), Imran et al. (2010) and Adhikari (2012), this study also uses the dose–response method to know about the association between the exposure of PM_{10} and health outcomes in the opencast coal belt of Odisha. This method relates the essence of a 'dose' (i.e., daily exposure to the concentration of pollutants) to the 'response' of the receptor (the response can be different types of respiratory illness [RI], mental stress and even death/mortality) and this intensity of effects can be considered as the proportion or the days of illness.

Our study employs the easiest form of the general 'health production function' proposed by Freeman, Herriges and Kling (1993). The notable literature including Grossman (1972), Cropper (1981), Gerking and Stanley (1986) and Harrington and Portney (1987) provide the fundamental base for the health production model which was expanded by Freeman in 1993. The basic health production function for an individual can be specified as follows:

$$H = H (Q, M, A, Z)............ \quad (1)$$

Here, H represents the health status (respiratory sickness) of the people that are directly correlated to the level of air ambient quality Q. M shows the mitigating expenses including all medical costs. A refers to the averting activities to avoid or reduce the pollution exposure and Z captures other socio-economic characteristics of an individual or individual's baseline health stock. For the purpose of the present study, we have taken into account only the relationship between respiratory health and air pollution (i.e., PM_{10}) level.

Data Source

The present study is mainly based on primary data. The air pollution (PM_{10}) data (considered as the main parameter for environmental pollution in opencast coal mines area) are collected from the OSPCB. Two-stage stratification sampling method was used for selecting households in the study. In the first stage, we selected the location of the air pollution monitoring station, that is, the MCL area for the study. Then in the second stage, an area of 4 kilometres radius was selected around the air monitoring station. Total of 10 villages were located within that radius. Thus, a total of 210 households from the 10 villages (for each village, 21 household were randomly chosen) and 855 household members were selected for survey. Out of the 855 selected, 254 members suffered from respiratory illness. These 254 household members are the focus of the study. Through primary survey we have collected the weekly health information (regarding weekly acute respiratory symptoms and related sick days) from respondents to control the impact of seasonal variation in air pollution levels. Thus, we have maintained health diary of 254 household members for six weeks repeatedly. Therefore, the survey concluded in a pooled data where we found only 932 (restrictive sample) observations who suffered from RI diseases. The study also collected other environmental, socio-economic and demographic information to control the health impact of air pollution.

Exposure to Air Pollution and Health Impact in Opencast Coal Mining Area

The analysis of the health impact of a marginal change in the air pollution level demands calculating the equation for sick days due to respiratory illness. By following the recent studies (Adhikari, 2012; Chowdhury & Imran, 2010; Gupta, 2006; Kumar & Rao, 2001), we estimated the ordinary least square (OLS) regression model to find out the relationship between the air pollution level and negative health outcome.

OLS Regression Model for Estimating Dose–Response Function

OLS is a method which estimates the unknown parameter in linear regression. The main aim of OLS is to reduce the sum of the squares of the differences between the observed variable in the data set and a set of explanatory variables. OLS as a linear regression model expresses the slope of coefficients as an absolute change in the expected outcome related with a unit change in the independent variables. OLS is a linear model for each and every sample, that is, n. If X_i are the k explanatory variables and Y is the dependent variable, then

$$Y_n = \sum_{i=0}^{k} \beta_i X_{ni} + \varepsilon_n \ldots\ldots\ldots\ldots\ldots \quad (2)$$

By minimizing the error of prediction, we can find the coefficient β. One of the important weaknesses of OLS regression is that it faces the collinearity problem among the independent variables (Wooldrige, 1984). Therefore, we have checked the collinearity diagnostics test among the independent variables. From the test, it is clear that the multicollinearity problem among the explanatory variables is not a critical concern. So the independent variables used in the model are relaxed from problem of multicollinearity (Table 9.2).

For empirical analysis of dose–response function, the restricted activity days or sick days due to RI are taken as the dependent variable

Table 9.2 Collinearity Diagnostics

Variable	VIF	SQRT VIF	Tolerance	R-squared	Eigen Value	Conditional Index
PM$_{10}$	1.05	1.02	0.9552	0.0448	11.5013	1.000
Age	1.42	1.19	0.7055	0.2945	1.2916	2.9841
Gender	1.69	1.30	0.5927	0.4073	0.9506	3.4783
HH-size	1.15	1.07	0.8680	0.1320	0.6297	4.2736
Exps_cldst	1.51	1.23	0.6617	0.3383	0.5118	4.7405
Awr_plhlt	1.66	1.29	0.6012	0.3988	0.4735	4.9283
Astm_cron	1.21	1.10	0.8285	0.1715	0.3844	5.4701
B.P_cron	1.52	1.23	0.6585	0.3412	0.3453	5.7710
Ind_smkng	1.64	1.28	0.6106	0.3894	0.2085	7.4267
Fuel_coal	1.37	1.17	0.7294	0.2706	0.1272	9.5077
PCI	1.54	1.24	0.6502	0.3498	0.0902	11.2948
Prvswk_ill	1.13	1.06	0.8879	0.1121	0.0539	14.6082
Prvsw_exp	1.02	1.01	0.9792	0.0208	0.0314	19.1294
Exercise	1.49	1.22	0.6730	0.3270	0.0002	244.5824
Mean VIF	1.37				Condition Number	244.5824

Source: Authors own calculation.

Note: It is a rule of thumb that a tolerance of 0.1 or less than 0.1 is a reason for the presence of multicollinearity. Equally, VIF of 10 or greater is also a cause of concern for multicollinearity. Here from the above diagnostics test, it is clear that the multicollinearity problem among the explanatory variables is not a critical concern. So the independent variables used in the model are relaxed from the problem of multicollinearity.

and the independent variable is air pollution level (i.e., PM$_{10}$), along with other socio-economic and control variables. The details about the independent variables are given further.

The study has focused on the daily PM$_{10}$ as the only important indicator for air pollution in the opencast coal mining area as regular exposure to PM$_{10}$ is considered to have the most harmful effect on respiratory health (Chowdhury & Imran, 2010; Gupta, 2006).

In the estimation part, we have taken some control variables including pre-existing illness (from previous week), chronic diseases, exposure to outdoor pollution, smoking and so on to ignore the over-estimation problem in a regression model. Apart from these control variables, the study also captured the socio-economic characteristics of individuals that may affect the health outcomes of human beings directly or indirectly such as age, gender, education, awareness about adverse health effects of pollution, per capita income level and exercise habits) and household characteristics such as size of household and medium of cooking, fuel or indoor pollution.

Results and Discussions

OLS regression result in Table 9.3 presents that the β value of PM_{10} is positive and p-value is significant at 1 per cent level. This depicts a direct relationship between sick days (due to respiratory illness) and pollution level. The coefficient of gender in OLS regression model is negative and significant at 5 per cent level, which reveals higher probability of RI for female individuals as the air pollution level increases (Imran et al., 2006). The coefficient value is positive and significant at 5 per cent level for chronic disease asthma, which presents that sick days increase as the chronic asthma increases. The illness of previous week has positive coefficient with 1 per cent level of significance which depicts that if any person has suffered from RI in the previous week, then the risk of suffering more RI-related sick days will increase for the same person in present time.

The control variable smoking habits of individual is also significant and positive. It indicates that the individuals who smoke are more likely to be affected by daily exposure to PM_{10} and therefore sick days due to RI increase for them.

Conclusion

Given that the level of PM_{10} is consistently increasing at a very frightening level in the study region, it is genuine to predict that the

Table 9.3 OLS Regression: Dependent Variable Number of Sick Days Due to RI

Independent Variables	OLS Regression Coefficient (P-value)	Standard Error
PM$_{10}$	**3.0419(0.000)***	0.6200
Age	−0.020(0.86)	0.1221
Gender	**−0.298(0.046)****	0.1493
HH size	**0.126(0.015)****	0.0518
Exposed_coaldust	−0.180(0.20)	0.1420
Awar_polutnhelth	−0.008(0.69)	0.1573
Asthma_cronic	**0.400(0.002)***	0.1257
B.P	−0.102(0.52)	0.1598
Indiv_smoking	**0.335(0.08)*****	0.1960
Fuel_coaldumy	0.092(0.49)	0.1362
Prevsweek_ill	**0.501(0.000)***	0.1193
Prevsweek_expend.	−0.095(0.40)	0.1179
Exercise	−0.044(0.71)	0.1533
PCI	0.023(0.83)	0.1132
Constant_	**−11.95(0.000)***	3.2548
	R^2 = 0.10, F = 6.25 **Prob. > F = 0.000**	
No. of observations	932	

Source: Authors own calculation.

Note: *, ** and *** indicate significance at 1%, 5% and 10% level, respectively.

health impact (particularly RI) will be very penetrating and extremely important in the nearness of the coal project area. This is also observed from the international and national literature. The air ambient quality in Angul–Talcher coal mining region is much higher than the standard limit prescribed by both the central and state pollution control boards. This study attempts to analyse the health impact of the coal mining induced air pollution in the Angul–Talcher coal mining area.

The result confirms that there is a direct and highly significant association between the level of air pollution (RSPM/PM$_{10}$) and RI-related sick days in the OLS regression model. The coefficient of pollution variable represents that a declining critical air pollution level (PM$_{10}$ level) causes a decline in expected number of RI-related sick days. The air pollution level (particularly the PM10) is very critical in opencast coal mining region. This critical air quality affects adversely the respiratory health status of human being near the coal belt. Thus, with these findings the authors suggest that green belts and proper afforestation in coal mining clusters should be a regular activity of the government of Odisha and the stock holders of mining company. Then this green zone will serve as an additional carbon sink and can contribute towards building local environmental benefits. At the same time, regional environmental impact assessment is to be periodically taken up. Since it is not an easy task for macro cases, particularly first more vulnerable mining clusters should be identified at micro level then a robust environmental monitoring system should be established there.

Acknowledgements

We are grateful to Professor Pulin B Nayak and Professor Binayak Rath and the other participants of the conference (*Health, Public Policy and Human Development: A Way Forward to Address SDGs* organized by the National Institute of Technology, Rourkela, 30–31 March 2017) for their valuable comments. I am thankful to the villagers of MCL area, Odisha who contributed a lot for this study.

References

Air Quality and Health Effects, World Health Organization Technical Report Series No-157, 2002
Air Quality Guidelines-Global Update 2005, WHO https://www.who.int/phe/health_topics/outdoorair/outdoorair_aqg/en/
A Rapid Assessment of Communitization Processes of the National Rural Health Mission in Jharakhand, Orissa and Bihar, Community Health Fellowship Programme, Public Health Resource Society, New Delhi, Jan–March, 2009
Adhikari, N. (2012). *Measuring the health benefits from reducing air pollution in Kathmandu valley* (Working Paper No. 69–12). Kathmandu: South Asian Network for Development and Environmental Economics.

Alberini, A., Cropper, M., Fu, T. T., Krupnick, A., Liu, J. T., Shaw, D., & Harrington, W. (1997). Valuing health effects of air pollution in developing countries: The case of Taiwan. *Journal of environmental economics and management, 34*(2), 107–126.

Banerjee, S. (2001). Economic valuation of environmental benefits and costs. In R. N. Bhattacharya (Ed.), *Environmental economics: An Indian perspective* (pp. 125–159). New Delhi: Oxford University Press.

Chowdhury, T. & Imran, M (2010). *Morbidity costs of vehicular air pollution: Examining Dhaka city in Bangladesh* (Working Paper No. 17–06). Kathmandu: South Asian Network for Development and Environmental Economics.

Cropper, M. L. (1981). Measuring the benefits from reduced morbidity. *The American Economic Review, 71*(2), 235–240.

Economic Survey, 2012–13, Govt. of Odisha

Epstein et al. (2011). Full cost of accounting for the life cycle of coal. *Annals of the New York Academy of Science, Feb; 1219,* 73–98.

Finkelman, R. B. (1999). Health impacts of domestic coal use in china. *Proceedings of the National Academy of Sciences, 96,* 3427–3431.

Frinkelman, R. B. et al. (2002). Health impacts of coal and coal use: possible solutions. *International Journal of Coal Geology, 50,* 1–4.59.

Freeman, A. M., Herriges, J., & Kling, C. (1993). *The measurement of environmental and resource values.* Washington, DC: Resources for the Future. Retrieved from http://econdse.org/wp-content/uploads/2016/07/Freeman-Herriges-Kling-2014.pdf

Garada, R. (2013). Dynamics of coal mining caused environmental crisis versus displaced people's question of survival; A case of Talcher coal belt, Odisha (India). *Global Journal of Human Social Science; Geography, Geoscience, Environmental Disaster management, 13*(6).

Gerking, S., Stanley, L. R. (1986). An economic analysis of air pollution and health: The case of St Louis. *Review of Economics and Statistics, 68,* 115–121.

Gowswami et al. (2010). Environmental degradation due to exploitation of mineral resources: A scenario in Orissa. *The Bioscan, special issue, 2,* 295–304.

Grossman, M. (1972). On the concept of health capital and the demand for health. *The Journal of Political Economy, 80*(2), 223–255.

Gupta, U. (2006). *Valuation of urban air pollution: a case study of Kanpur city in India.* (Working Paper No. 17–06). Kathmandu: South Asian Network for Development and Environmental Economics.

Harrington, W., Portney, P. R. (1987). Valuing the benefits of health and safety regulation. *Journal of Urban Economics, 22*(1), 101–112.

Hendryx, M. (2009). Mortality from heart, respiratory & kidney disease in coal mining areas of Appalachia. *In Occup Environ Health, 82,* 243–249.

Kumar, S., & Rao, D. N. (2001). Valuing benefits of air pollution abatement using health production function: a case study of panipat thermal power station, India. *Journal of Environmental & Resource Economics, 20,* 91–102

Mishra, P. P. (2009). Coal mining and rural livelihoods: case of the IB valley coalfield, Orissa. *Economic and Political Weekly, 44*(44), 117–123.

Mishra, S. K. (2012). Coal mining externalities: a study of Basundhara coal field in India. Council for social development, Hyderabad. http://www.csdhyd. org/HSDP%201.pdf.

Murthy, A. et al. (2006). Ecological, socio-economic & health impact assessment due to coal mining: A case study of Talabira coal mines in Orissa. *Conservation & Livelihood Team*, January-April.

Ostro, B. (1994). *Estimating the health effects of air pollutants: A method with to Jakarta* (Working Paper No. 301). Washington, DC: World Bank, Policy Research Department. Retrieved from http://documents.worldbank.org/ curated/en/355391468752348015/pdf/multi0page.pdf

Pope, C. A. (2007). Mortality effects of longer term exposures to fine particulate air pollution: Review of recent epidemiological evidence. *Inhalation Toxicology, 19* (Supplement 1), 33–38.

Pope, C. A., Bates, D. V., & Raizenne, M. E. (1995). Health effects of particulate air pollution: Time for reassessment. *Environmental Health Prospective, 103*(5), 472.

Saha, S., Pattanayak, S. K., Sills, E. O., & Singha, A. K. (2011). Under-mining health: Environmental justice and mining in India. *Health & Place, 17*(1), 140–148.

Sarkar, D. et al. (2004). Optimal health care strategy in coal mines: An economic analysis. *Indian Journal of Occupational and Environmental Medicine, 8*(2): 38–49.

Singh, P.K. et al. (2010). Impact of coal mining & industrial activities on land use pattern in Angul-Talcher region of Orissa, India. *International Journal of Engineering Science & Technology, 2*(12), 7771–7784.

Singh, G. (2007). Mitigating environmental & social impacts of coal mining in India. 1st International Conference on "Managing the social environmental consequences of coal mining in India" November: 19–21, New Delhi.

Zullig, K.J., & Hendryx, M. (2010). A comparative analysis of health-related quality of life for residents of U.S. counties with and without coal mining. *Public Health Reports, 125*, 548–555.

CHAPTER 10

Global Sustainability Shift and Hydropower Development

Bhartendu Kumar Chaturvedi, Atri Nautiyal and Mohammed Yaqoot

Introduction

Globally, sustainable development has become the guiding principle for achieving socio-economic progress. Sustainable development is the development that meets the needs of the present without compromising the ability of future generations to meet their own needs (UN, n.d.). To achieve sustainable development, it is imperative to have synergy between economic growth, social inclusion and environmental protection. On 25 September 2015, United Nations adopted 17 Sustainable Development Goals aimed at ending poverty, protecting the planet and ensuring prosperity for all by 2030. Affordable and Clean Energy, and Climate Action are 2 of the 17 Sustainable Development Goals that are focused on accelerated integration of affordable and clean renewable power to the electric grid to combat climate change (UN, n.d.). Utilization of renewable energy sources was also promoted under various mechanisms of the Kyoto Protocol that ended in 2012. Subsequently, to combat climate change, the Paris Agreement was adopted in 2016. About 160 countries have signed the Paris Agreement and aimed to reduce their greenhouse gas emissions through renewable energy utilization, energy efficiency improvement and afforestation. Hence, Sustainable Development Goals and the Paris Agreement have shifted the focus on enhanced renewable energy utilization (UNFCCC, n.d.). Several countries have already added large renewable power capacities to their grid. Power generated from inexhaustible energy sources namely hydro, wind, solar, biomass, geo-thermal and ocean are considered renewable power. In many studies, hydropower has been considered distinct from renewable power as it constitutes a big part of renewable power capacity and its inclusion can mask developments in other renewable energy technologies (REN21, 2017). Similarly, in this study, hydropower has been treated separately from renewable power. China, United States, Germany, Japan, India and Italy were global leaders in renewable power with 258, 145, 98, 51, 46 and 33GW installed capacity respectively by the end of year 2016 (REN21, 2017). In 2016, renewable power generating capacity experienced its largest annual growth with capacity addition of 161GW that constituted 62 per cent of net global power capacity addition. Wind power and solar photovoltaics (PV) are the main constituents of the renewable power capacity installed globally. Fall in prices of renewable energy technologies (especially solar PV and wind) and targeted renewable energy support mechanisms have been the main drivers behind increased renewable power capacity addition and the trend is expected to continue (IEA, 2015; IRENA, 2017; REN21, 2017; Sahu, In Press). A projection by International Renewable Energy Agency suggests that by the year 2050, the share of solar PV and wind power would be about 52 per cent of the global electricity generation (IRENA, 2017).

Hydropower is a clean and renewable source of energy that can be harnessed for large-scale power generation (Li, Li, Ji, & Yang, 2015; Tahseen & Karney, 2017). Greenhouse gas emissions during the construction and operation of hydropower plants are quite low compared to that from fossil fuel-fired power plants. On life cycle basis, a typical hydropower plant emits 2–18 kt CO_2 equivalent per TWh in comparison to 389–1272 kt CO_2 equivalent per TWh released by fossil fuel-fired power plants (Gagnon, Bélanger, & Uchiyama, 2002; IEA, 1998; Tahseen & Karney, 2017; Zhang, Karney, MacLean, & Feng, 2007). Assessment studies suggest that by utilizing 50 per cent of global hydropower potential, greenhouse gas emissions could be reduced by 13 per cent, along with added benefit of substantially reduced SO_2 and NO_x emissions (Bates Kundzewicz, & Wu, 2008; Swingland, 2003). With significantly higher useful lives that can be further extended up to 100 years through appropriate renovation and modernization, and zero fuel cost, electricity generated by hydropower plants is generally cheaper (NG, n.d.; PwC, 2016; WB, 2017). Often, hydropower projects are multi-faceted and are used for power generation, water supply, flood control and recreational benefits (Capik, Yilmaz, & Cavusoglu, 2012; Evans, Strezov, & Evans, 2009; Kaygusuz, 2009). Storage dams of hydropower projects have substantial energy storage capacity that enables flexible operation of electric grid (Maxim, 2014; Rehman, Al-Hadhrami, & Alam, 2015; Zhang, Andrews-Speed, & Perera, 2015). The energy storage capacity of hydropower plants can be utilized to address inter-mittency issues associated with renewable power from wind or solar energy (Ayodele & Ogunjuyigbe, 2015; Caralis, Papantonis, & Zervos, 2012; Kusakana, 2015; Steffen, 2012). Thus, reliable, clean and cheap hydropower can facilitate integration of more renewable power (wind or solar) to the grid. Hydropower projects often bring investments in roads, dams, canals, schools, hospitals and communications to remote locations leading to economic development of the area. However, these projects involve dislocation of project-affected people, along with irreversible impact on environment that often hinders their development (Tahseen & Karney, 2017). In light of universal adoption of Sustainable Development Goals and the Paris Agreement, and consequent commitment to enhance integration of renewable power to the grid, it is imperative to assess opportunities and risks of hydropower. In this study, an attempt has been made to assess the opportunities and risks of hydropower as a facilitator to sustainable development.

Global Trends in Hydropower

Globally, during 2005–2016, hydropower generation grew at a compound annual growth rate of 2.7 per cent per annum, whereas wind and solar power generation registered compound annual growth rates of 17.35 per cent and 38.31 per cent respectively (Figure 10.1).

With an addition of 25 GW during 2016, global hydropower capacity reached 1,096 GW by the end of year 2016 that contributed 16.6 per cent to global electricity generation (Table 10.1). In terms of installed hydropower capacity, China, Brazil, United States, Canada, Russian Federation and India are leaders with a total share of about 60 per cent of global capacity (Table 10.1). During 2016, global pumped storage capacity (counted separately) also increased to 150 GW with an addition of 6.4 GW (REN21, 2017). In the year 2016, China commissioned about 33 per cent of the new global hydropower capacity followed by substantial capacity additions in Brazil, Ecuador, Ethiopia, Vietnam and Peru (Table 10.1). In pumped storage capacity addition during the year, China once again emerged as the leader followed by South Africa, Switzerland, Portugal and Russian Federation. With an addition of 8.9 GW of hydropower capacity and 3.7 GW of pumped storage capacity in 2016, China achieved cumulative capacities of 305 GW and 27 GW respectively. The hot spots of growth in hydropower generation were China and Brazil with 6 per cent and 7.4 per cent annual increase during 2016 (REN21, 2017).

In addition to new hydropower capacity addition, modernization and retrofitting have been an integral part of the hydropower industry. Generally, modernization and retrofitting extend useful life of the hydropower plants, along with significant improvement in their performance. In 2016, modernization and retrofitting of Kamskaya Plant in Russian Federation increased the plant's capacity by 14 per cent, along with improved reliability and safety (REN21, 2017). Apart from technological improvements in mechanical equipment of hydropower plants, integration of advanced control systems to the plant and data analytics are optimizing plant operations resulting in enhanced reliability, improved efficiency and smoother integration to grid.

Global Sustainability Shift and Opportunities for Hydropower

Adoption of Sustainable Development Goals by the United Nations in 2015, along with ratification of the Paris Agreement in 2016 has

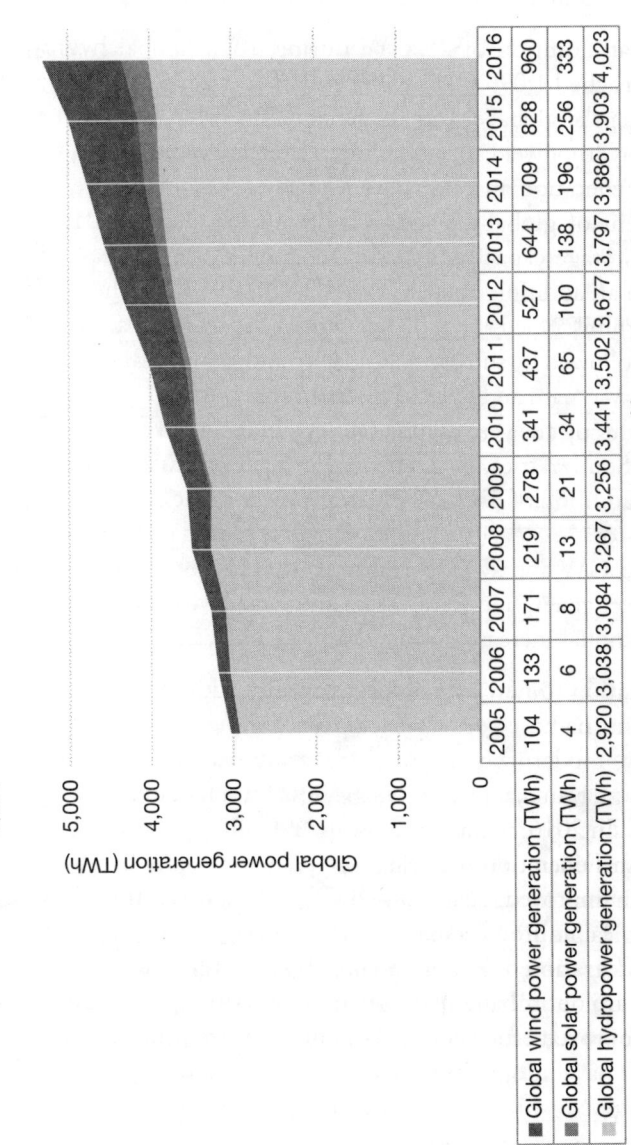

	2005	2006	2007	2008	2009	2010	2011	2012	2013	2014	2015	2016
■ Global wind power generation (TWh)	104	133	171	219	278	341	437	527	644	709	828	960
■ Global solar power generation (TWh)	4	6	8	13	21	34	65	100	138	196	256	333
■ Global hydropower generation (TWh)	2,920	3,038	3,084	3,267	3,256	3,441	3,502	3,677	3,797	3,886	3,903	4,023

Figure 10.1 *Growth of Hydro, Solar and Wind Power Generation during 2005–2016*

Source: BP (2017).

Table 10.1 *Top Six Countries by Hydropower Capacity and Capacity Addition in 2016*

	Capacity Added in 2016 (GW)	Cumulative Capacity (GW)
Top Countries by Total Capacity		
China	8.9	305
Brazil	5.3	97
United States	0.4	80
Canada	–	79
Russian Federation	0.2	48
India	0.6	47
World	25	1,096
Top Countries by Capacity Addition during 2016		
China	8.9	305
Brazil	5.3	97
Ecuador	2.0	4
Ethiopia	1.5	4
Vietnam	1.1	16
Peru	1.0	5

Source: REN21 (2017).

resulted in global shift towards sustainability. The sustainability shift has created huge opportunities for renewable energy options as they are clean and sustainable. Worldwide nations have fixed renewable power targets intending to achieve large-scale integration of renewable power to the grid. Table 10.2 presents the renewable energy targets of some countries. The same trend of enhanced renewable power addition to the grid is visible globally. Few countries such as Canada and United States have no national renewable power targets although several of their states have adopted renewable power targets (REN21, 2017). Thus, the global shift towards sustainability will lead to substantial renewable power capacity addition to the grid.

Increased shares of variable renewable energy for power generation have stimulated the growth in electricity storage capacities as they

Table 10.2 Renewable Energy Targets of Some Countries

Country	Targeted Share of Electricity Generation from Renewable Sources	Targeted Renewable Power Installed Capacity
Algeria	27% by 2030	1 GW from bio-power; 15 MW from geothermal power; 13.5 GW from solar PV; 2 GW by concentrated solar power; 5 GW from wind power by 2030
Bhutan	100% by 2050	5 MW from bio-power; 5 MW from solar PV; 5 MW from wind power by 2025
Brazil	23% by 2030	18 GW from bio-power; 125 GW from hydropower; 24 GW from wind power; 7 GW from solar by 2024
China	No declared target	340 GW from hydropower; 110 GW from solar power; 210 GW from wind power by 2020
Denmark	50% by 2020 100% by 2050	No declared target
Finland	33% by 2020	13.2 GW from bio-power; 14.6 GW from hydropower; 884 MW from wind power by 2020
Germany	40–45% by 2025 55–60% by 2035 80% by 2050	100 MW addition per year from bio-power; 2.5 GW addition per year from solar PV; 2.5 GW addition per year from wind power (onshore); and 6.5 GW from wind power (offshore) by 2020
India	40% by 2030	100 GW from solar power; 60 GW from wind power; 10 GW from bio-power and 5 GW from hydropower (small-scale) by 2022
Japan	24% by 2030	1.5 GW from ocean power (wave and tidal) by 2030
Mexico	35% by 2024 50% by 2050	20 GW from renewable power by 2030, of which 10 GW from wind power
South Africa	9% by 2030	17.8 GW from renewable power by 2030

(Continued)

Table 10.2 *Continued*

Country	Targeted Share of Electricity Generation from Renewable Sources	Targeted Renewable Power Installed Capacity
Turkey	30% by 2023	1 GW from bio-power; 1 GW from geothermal power; 34 GW from hydro-power; 5 GW from solar PV; 20 GW from wind power by 2023
United Kingdom	No declared target	39 GW from wind power (offshore) by 2030
Yemen	15% by 2025 100% by 2050	6 MW from bio-power; 200 MW from geothermal power; 4 MW from solar PV; 100 MW from concentrated solar power; 400 MW from wind power by 2025

Source: REN21 (2017).

help to keep the grid stable. Pumped hydro storage, battery, flywheel, compressed air and thermal storage (molten salt) are the various electricity storage options. Of the total global power storage capacity of 176 GW installed till mid-2017, pumped hydro storage accounts for 96 per cent followed by thermal storage (1.9%), battery (1.1%) and mechanical storage (0.9%) (IRENA, 2017). Pumped hydro storage is the most matured large-scale electricity storage technology that can keep the grid stable while integrating variable renewable power to it (Foley, Leahy, Li, McKeogh, & Morrison, 2015; Kocaman & Modi, 2017; Rehman et al., 2015; Steffen, 2012). As depicted in Figure 10.2, a pumped hydro storage system stores energy in the form of potential energy of water that is pumped from a lower reservoir to a higher reservoir. Surplus and cheap electric power available during off-peak period is used to run the pumps to raise water from lower reservoir to the upper one. During peak power periods with high power demand, the stored water is released through hydro turbines to generate power. In the pumped hydro system, reversible turbine generator can act as a pump or turbine as per the need (Rehman et al., 2015).

During 2016, global pumped hydro storage capacity increased by 6.4 GW that was double of previous year's capacity addition (IHA,

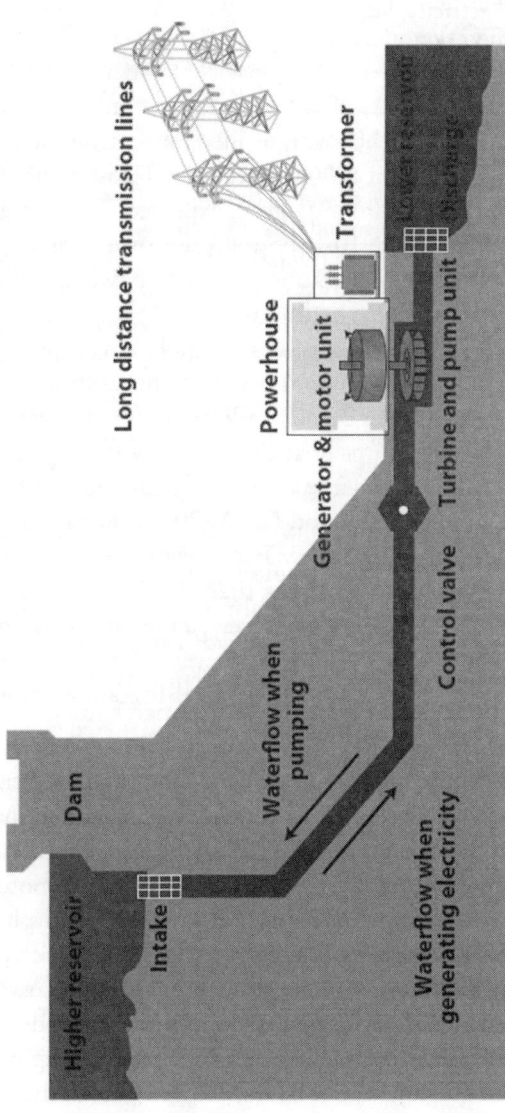

Figure 10.2 *Schematic of Pumped Hydro Storage System*

Source: Luo, Wang, Dooner and Clarke (2015).

2017). These capacities were primarily added in China, South Africa and Europe (REN21, 2017). Currently, China, Japan and United States are the global leaders in pumped hydro storage installed capacity with 32.0 GW, 28.3 GW and 22.6 GW respectively (IRENA, 2017). In addition, 20 GW of pumped hydro capacity is under various stages of construction globally (IHA, 2017). As many countries are striving to substantially increase the share of intermittent renewables in their electricity mix, significant growth in multi-purpose hydropower plants especially pumped hydro storage is expected. Reflecting the trend, data presented in Figure 10.1 show strong correlation between growths in solar/wind power generation and hydropower generation. Correlation coefficient for global hydropower and solar power generation is estimated as 0.91 whereas it is 0.98 for global hydropower and wind power generation. Thus, several countries have declared their plans for enhanced hydropower capacity addition. For example, in its 13th Five-Year Plan, China aims to achieve 40 GW pumped storage capacity by 2020 to balance the large volume of solar and wind power that are getting integrated to the grid (IHA, 2017). For the last five years, annual investment in new renewable power capacity (including hydropower) has been about two times than that in new fossil fuel power plants. During 2016, solar power received the maximum investment followed by wind power and hydropower. Overall, renewable power accounted for 63.5 per cent of the total investments in new capacity during 2016 (REN21, 2017).

Widespread development of pumped hydropower storage capacities are leading to its evolution as a storage system with improved operational flexibility to balance fluctuations in the grid. Traditionally, in pumped hydropower systems, power regulation was only available during generation. However, contemporary variable speed pumped hydropower systems increase plant efficiency and flexibility with power regulation option in both pumping and generation mode (IHA, 2017). Ternary systems having a motor generator, and distinct pump and turbine set can allow for simultaneous generation and pumping that provides improved frequency control (IHA, 2017). Some of the hydropower plants are experimenting with floating PV panels on reservoir surface that increase electricity generation with reduced evaporation and no additional land requirement (IHA, 2017).

In addition to directly fulfilling two Sustainable Development Goals of Affordable and Clean Energy, and Climate Action through supplying affordable, reliable, flexible and renewable hydropower and facilitating integration of other renewable energy sources to the grid, hydropower projects help achieve many other Sustainable Development Goals. Irrigation, flood control, water supply and tourism are some of the multiple purposes of reservoir-based hydropower projects that directly or indirectly help to achieve Sustainable Development Goals of Clean Water and Sanitation, No Poverty, Zero Hunger, Good Health and Well-being, Decent Work and Economic Growth, Life below Water, and Sustainable Cities and Communities. Thus, as hydropower helps to achieve many Sustainable Development Goals, the global sustainability shift will lead to enhanced hydropower capacity addition throughout the world.

Risks Associated with Hydropower

Hydropower, along with it all its merits, has several risks attached to it that impede the development of hydropower projects. Hydropower projects pose environmental and social risks as their development leads to irreversible change in landscape and rivers' natural flow (Berkun, 2010; Charoenngam & Yeh, 1999; De Faria & Jaramillo, 2017; Holdren, 2008; Olabi, 2012; Piao et al., 2010; Ranasinghe, 2002; Tang, Qiang, Duffield, Young, & Lu, 2007; Vörösmarty et al., 2010). This results in large-scale land inundation, disruption of human settlement, loss of aquatic life and biodiversity, geological damage and changes in aquatic sediment distribution (Berkun, 2010; De Faria & Jaramillo, 2017; Ranasinghe, 2002; Sarkar & Karagöz, 1995; Sternberg, 2008; Yuksel, 2010). Due to these environmental and social risks, development of hydropower projects faces resistance from local communities that leads to project delays and cost overruns (Li et al., 2015; Tang, Li, Qiang, Wang, & Lu, 2013). The 1,000 MW Tehri Dam project in India got delayed by more than 25 years as it faced mass protests on the issues of safety, environment and rehabilitation leading to cost overruns (PwC, 2016). Development work in Hook Canyon Pump Storage and Olivenhain–Hodges Pumped Projects in United States were stopped as it was perceived that the projects could adversely affect water quality and aquatic life (Yang & Jackson, 2011). Reportedly, mean cost overrun for hydropower projects is 96 per cent compared to 6 per cent for its thermal counterparts (Ansar, Flyvbjerg, Budzier, & Lunn, 2014). Additionally, due to the requirement of higher upfront cost in order to account for complexities in engineering, environmental and social impact mitigation along with frequent time and cost overruns resulting in uncertain cash flows, hydropower project developers are charged higher risk premiums increasing their financial risk (PwC, 2016). Results of a survey conducted in China indicate that resettlement of migrants, incompetence of sub-contractors, project delay, inadequate or correct design, premature failure of facilities, and ecological and environmental impacts are the most critical risks associated with hydropower projects (Tang et al., 2013). Extensively following Michael Cernea's Impoverishment Risks and Reconstruction model has exhibited linkage between eight interlinked potential risks that are inherent to displacement caused by large projects such as hydropower projects. The eight risks are landlessness, joblessness, homelessness, marginalization, increased morbidity and mortality, food insecurity, loss of access to common property and social disarticulation (Cernea, 1997). Thus, hydropower projects face environmental, social, engineering, project management and financial risks that need adequate redressal for their accelerated development.

Discussion

The worldwide sustainability shift and consequent large-scale integration of variable renewable power to the grid has made hydropower a desirable constituent of electricity mix as it is clean, renewable and provides flexibility to the grid by facilitating electricity storage. Additionally, hydropower serves multiple purposes such as irrigation, water supply and flood control. Hence, with increased renewable power in electricity mix, worldwide hydropower capacity is expected to increase. However, hydropower projects face environmental, social, engineering, project management and financial risks that often result in project delay and cost overrun making projects unviable. Therefore, considering the benefits of hydropower in promoting sustainable development, it is imperative to assess and address risks associated with hydropower projects. The World Bank has emphasized on harnessing hydropower resources in a sustainable manner adequately considering resettlement issues, flooding of land and alteration of river ecosystems, and adopting suitable risk mitigation measures (IHA, 2017). Based on a joint research project of UNESCO and International Hydropower Association that began in 2008, scientists have developed G-res Tool that utilizes a new conceptual approach to estimate carbon footprint of hydropower projects (IHA, 2017). The World Bank is working with International Hydropower Association to develop widely acceptable guidelines for assessing climate resilience of hydropower projects and associated risks that will help the investors and financial institutions in project appraisal (REN21, 2017). Estimation of carbon footprint and assessment of climate resilience of hydropower projects help the investors in channelling their funds to combat climate change through climate finance mechanisms. Recently, apart from multilateral development banks, countries such as Poland and France have started issuing green or climate bonds to finance climate-resilient projects. These bonds are fixed income loans that aim to support projects that help reduce emissions and combat climate change. Hydropower has been one of the biggest beneficiary of green bonds as it has attracted one-third of US$130 billion energy linked green bonds issued so far (IHA, 2017). Thus, with widely accepted guidelines and tools for assessment of climate resilience and sustainability, and availability of green bonds, hydropower projects can address environmental, social, engineering, project management and financial risks making them more viable. Considering the importance of hydropower in promoting sustainable development and grid stability, it is necessary to adopt new mechanisms that enable risk mitigation and help accelerated development of hydropower projects.

Conclusion

Post global sustainability shift, trends indicate substantial growth in hydropower capacity addition, along with increased solar and wind power capacities. With increased share of variable renewable power in electricity mix, hydropower becomes desirable as its electricity storage capability provides operational flexibility to the grid. However, hydropower projects encounter environmental, social, engineering, project management and financial risks that lead to project delays and cost overruns. For sustainable development, it is necessary to assess and address the risks to reap the benefits of hydropower. International agencies and research organizations are developing new climate resilience guidelines and tools for estimation of carbon footprint of hydropower projects to assess their sustainability. Widespread adoption of these guidelines and tools can help mitigate risks associated with hydropower and make the projects more viable and sustainable.

References

Ansar, A., Flyvbjerg, B., Budzier, A., & Lunn, D. (2014). Should we build more large dams? The actual costs of hydropower megaproject development. *Energy Policy, 69*, 43–56.

Ayodele, T. R., & Ogunjuyigbe, A. S. O. (2015). Mitigation of wind power intermittency: Storage technology approach. *Renewable and Sustainable Energy Reviews, 44*, 447–456.

Bates, B., Kundzewicz, Z. W., & Wu, S. (2008). *Climate change and water: Paper VI* (IPCC technical paper). Geneva: The Intergovernmental Panel on Climate Change.

Berkun, M. (2010). Hydroelectric potential and environmental effects of multidam hydropower projects in Turkey. *Energy for Sustainable Development, 14*, 320–329.

BP. (2017, June). *BP Statistical Review of World Energy 2017*. London: Author.

Capik, M., Yilmaz, A. O., & Cavusoglu, İ. (2012). Hydropower for sustainable energy development in Turkey: The small hydropower case of the Eastern Black Sea Region. *Renewable and Sustainable Energy Reviews, 16*, 6160–6172.

Caralis, G., Papantonis, D., & Zervos, A. (2012). The role of pumped storage systems towards the large scale wind integration in the Greek power supply system. *Renewable and Sustainable Energy Reviews, 16*, 2558–2565.

Cernea, M. M. (1997). The risks and reconstruction model for resettling displaced populations. *World Development, 25*(10), 1569–1589.

Charoenngam, C., & Yeh, C. (1999). Contractual risk and liability sharing in hydropower construction. *International Journal of Project Management, 17*(1), 29–37.

De Faria, F. A. M., & Jaramillo, P. (2017). The future of power generation in Brazil: An analysis of alternatives to Amazonian hydropower development. *Energy for Sustainable Development, 41*, 24–35.

Evans, A., Strezov, V., & Evans, T. J. (2009). Assessment of sustainability indicators for renewable energy technologies. *Renewable and Sustainable Energy Reviews, 13*, 1082–1088.

Foley, A. M., Leahy, P. G., Li, K., McKeogh, E. J., & Morrison, A. P. (2015). A long-term analysis of pumped hydro storage to firm wind power. *Applied Energy, 137*, 638–648.

Gagnon, L., Bélanger, C., & Uchiyama, Y. (2002). Life-cycle assessment of electricity generation options: The status of research in year 2001. *Energy Policy*, 30, 1267–1278.

Holdren, J. P. (2008, January 25). Science and technology for sustainable well-being. *Science*, *319*, 424–434.

IHA (International Hydropower Association). (2017). *Hydropower status report 2017*. London: IHA.

IEA (International Energy Agency). (1998). *Benign energy? The environmental implications of renewables*. Paris: IEA.

IEA (International Energy Agency). (2015). *Renewable energy medium–term market report 2015: Market analysis and forecasts to 2020*. Paris: IEA.

IRENA (International Renewable Energy Agency). (2017). Electricity storage and renewables: costs and markets to 2030. Abu Dhabi: IRENA.

Kaygusuz, K. (2009). The role of hydropower for sustainable energy development. *Energy Sources (Part B), Economics, Planning, and Policy*, *4*, 365–376.

Kocaman, A. S., & Modi, V. (2017). Value of pumped hydro storage in a hybrid energy generation and allocation system. *Applied Energy*, *205*, 1202–1215.

Kusakana, K. (2015). Feasibility analysis of river off-grid hydrokinetic systems with pumped hydro storage in rural applications. *Energy Conversion and Management*, *96*, 352–362.

Li, Y., Li, Y., Ji, P., & Yang, J. (2015). The status quo analysis and policy suggestions on promoting China's hydropower development. *Renewable and Sustainable Energy Reviews*, *51*, 1071–1079.

Luo, X., Wang, J., Dooner, M., & Clarke J. (2015). Overview of current development in electrical energy storage technologies and the application potential in power system operation. *Applied Energy*, *137*, 511–536.

Maxim, A. (2014). Sustainability assessment of electricity generation technologies using weighted multi-criteria decision analysis. *Energy Policy*, *65*, 284–297.

NG (National Geographic). (n.d.). Hydropower. Retrieved from http://www.nationalgeographic.com/environment/global-warming/hydropower/

Olabi, A. G. (2012). Developments in sustainable energy and environmental protection. *Energy*, *39*(1), 2–5.

Piao, S., Ciais, P., Huang, Y., Shen, Z., Peng, S., Li, J. (2010). The impacts of climate change on water resources and agriculture in China. *Nature*, *467*(2), 43–51.

PwC. 2016. Hydropower at crossroads. Retrieved from https://www.pwc.in/assets/pdfs/publications/2016/hydropower-at-crossroads-pwc-assocham-report.pdf

Ranasinghe, M. (2002). Risk and uncertainty analysis of natural environmental assets threatened by hydropower projects: Case study from Sri Lanka. *Energy for Sustainable Development*, *6*(1), 56–62.

Rehman, S., Al-Hadhrami, L. M., & Alam, M. M. (2015). Pumped hydro energy storage system: A technological review. *Renewable and Sustainable Energy Reviews*, *44*, 586–598.

REN21. (2017). Renewables 2017 global status report. Retrieved from http://www.ren21.net/wp-content/uploads/2017/06/17–8399_GSR_2017_Full_Report_0621_Opt.pdf

Sahu, B. K. (2018). Wind energy developments and policies in China: A short review. *Renewable and Sustainable Energy Reviews, 81*, 1393–1405.

Sarkar, A. U., & Karagöz S. (1995). Sustainable development of hydroelectric power. *Energy 20*, 977–981.

Steffen, B. (2012). Prospects for pumped-hydro storage in Germany. *Energy Policy, 45*, 420–429.

Sternberg, R. (2008). Hydropower: Dimensions of social and environmental coexistence. *Renewable and Sustainable Energy Reviews, 12*, 1588–1621.

Swingland, I. (2003). Capturing carbon and conserving biodiversity: The market approach. London: Routledge Publisher.

Tahseen, S., & Karney, B. W. (2017). Reviewing and critiquing published approaches to the sustainability assessment of hydropower. *Renewable and Sustainable Energy Reviews, 67*, 225–234.

Tang, W., Li, Z., Qiang, M., Wang, S., & Lu, Y. (2013). Risk management of hydropower development in China. *Energy, 60*, 316–324.

Tang, W., Qiang, M., Duffield, C. F., Young, D. M., & Lu, Y. (2007). Risk management in the Chinese construction industry. *Journal of Construct Engineering and Management, 133*(12), 944–956.

UN (United Nations). (n.d.). *The sustainable development agenda.* Retrieved from http://www.un.org/sustainabledevelopment/development-agenda/

UNFCCC (United Nations Framework Convention on Climate Change). (n.d.). *The Paris Agreement.* Retrieved from http://unfccc.int/paris_agreement/items/9485.php

Vörösmarty, C. J., McIntyre, P. B., Gessner, M. O., Dudgeon, D., Prusevich, A., & Green, P. (2010). Global threats to human water security and river biodiversity. *Nature, 467*(30), 555–561.

WB (World Bank). (2017). Topics. Retrieved from http://www.worldbank.org/en/topic/hydropower/overview#1

Yang, C., & Jackson, R. B. (2011). Opportunities and barriers to pumped-hydro energy storage in the United States. *Renewable and Sustainable Energy Reviews, 15*, 839–844.

Yuksel, I. (2010). As a renewable energy hydropower for sustainable development in Turkey. *Renewable and Sustainable Energy Reviews, 14*, 3213–3219.

Zhang, Q., Karney, B., MacLean, H. L., & Feng, J. (2007). Life-cycle inventory of energy use and greenhouse gas emissions for two hydropower projects in China. *Journal of Infrastructure Systems, 13*, 271–279.

Zhang, S., Andrews-Speed, P., & Perera, P. (2015). The evolving policy regime for pumped storage hydroelectricity in China: A key support for low-carbon energy. *Applied Energy, 150*, 15–24.

CHAPTER 11

Man–Nature Relationship in South Asia

Shakir ul Hassan

Introduction

Environmental history is the exploration of past dynamics between two entities, that is, human society and the natural environment. This study covers a *longue duree* of transformations that took place from the post-Pleistocene period through early state societies to late colonial period. The exploration into pasts is based on themes and temporal frames to examine human alteration in ecology and natural environment, and development of human modes of subsistence from hunting and gathering, foraging, settled Neolithic man to urban state systems. Major focus has been put on three processes: firstly, proliferation of agriculture and lateral state expansion from settled perennial regions to cul-de-sac areas or regions of relative isolation; secondly, it discusses human perception, value and ideology concerning environment and the instrumentalist role played by the pre-modern society in transformation of physical landscape which they shared. Lastly, the study takes into account treatment meted out to forest tribal communities by settled states from early archaic states to early colonial states. The study also underlines rise and expansion of the agrarian society in Rajasthan, Sindh and Tamilkam in early medieval period and role of Mughal state in land reclamations in the 17th century. Lastly the study takes into account colonialism as environmental watershed in the history of south Asia.

Emergence of Settled Societies and Archaic State

Central to the archaeologists' theoretical oeuvres in relation to cultural evolution are the origins of agriculture and civilization, both characterized a major transition in long-term human history. Anthropologists and archaeologists have directed vast energies to marshal those necessary processes that led to the evolution of agriculture and ensuing political formations in a variety of cultural zones. Likewise, in south Asia these perennial questions such as under what conditions the prehistoric foraging tribes transformed into farmers, and how and where did the early larger states arise have been greatly explored and debated. In the interglacial Holocene epoch (at the end of Pleistocene about 10,000 years ago), humans made a pronounced departure from being mere foragers to settled farmers by clearing away natural vegetation over plots of land to grow food grains. Lands that would receive fresh alluvial deposits periodically were preferred in different geographical contexts. These overarching transformations in human adaptive behaviour by becoming permanently settled communities, improving tool technology and entering into relations with environment have been widely mentioned as the Neolithic revolution (B. Allchin & Allchin, 1982).

Domestication of Food Grains in South Asia

Almost in five major cultural zones—Mehrgarh, Kashmir, Chirand and so on the so-called Neolithic cultures appeared discretely, leading to domestication of certain species of plants and animals, restriction of routine life to permanent settlement patterns, usage of ceramic potteries accompanied by corresponding diminutions in the stone tool size used by grain-producing farmers. The Neolithic farmers adopted sedentism at the cost of nomadic pastoralism for it depended on immediate individual act—whether foraging or pasturage of herds—of a given band, whereas labour-intensive, settled farming-based communities had enough resource base resulting in self-sufficient food production. These farming communities possessed means of storing grains within pottery utensils. Livestock maintained by farmers not only ensured food supply in time of need but also domesticated animals were tied to the process of farming activities.

Among these Neolithic agricultural regions within a food-producing economy, only the pre-Harappan settlements ably evolved into a spatially and temporally enormous urban culture. This urban culture is illustrated by the vast magnitude of material artefacts recovered from the Harappan settlements belonging to the Mature phase. The entire geographical zone was culturally integrated: Harappans made use of uniform and standardized bricks and pottery, steatite weights and seals, copper and bronze metallic implements, carnelian beads, monumental city architecture and writing script—often associated with the early states.

Emergence of Urbanism in Harappan Settlements

The Harappan urbanism flourished in cities of Harappa, Mohenjo-daro, Kalibangan, Lothal and Dholavira around the 3rd millennium to mid-2nd millennium BCE on the solid basis provided by agriculture, animal domestication, forest produce and urban economy sustained by the Indus and its tributaries. The Indus was the lifeline of the Harappan urbanism. The northern plains of the Indus are comprised of five main tributaries, while its southern alluvial plains drain the regions of Sindh. Most of the interpretative analyses of the urban Harappan settlements are based more or less on the central place theory—which assumes that the upper stategraphic levels contain all those cultural characteristics present in the lower ones.

In the Mature Harappan period (2600–1900 CE) a boom occurred in production of copper and its alloy bronze metallurgy. Bronze was

Table 11.1 *Harappan Chronology after Upinder Singh, 2008*

Harappa Chronology		
Early Harappan		
Period 1A/1B	Ravi aspect of Hakra Phase	> 3700 BC – 2800 BC
Period 2	Kot Diji Phase	c. 2800 BC – 2600 BC
Harappan (Indus)		
Period 3A	Harappa Phase A	c. 2600 BC – 2450 BC
Period 3B	Harappa Phase B	c. 2450 BC – 2200 BC
Period 3C	Harappa Phase C	c. 2200 BC – 1900 BC
Late Harappan		
Period 4	Late Harappa Transition Phase	c. 1900 BC – 1800 BC
Period 5	Late Harappa/Cemetery H Phase	c. 1800 BC – 1300 BC

Source: http://ww2.comsats.edu.pk/hic/HarappaCivilization.aspx

widely produced through two-piece mould or the lost-wax casting. The bronze Dancing Girl in Mohenjo-daro was produced by lost-wax casting technique. Vasant Shinde (2016), while mentioning about Harappan metallurgy, has observed:

> They used copper and bronze to manufacture axes, adzes, knives, fish hooks, chisels, pots and pans and jewelry in form of bangles, beads, or diadem strips...Besides copper, the Harappans worked with gold, silver and lead...Copper artifacts are found at larger and more economically developed settlements. A few copper vessels and beads have been found in hoards but, unlike other metal objects, especially gold and silver, more than 75% of copper artifacts, ornaments, and vessels have been found in non-hoard contexts, including burials.

Harappan-crafted beads were exchanged in trade as objects of royal consumption most prominently with distant regions of Mesopotamia connected to Arabian Sea and Persian Gulf through waterways. Lapis lazuli was a semi-precious stone imported from Shortugai (Afghanistan). The Harappans surely altered physical landscape around the River Indus, which in turn shaped their lifestyle by recurring floods and shifting of the greater Indus watercourses. Here I will draw the attention towards two fundamental concerns of the Harappan landscape archaeology: firstly, subsistence economy in which man and environment interactions occurred within site catchment areas during the mature Harappan period; secondly, to what extent the Harappans altered the local natural ecosystem of the given inhabited space (B. Allchin & Allchin, 1982).

Agriculture: The Harappan culture was a bronze and riverine culture. In relation to rainfall, river regimes, groundwater, alluvial soils and mineral resources, the Harappan farming communities had a comparative advantage compared to pastoral communities. The predominant population of Harappan civilization was involved in farming and related sources of subsistence as compared to pastoral activities. According to B. Allchin and Allchin (1982), specialists of Harappan archaeology, the Harappan urbanism was based on agriculture, which was exploited for food. They practiced double cropping. The people cultivated a range of crops grouped into the following:

1. Rabi crops: They included cereals
2. Kharif crops: They included crops such as cotton and grapes

Wheat and barley were certainly important components of Harappan subsistence strategy. In Mohenjo-daro and Harappa the limiting factors to agricultural crop production were recurrent summer floods and rains. The main Harappan habitation centres located in Indus plains were sparsely populated interspersed by pastoral communities. These plains received highly unpredictable natural precipitation which 'did not offer potential for unlimited agricultural growth' (Ratnagar, 2001).

Domestication: Paleoecology of Harappan culture is still in its rudimentary stage. Archaeological data recovered so far from excavation and representation of animals on figurines and pottery are only direct evidences of the Harappan domestication. The Early and Mature Harappan archaeological clumps demonstrate an evolutionary tendency when it comes to herding and domestication of bovids. The Harappan subsistence economy was supplemented by exploitation, animal husbandry and domestication of animals particularly of zebu cattle, camel, dog, cats, buffalo and so on. The archaeological data suggests that goat (*Capra hircus*), sheep, zebu (*Bos indicus*), camel, water buffalo (*Bablus bublis*) and ass (*Equus asinus*) were domesticated. Human exploitation of the lush natural environment in the Harappan phase took four forms: cultivation of crops for consumption, intervention by domestication of *bovidae*; though the river Indus repeatedly shifted its course, alteration of its natural course of water surface run-off occurred by building of dams, channels and bunds; and lastly extraction of copper and production of bronze through lost-wax technique. It is more certain that the Harappans were the dynamic participants in forging of material space of the Harappan Civilization; they gradually transformed its natural ecological patterns by intensifying agriculture of specific crops and the phenomenon of domestication of large and small locally existing bovid animals. In contrast to the pre-Harappan cultures, the Harappans used and circulated copper and bronze metallic implements more extensively that ensured efficient control over resource base. The mature phase 2600–1900 CE illustrated a boom in the production and circulation of copper and bronze artefacts.

Human Colonization of the Gangetic Basin in Early Historic Times

In the Early Historic period, two gradual changes took place in northern India: firstly, formation of imperial state system in Gangetic basin watershed, which was development over the lineage-based social organization. These states successfully consolidated structures of relations with people by means of collecting revenues and creating armies to wage wars against neighbouring territories for war booty. The use of elephants and horses became a factor of kingship in fulfilling multiple functions particularly in battle. The concept of war elephant was created in the Early Historic period. Elephant was conceived as the supreme 'imaginable gift' to the king in the Buddhist canonical texts such as *Digha Nikaya*. Trautmann (2015) contended that the hegemony of the Magadha Empire mainly sprouted from relatively better control of elephants and horses:

The outstanding political development over the following two centuries, 500–300 BCE, was intense interstate warfare among the principal polities, called the Mahajanpadas, in the sources resulting in their unification under one of them, the kingdom of Magadha. This kingdom absorbed its neighbors and grew to a larger empire encompassing nearly the whole of India...in India the interstate warfare was the classic period of the fourfold army, including war elephants and there is every reason to think that the control of horse and elephants was crucial to the outcome.

Secondly, these imperial states, particularly the Mauryas began claiming universal empire under Ashoka and either directly or indirectly held control over both the settled population and forest-dwellers. In his Rock Edict XIII, Ashoka boasts the claim, 'And even the forest dwellers are included in the dominion of the Devanampiya (i.e., Ashoka).'

The Mauryan state even though being a sub-continental empire, was not so ambitious as to uproot the local tribal societies. In his royal Edicts, Ashoka mentioned about the gold-bearing regions of deep south specifically of the Cholas, Cheras and Pandyas basically as tribal polities (Thapar, 2002). Several political oligarchies in the extreme north of the Mauryan Empire existed, which were lucrative in providing the forest produce to the Mauryas. In the contemporary text of *Arthashastra*, guidelines are drawn for forest-dwellers and forest management for the supervision of the forest produce such as timber and honey and it declares to impose fines on poaching in forests.

Spread of Wet Rice Agriculture in Mid-Ganga Plains

Donald Worster, a leading theorist of environmental history, has argued that among the ways of doing environmental history exploring the human mode of production and subsistence is fundamental apart from equally significant components such as human interaction with ecology and human perception of nature (Worster, 1994). R. S. Sharma (2007) has pinpointed the iron tool technology and wooden ploughshare equipped with iron coulter to be the prime mover linked to the eastward migration of the Later Vedic people along erstwhile banks of the river Ganges, subsequent agricultural expansion, silver punch-marked coinage, emergence of urban cities (nagara) in Middle Ganga valley and inchoate territorial states called as 'Mahajanapada' in Pali texts in the 6th century BCE. Several royal capitals like the powerful state of Magadh emerged under the Haryankas.

However, D. Chakrabarti (2001) persuasively argues that spread of iron technology for the production of functional agricultural implements undoubtedly was a 'necessary condition' for agrarian expansion. But he contends that it was not singularly a 'sufficient condition' for foundation of urban life in the Gangetic plains. He is of the opinion that previously dense forested areas could have been cleared through fire since agricultural iron tool implements were not used in great widespread proportions.

In Atranjikhera, Jakhera, Hastinapura, Rupar and Ahichhatra only few chisels and sickles were discovered. Hoes have been found in Chirand and Jakhera. Axes and adzes have been found in Pataliputra and Kausambi, and most important, a ploughshare was reported to be found in Jakhera.

Rise of Territorial Units (Mahajanapadas)

The dominant characteristic feature indicated in the literary sources of the Early Historic times (800–200 BCE) was rise of powerful monarchical ideology in the Gangetic plains. Within these large territorial states in the Early Historic period, there emerged new urban settlements called either nagara or mahanagara. These complex urban settlements were primarily located in the mid-Gangetic plains, which was the nerve centre of the early Historic political upheavals in northern India.

'Kings (samrat) are anointed for imperial rule (samrajya); oh Emperor (Samrat) they style him anointed.' (Kieth, 1920)

The 16th territorial ethnic entities or the 16 mahajanapadas as mentioned in Buddhist texts were Kasi, Kosala, Anga, Magadha, Vajji or Vriji, Malla, Chedi, Vatsa, Kuru, Panchala, Matsya, Surasena, Assaka or Ashmaka, Avanti, Gandhara and Kamboja. Some on these followed efficient monarchial state system, while some like Vajjis were a powerful oligarchic confederacy (Thapar, 1991).

Early Medieval State and Peasantization in Periphery and Deep South

Around mid-1st millennium CE, among many fundamental historical processes which occurred that were initiated in the post-Gupta period, three manifested in Indian subcontinent clearly: first, they consciously inaugurated the peasantization or penetration of agriculture into thus far peripheral regions; two, lateral expansion of regional state societies outside the Madhyadesha and finally, influx of Brahmans and complimentary Brahmanical hegemony into hitherto inaccessible territories in deep south India and beyond. All these process are accommodated within a historical period called the Early Medieval. Periodization implies more than temporal grouping of discrete events into periods, but it encompasses ideas into its canopy. The traditional and simple tripartite periodization into Ancient, Medieval and Modern Indian history, enthralled by political events such as wars and battles and so on concentrating on dynastic shifts, trivialized socio-political continuities and processes render the study of environment redundant.

The state formation, marked by petty court bureaucracies, was the dominant feature of the Early Medieval historical period since it brought in a markedly perceptible way: a 'measure of cohesion among local elements of culture by providing them a focus' (Chattopadhyay, 2005).

Manuals on the subjects of cattle rearing, agriculture tool making such as sickles and ploughs, stages of harvesting of crops and timings of rainfall were produced in this period (Guha, 1999). The Sanskrit text *Krishi-Parashara* is a peasant's almanac for time keeping and calendar making is equally important for organization of agrarian economy. Seemingly of early origin, it is composed in the Vedic meter (*Anushtamba*) as it gives details about seasons, schedule of crops, harvesting techniques specifically for rice. Similarly another Sanskrit treatise on agriculture—*Kashyapiyakrishisukta* (700–800 CE) contained suggestions and adages on the agricultural related phenomenon: such as procurement of farming implements, construction of canals, protective embankments and dams, division of land, procurement of seeds, a good farmer and characteristics of good cows. This text contains a detailed section on season of farming and determining land for rice and pulses. For example, 'Production of grains and other vegetation are the sole purpose for highest fulfilment of the earth' (Ayachit, 1999). Fertile land suitable for agriculture came to be perceived in opposition to other different types such as forests, oceans, rivers and mountains. In the third section of the treatise, the following saying qualifies people of all castes entitled to agriculture: 'People of all classes-Brahmans, Kshatyriya, Vaishya and Sudras as also others-acting on the orders of ruler should cultivate diverse crops in a manner thus indicated especially in the fertile fields' (Ayachit, 1999).

Brahmadeyas: Changing Landscape of Deep South from 6th–9th Century

This period witnessed ruralization of economy in the sense that rise of state-societies into previously historical backwaters coupled with transformation of their natural environments through rapid spread of agricultural economy by means of the institution of generous land grants (*brahmadeya, agrahara*) into fringe zones such as Bengal, Kashmir, Tamilkam, Andhra and Orissa. These brahmadeya grants were established in proximity to the tribal communities. Upinder Singh (2008) claims, 'Brahmadeyas functioned as nodes of reciprocal interaction between Brahmanical and tribals religion resulted in the Brahmanization of tribal deities'.

In the valley of Vagai-Tamraparni and Palay-Cheyyar by Pallavas and Pandyas were their territorial strangleholds by putting in solid foundations to their political authority respectively. Following the 6th century AD the Brahmans started to migrate far south and far east such as to Tamilkam, West Bengal, Sindh, Kashmir and Rajasthan which were previously least influenced by Brahmanical world view. They brought with them the Puranic cosmological worldview too.

Prior to the 6th century there existed in south Indian Sangam Tamil texts division of Tamilkam into five eco-zones: Kuruji, Mullai,

Marutam, Neytal and Palai. Attested by literary and epigraphic sources, by the 7th century CE Tondai Nadu the symbiotic and harmonious man–environment relationship of the Sangam period was replaced by tripartite classification of land into wet, dry and mixed based on organization of artificial irrigation. It was under the regional kingdoms of Pallavas and Pandyas that the process of colonization of tribal spaces inhabiting natural ecosystem occurred through the institution of temple and brahmadeya. Along with that the discreet kinship-based peasant units (*nadu*) were integrated. The kingdoms also vied with each other for control over the Kaveri valley in Tamil Nadu (Sinha, 2011).

Temples, located within the premises of brahmadeya, were symbols of the Brahmanical ideology and royal control. The Pallava polity inaugurated transition to Brahmanical socio-political order and brahmadeya grants in Tondai Nadu. These Brahmans accorded Kshatriya status to Pallava and Pandya kings by means of Puranic genealogies, thus legitimizing their claim to sovereignty through performance of Vedic rituals. Post the 6th century state formation in deep southern India transformed the physical landscape in which overarching construction of irrigation networks, integration of peasant units and institutions of temples dominated.

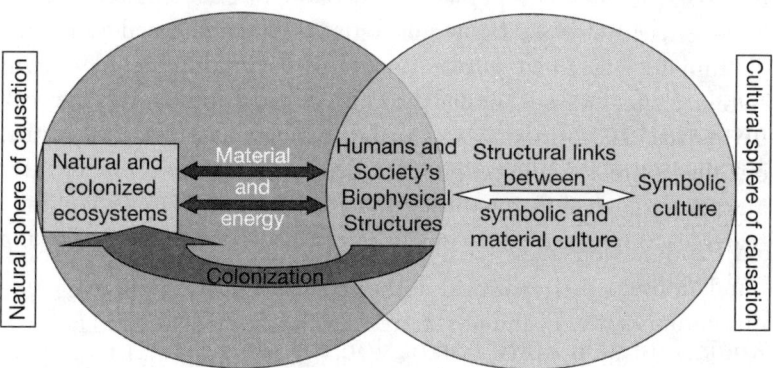

As also indicated in the figure, Richard Hoffman (2014), a well-known medievalist of environmental history, in his book *An Environmental History of Medieval Europe*, argues, 'Humans not only interact with natural sphere, they consciously seek to use elements of it for their cultural purposes and in doing so, they modify it consciously or not.' Likewise, the farming peasants in Tamil Nadu around the 7th–8th century made their way into tribal forest for turning it into cultivable field.

This state formation under Pallavas of Kanchi and Pandyas of Madurai in early medieval south was marked by enormous social, political and ecological transformations. Kinship-based social ties gave way to Brahmanical caste and ritual ranking in Tamil region. Property relations evidenced transformations since the 9th century under the imperial Cholas introduced sluice-based irrigation networks in Kaveri river basin. As a result, individual private holdings and *kani* and *pattru* holdings were recognized and social stratification surfaced among peasants, priests, traders, administrators and so on (Kulke, 2004). The institution of temple gained supremacy over resources. The Saiva Siddhanta movement emerged to take control over temple resources and Shiva Lingayats of Basavana challenged the Brahmanical *varna* ideology (Flood, 1996). Five *Tinai* (ecological zones) disappeared and three types of lands existed—dry, wet and mixed. Gradual peasanti- zation of tribes, accommodated within caste of *antajaya*, encouraged more reclamation of land. As a result, as social stratification started to grow, merely a complimentary ideology of caste could maintain social order; therefore *Varna* ideology consolidated social hierarchy. To sum up, it was merely after the 6th century CE that in deep south state-societies emerged under the Pallavas and Pandyas who not only patronized the cosmopolitan Sanskritic kingly and *Dharmic* norms, but the entire Puranic religion (bhakti form) had become an inte- grative ideological factor through varna paradigm, temple-building, material-art representations of deities and associated rituals of dancing and singing.

Regional Local State Formation through Peasantization Sind and Rajasthan

Peasantization of pre-state and pre-literate tribal and pastoral nomads in Punjab, Rajasthan, Tamil Nadu and Sindh was a long-drawn process which began within the Early Medieval period when they were transformed into agrarian-based states. Prior to their colonization and gradual encroachment of peasant agriculture into previously tribal regions, these regions were inhabited predominantly by martial warrior tribal, whose relationship with environment was harmonious.

Jats started to migrate as transhumant migrants to Sindh by the 8th century. These Sindi tribal Jats dominated the southern Indus region. By the 11th century, these tribal Jats had become peasants par excellence. Irfan Habib remarked that such a dramatic transformation was the end product of spread of the Persian wheel in the Indus basin environment. It drove the previously mobile pastoralist groups into ranks of peasantry. These tribal over a period of 500 years developed into a settled and stratified society.

Concerning the historical period of Early Medieval, the Marxist historians such as Kosambi and Sharma formulated the *Indian Feudalism* hypothesis to encapsulate overall *changes* in the form of political fragmentation or parcelizaton of power, rise of samantas, proliferation of *jatis*, subjection of peasantry and general decline of older urban spaces and money, especially copper coinage (Chattopadhyay, 1985). Sharma's construct was backed by immense inscriptional storehouse and Puranas, chronicles and political biographies referring respectively to intuitions of Brahmadeya and degeneration of social and moral ethics—Kaliyuga. The kernel of change ensured by the Gupta polity was the 'excessive preoccupation of people with land' that spawned a series of related practices and intuitions chiefly agricultural expansion through land grants to Brahmans (dominance of Brahmanical ideas) in peripheral forested areas and growth of private rights in land, which led to new fiscal and administrative arrangements. This tool of analysis (feudal) has reached an impasse since a range of alternative ways of thinking about the early medieval, post 1970s, have focused on processes such as lateral expansion of state society and local state formation through spread of clan-polities, peasantization of tribes, emergence and integration of cults. Similarly, the historically significant process of state formations in the forms of either vertical or horizontal local polities such as Paramaras of Malwa, Chahmans of Ajmer, Chalukyas of Gujarat, Ghadvalas of Kanauj, Guhilas of Mewar, Chahmans of Dholpur, Chahmans of Nadol, Prathiharas of Kanauj, Gurjaras of Nandipuri also occurred in Western India (Chattopadhyay, 2005).

The expansion of these local polities occurred corresponding to the peasantization of tribes and proliferation of settlements with artificial irrigation techniques as stepwells (*vapi*), *araghatta* wells, tanks, reservoir (*tadaga*). In these regions of present-day Rajasthan and eastern Gujarat, agriculture of cereals expanded and crops cultivated were *godhuma* (wheat), *jawar* (millet), *mung* (pulses), *cana* (gram), oilseeds and *cokha* (rice). Therefore the peasantization of tribes, territorial expansion of Rajput polities and artificial irrigation-based agriculture were connected to give way to newer forms of social formations.

Medieval Empires, Famines, Plagues and Reclamations from the 14th–17th Century

Most of the Indian historical literary text contains huge descriptions of destructive diseases and plagues wiping out vast magnitude of people and settlements. The 12th century Sanskrit chronicle *Rajatrangini* is rife with devastating instances of harvest failures either from famines owing to inordinate exactions in kind from the peasants or from natural calamities such as hailstorms, unseasonal floods and unnecessary excessive rains. The *Arthashastra*, Sangam literature, regional chronicles and epics are full of such references to famines and floods causing starvation and plagues. In the Sangam period Tamil epic *Manimekhalm* has reference to a 12-year long famine. Though the Pallavas inaugurated an all-out agrarian expansion in deep southern India, constructed dams and embankments, the famines and plagues struck as ever with regularity the in the early period of the reign of Narasimhavarman I (630–668 CE). Ibn Battuta in his memoirs *Rihla* cites a remarkable depiction of the city of Mathura (present Madura) susceptible to frequent famines, disease epidemics and plagues:

> Mathura is a large city, with broad streets. The first person to make it the capital was my father-in-law, Sultan Sharif Jalal ud

Din Ahsan Shah. He built the city to resemble Delhi and it is well constructed. When I went to the city there was an outbreak of cholera and people were dying fast... {The Sultan res} returned to Mathura and found his wife, mother and child ill. He remained in the city for three days and then moved to the bank of the river situated one parsang from the town. At this place there is a temple of the infidels. (Shokoohy, 2013)

At the same time conditions in Europe and central Asia were exacerbated by the well-known pandemic, the Black Plague (1347–1352 CE), caused by rats, which marked a watershed in European history, affecting socio-economic structures entirely. Regular famines and plagues visited the Mughal cities also. While famines were occurring regularly, in the 13th century CE north India, Alauddin Khilji sensing the alarming consequences of the Mongols devastating series of campaigns, compelled peasants to pay revenue in kind. This was done to maintain continuous supply in the market and to ward off danger of famine-like situation. Earlier the Delhi Sultans shifted their capital from the Qutub Complex to Purana Qila due to scarcity of water supply in the former place. The Mughals often changed their capital cities. Shah Jahan shifted the capital to Delhi where he constructed the marvellous city of Shahjahanabad on the banks of River Yamuna to evade from the scarcity of water in Agra.

Karl Wittfogel came up with a hypothesis that Asian societies are static. Owing to the environmental conditions being semi-arid, these societies spawned a natural mode of production called Asiatic mode of production that was based on management of irrigation in hydraulic societies like India where the state had to perform functions of maintaining irrigation to fields. These countries were ruled by qualified priests. According to Wittfogel (1976), 'Agrarian despotism always keeps the dominant religion integrated in its power system.' He dubbed the oriental modes of subsistence as 'hydraulic economies' and hydraulic state as genuinely managerial state. A specific organization of labour was required to increase cultivation, cooperation and control over population at a large scale territorial level in agriculture. Kin-based groups are leaders that maintain internal order and protect

the commonwealth territory from external aggression. Wittfogel enu-
merated the following functions of irrigation managerial state in India:

Hydraulic Works	Non-hydraulic Works
1. Productive installations (canals, aqueducts, reservoirs, sluices and dykes for the purpose of irrigation) 2. Protective installations (drainage canals and dykes for flood control) 3. Aqueducts provide drinking water 4. Navigation canals	1. Works for defence and communication (walls and other structures of defence and highways) 2. Edifices serving the public and personal needs of the secular and religious masters of hydraulic society (palaces and capital cities, tombs and temples)

Mughal State Agrarian Structure

The Mughals (1526–1707 CE) established political rule over nearly
whole of the Indian subcontinent. The Mughals confronted an unbridled resistance from the regional political elites in the beginning, but
later negotiated with their rights and privileges and incorporated these
rajas and zamindars into the imperial administrative framework of the
Mansabdari system. The Indian society from the late 16th century
witnessed many interrelated socio-economic processes such as commercialization of agriculture, land reclamations in eastern regions of
the Mughal Empire (Bihar and Bengal) by approaching fertility bearing rivers and introduction of new animals and crops into the Indian
subcontinent by European merchants and traders. Commercialization
of agriculture followed since the Mughals realized agrarian revenues
in cash called *Jama-Dami* (Cash in copper coins). Mughal authorities
used forced labour (*begar*) in Kashmir to procure saffron produce. In
the 17th century, agricultural production had intensified for eastern
Bengal witnessed the influx of the Mughal mansabdars and *Madad-i-
Mash* holders, and on top of that sophisticated canal irrigation, dams
with sluices and in great measure reclamations of land. In the Mughal
period, fairly documented in literary texts and visual cultures, central
Asian melons, flowers, trees and animals were introduced in the

Indian subcontinent. At the same time, Europeans also brought the Turkey bird to India. Apart from tobacco, several vegetables such as cauliflower, cabbage and potato were adopted for cultivation in India.

Mughal State and Frontiers Tribals Communities

The tribal communities would often through social banditry and raiding disturb political order in frontier regions of the imperial Mughals from every corner such as the Gakhars, Arghuns of Sindh, the Naga, the Ahoms of Assam, Afghani Roushaniyan, Kolis of Maharashtra, the Mundas and Santhals of Chota Nagpur. Further the recalcitrant nobles and rebellious people resorted to living into forests to evade tributes. In his memoirs Babur bewailed the 'forests of thorny trees in which the people. ...hole up and obstinately refuse to pay tribute' (Thackston, 2007). The situation in Chota Nagpur from the 13th century till the Mughal annexation of these territories was that brave, chivalrous warriors and scholarly people as well as 'priests were invited from distant places to serve the region in their various capacities. Refugees and military invaders also came and settled down in the region from time to time' (Ghosh, 1991). These people were called *diku* (outsider) immigrants who had infiltrated tribal territory and controlled the cultural life of native tribals. With the Mughal east-ward expansion, it resulted in the 'influx of immigrants which continued till the Mughal era, upsetting the demographic pattern of the region, however, did not result in any major protest from the aborigines at that time'.

However, the Mughals from the last decade of the 16th century initiated a process of bringing the tribal chief leader (*manki*) of central India (Chota Nagpur) and Sindh within the Mughal system of revenue gathering. In the early 17th century, the Mughals successfully captured the Oreans and rebel chiefs and imprisoned them in the Gwalior fort. To persuade them into a tributary state of the Mughals in 1585, Chota Nagpur Raj was practically controlled by the Mughal rulers, though these tribal domains were not brought under the Mughal methods of governance. It was in 1680 CE that the *manki* Durjansal was put into prison by the Mughals since he failed to pay tributes. In the late 17th century the tribal chiefs were freed on the condition that they would to pay tributes and made the allowed the following:

> The Hindu courtiers and mercenaries whom he made 'jagirdars' of Munda and Oraon villages with the right to collect and enjoy taxes from those villages. The immigrant 'jagirdars' and 'thikadars' in course of time, introduced land rent in the Chotanagpur region and gradually ousted many of the original in-habitants of the land for their inability to pay rent or reluctance to render 'begar' or forced labour to the new masters. Thus, the transfer of ancestral tribal lands to outsiders began as early as the 17th century reducing the tribal peasants to mere cultivators of land, paying rent to the non-tribal 'diku' land-lords, who in turn paid a share to the Maharaja of Chotanagpur, who then paid a share to the Mughal emperor. (Ghosh, 1991)

When the British East India Company obtained the right to *Diwani* from Shah Alam in 1765 following the defeat in Buxar, the Chota Nagpur Raja Gopal Rai accepted British authority and therefore agreed to pay tribute of three thousand rupees annually. Within two decades the British colonial authorities introduced institution of control and supervision into tribal as *Thana* (Roy, 1928). Though the British were expected to bring respite to local tribal, they miserably failed. In the 19th century a new class of Thakidars (*diku*) emerged, who deliberately encroached the rights of these poor tribal which resulted in a series of tribal rebellions against the authorities. The British dubbed these rebellious tribes as 'criminals' (Roy, 1915).

Colonial Modernity: Tribalism, Capitalism and Environmentalism in India

India came into the canopy of the forces of modernity through the agency of British colonialism. Among its many salient characteristics Michel Foucault (1984) has highlighted 'heroization of present and consciousness of discontinuity of time' as the dominant of all features of modernity. British colonial government introduced in India 'modern' institutions such as education, property-rights regime, railway transportation, political system, legal system and capitalism. The establishment of these institutions had either direct or indirect forward and backward linkages to working of the British capitalist system. As their home markets had reached a point of saturation, they began establishing railway networks which was determined and necessitated by linking of regions producing raw materials and connecting them to markets. When the Indian subcontinent was colonized by the British, the *telos* of colonization had changed from land grabbing by dispossession (represented Colonization of American) to control of markets and raw materials. Widespread network of railways, established by colonial state in mid of nineteenth century, to a great measure positively benefitted Indian producers for inter-connecting them to larger regional and global markets, however, the same channels of communication symbolized arteries through which for nearly a century the Indian resources and wealth would be drained out to the metropolitan core of the British empire.

The British colonialism was an ecological watershed as it exterminated indigenous forests population, dispossessed the tribal of rights in forests and land and initiated forced commercialization of agriculture. Richard Grove initiated the debate that British colonial state had from the beginning attempted to adhere to forest policy for conservation since the British quickly felt the connections between deforestation and environmental desiccation. Similarly, David Hardiman though agreed to hold Colonial policies responsible for the massive deforestation carried out by the British colonial state, however, interestingly he moves further and claims that such policies endured even under the post-colonial governments. The mainstream modern environmental discourse in India is based on the premise of Madhav Gadgil and Ramachandra Guha (2013).

> The British government established an autocratic forest department... which sought fulfilling of immoral needs by enclosing the forests and excluding the peasantry from using them as a resource base. This gave rise to disparate protests in the late 19th century and later nationalist-led forest protests of the Gandhian period.

The British colonial state introduced modern scientific forestry in south Asia with the objective to ruthlessly produce large commercial timber. However, the same motivations were continued by the post-colonial governments in the National Forest Policy 1952 in which forest resources were called 'national assets'.

While looking at the big picture and circumstances prevailing in the late 19th century, the famine report *A Narrative of the Drought and Famine Which Prevailed in the North West Provinces (1868, 1869 and the beginning of 1870)* deliberately makes light of terrifying repercussions of commodification of rice in Orissa and shrewdly underestimates the role played by the forced commercialization. It was this series of unsurpassing famines which compelled the colonial government into framing of Famine Code in 1880 (applied only in 1900). Different regions and divisions experienced the famine in varying degrees in terms of severity, mortality and magnitude based on, as per the reporter, soil fertility and retention, availability of irrigation as well as means of transport and communication. Though the famines occurred due to natural reasons, lack of traffic communication also created problems in the 19th century. Therefore, regions better in road communication were less subjected to severity of drought and famine.

References

Allchin, B., & Allchin, R. (1982). *The rise of civilization in India and Pakistan.* Cambridge: Cambridge University Press.

Ayachit, S. M. (1999). *Kashyapiya Krishisukti: A treatise on agriculture.* Secundrabad: Asian Agri-Foundation.

Chakrabarti, D. K. (2001). *Archaeological geography of the Ganga plain: The lower and the middle Ganga.* New Delhi: Permanent Black.

Chattopadhyay, B. D. (1985, June). Political processes and structure of polity in early medieval India: Problems of perspective. *Social Scientist, 145,* 4–9.

Chattopadhyay, B. D. (2005). *The making of early medieval India.* New Delhi: OUP, 18–20.

Flood, G. D. (1996). *An introduction to Hinduism.* Cambridge: Cambridge University Press, 168.

Foucault, M. (1984). What is enlightenment. In P. Rabinow (Ed.), *The Foucault reader* (32–50). New York, NY: Pantheon Books.

Gadgil, M., & Guha, R. (2013). *This fissured land: An ecological history of India* (2nd ed.). New Delhi: OUP.

Ghosh, A. (1991, 4 May). Probing the Jharkhand question. *Economic and Political Weekly, 26*(18), 1173–1181.

Guha, S. (1999). *Environment and ethnicity in India 1200–1991.* Cambridge: Cambridge University Press, 46–48.

Hoffman, R. (2014). *An environmental history of medieval Europe.* Cambridge: Cambridge University Press.

Kulke, H. (Ed.). (2004). *The state in India 1000–1700.* New Delhi: Oxford University Press.

Petraglia, M. D., & Allchin, B. (2007). *The evolution and history of human populations in south Asia.* Dordrecht: Springer.

Rangarajan, M. (2009). *Environmental issues in India: A reader.* New Delhi: Pearson Longman.

Ratnagar, S. (2001). *Understanding Harappa.* New Delhi: Tulika, 40.

Roy, S. C. (1915). *The Oraons of Chotanagpur.* Ranchi: Crown Publications.

Roy, S. C. (1928). *Oraon religion & customs.* Ranchi: Man in India Office, 316.

Sharma, R. S. (2007). *Material culture and social formations in ancient India.* New Delhi: Macmillan, 200–205.

Shinde, V. (2016). *Current perspectives on the Harappan civilization.* Wiley Online. Retrieved from http://www.sindhulogy.org/cdn/articles/harappan-civilization-current-perspective-and-its-contribution-vasant-shinde/

Shokoohy, M. (2013). *Muslim architecture of south India: The sultanate of Ma'bar and the traditions of the maritime settlers on the Malabar and Coromandel coasts.* London: Routledge Curzon.

Singh, U. (2008). *A history of ancient and early medieval India: From the stone age to the early medieval India,* New Delhi: Pearson Longman, 580–581.

Sinha, N. K. (2011). *Environmental history of early India: A reader.* New Delhi: OUP, 23–27.

Thackston, W. R. (2007). *The baburnama: Memoirs of Babur, prince and emperor.* New York, NY: Random House.

Thapar, R. (1991). *From lineage to state: Social formations of the mid-first millennium BC in the Ganga Valley.* New Delhi: OUP.

Thapar, R. (2002). *Penguin history of early India: From the origins to AD 1300.* New Delhi: Penguin India, 185–190.

Trautmann, T. R. (2015). *Elephants and kings: An environmental history.* Chicago, IL: University of Chicago Press, 184.

Worster, D. (1994). *Nature's economy: A history of ecological ideas.* Cambridge: Cambridge University Press.

CHAPTER 12

Domino-Effect of Climate Change on Biodiversity, Food Security and Oceanic Acidification

Rakhi Dawar, Mohammad Younus Bhat and Aswani R. S.

Introduction

Climate change is inarguably the biggest challenge the world is facing today as it comes with an array of consequences for the life on Earth. Climate change is defined as, 'a change in the state of climate that can be identified by alterations in the mean and/or the variability of its properties and that remains for decades or longer'. Natural and man-made causes instigate these changes in the rise in surface and sea temperatures, and this leads to rapid loss in ecosystems and biodiversity. Hence, this chapter analyses the current state of global climate change, its impacts and ways to mitigate it. Climate change is a global phenomenon, with stark consequences for the lower-middle income countries, due to socio-political volatilities. Climate change is not considered as a regional concern but a global one majorly since greenhouse gas (GHGs) are highly permeable in the atmosphere and no matter where they are emitted they are absorbed into the atmosphere and dispersed equally, thereby arousing the need for a cooperative mechanism of climate change adaptation. Due to this occurrence and also due to fewer resources to adapt, the developing countries are at the receiving end. This chapter also studies the scenario of climate change vulnerabilities in the developing countries.

With the steady rise in population, the bearing of climate change on food production is alarming. Ironically, agriculture is both on the contributing and receiving side of the spectrum of climate changes, whereby intensive single cropping and farm animals have led to a 21 per cent increase in carbon dioxide (CO_2) emissions from 2000 to 2010. The impact of global warming on agriculture is evident through the Intergovernmental Panel on Climate Change's (IPCC) reports that climatic changes will lead to 10–25 per cent reduction in agriculture outputs. According to Dobell and Gourdji (2012), through a strengthened hydrological cycle, an increase in the ozone (O_3) levels in the atmosphere and high levels of CO_2, this declination in crop productivity could be achieved. Texivia (2012) states that the increase in average surface temperatures could result in infertility, poor harvests and a major risk of yield failure, as such an upsurge in heat could hamper the reproductive duration of plants and climate change can directly damage the plant cells. Thus, this chapter tries to understand the potential and limits of addressing climate change in the field of agriculture and to explore the consequences of such impacts on agriculture and human security.

Responding to climate change is a profound challenge. However, the urgency for climate adaptation is highly precarious for the continuing existence of humans in the planet. If the present conditions persist, by the end of 2030, GHGs are predicted to increase by 25–90 per cent, increasing the global temperatures, leading to extreme climatic calamities (IPCC, 2007). Thus, mitigating climate change should become a policy priority for countries as it is not a phenomenon that can be addressed in isolation. It requires an international level of cooperative remedial action to assess these issues and to arrive at corrective measures. Hence, this chapter also aims to provide constructive suggestions towards policy creation to mitigate these wider concerns of humanity.

The reasons for global warming are changes in solar cycles, volcanic eruptions, gases in the atmosphere or in land use. Globally, the average temperature of the Earth has gone up by more than 0.8 °C since the middle of the 19th century. The Earth is warming now by a frequency of more than 0.1 °C a span of every 10 years. That thermal blanket of greenhouse gases around the planet has been attributed as the major cause of global warming. According to Food and Agricultural Organization (FAO), global atmospheric temperature is likely to exceed 1.5 °C relative to the average of the 1850 to 1900 period. Surface waters (0 to 700m deep) warmed up by an average of 0.7 °C per century globally from 1900 to 2016. North Atlantic region is the warmest of all regions on earth. FAO envisions increasing the food production of the world by a rate of 60 per cent in order to cope up with the demographic variations of the 21st century. This demonstrates how food production is under major risk due to climate change.

Impact on Agriculture and Food Security

According to IPCC, production of crops will decline by 10–25 per cent due to climate change. It is predicted that around 40 per cent of the rare species of fish will be reduced due to the impact of climate change on aquatic life. Deforestation and forest degradation could lead to about 11 per cent of global GHG emissions. As a result, FAO has stated that such harmful GHG emissions due to unhampered degradation of the green cover have increased from 0.4 Gt CO_2 in 1990 to 1.0 Gt CO_2 in 2015. There is a threat to public health because of food-borne diseases accruing to climate change. Global food wastage creates about 8 per cent of GHG emissions annually. Climate change can also have alarming impacts on aquaculture. Some examples of short-run impacts are losses of production and infrastructure arising from fatal events such as floods, and increased risk of parasites due to negative impacts on farming conditions. Reduced availability of wild seed and reduced precipitation leading to increased competition for fresh water are some of the long-term impacts. Aquaculture is ought to face long-term impacts due to changes in temperature, precipitation and ocean acidification. Even crop productivity is hampered due to climate change. Crop production will have a serious impact in the long term in the following ways: An intensified hydrological cycle and greater level of CO_2, coupled with elevated O_3 levels (Dobell & Gourdji, 2012).

It is observed that global warming causes an increase in vapour pressure of air. Furthermore, climate change can directly damage the plant cells. Warming increases heat stress during the critical reproductive period and results in sterility, lower yields and the risk of crop failure altogether. The worst consequence is that rising Temperature and CO_2 favour pests and diseases. Heavy rainfall will result in flooding and waterlogged soils, causing damage to crop production. It is estimated that warming will slow yield growth by 1.5 per cent per decade globally. For wheat, maize and barley, there is a pessimistic response of global yields to high temperatures (Lobell & Field, 2007). The major impacts of climate change are risks of lower agricultural production, sea level rise and extreme events. Parekh & Parekh, Kumar & Pankh (2001) estimated that climate change will lead to loss in yields of rice and wheat would vary between 32 and 40 per cent, gross domestic product (GDP) would drop by between 1.8 and 3.4 per cent, and farm level total net revenue would fall by 9 per cent. Global warming could result in the submersion of coastal lines resulting in large-scale emigration. As a result, there will be increased numbers of environmental refugees. If the sea level rises by one meter today, it would leave 7 million persons without a dwelling in India. India will be unable to pay for protective measures as it will involve a large share of its GDP.

Apart from that, CO_2 emissions reduce GDP and lead to higher poverty. All models present a view that higher temperatures in summer and winter are harmful for crops and same is the case with fall in rainfall (Mendelsohn, Nordhaus, & Shaw, 1994). As far as yields of rice are concerned, the grain yield declined by 10 per cent for each 1°C increase in growing minimum temperatures in the dry season. However, there is an insignificant effect on crop yield at maximum temperatures. A day temperature of 33°C and increasing night temperatures from 25°C to 33°C had a resultant high reduction in grain filling percentage and yield of grain. Global yields of wheat, maize and barley showed a negative impact of increased temperatures. Since 1981, the annual combined losses of these three crops representing roughly 40 meters or US$5 billion annually as of 2002 are the result of global warming (Lobell & Field, 2007).

Due to the exposure to increased CO_2 concentrations, photosynthesis rate increases among plants and it stimulates biomass growth. Higher biomass needs higher energy supply for maintenance needed in higher respiration, partly compensated by lower specific respiration. Stomatal conductance is reduced and transpiration rates are enhanced due to global warming. Furthermore, CO_2 levels increased sharply in the atmosphere leading to increased root/shoot ratios. The concentrations of mineral nutrients and proteins are reduced. On the other hand, higher temperatures may intensify pest and disease problems, leading to crop losses. Increased water shortage also affects the crop yields. Global warming leads to increase in sea levels which will bring salinization and an intrusion of sea water into fresh water sources, flooding and loss of soil fertility. The IPCC inferred that the agricultural productivity will decrease in the tropics as increasing temperatures of 2.5°C lead to a hike in food prices.

Human land use/land cover change has changed one-third to one-half of Earth's ice-free surface (Vitousek, 1994). Even the farm values on an average have been reduced due to warming (Mendelsohn et al., 1994). Climate change also results in natural calamities like tropical storms leading to loss of crops, demolition of houses and physical capital. Average prices for food will rise moderately with moderate increase in temperatures (until 2050) (Schmidhuber & Tubiello, 2007). It has been estimated that the change in temperatures would range from a fall of −1.5 per cent to a rise of +2.6 per cent by 2080 (Schmidhuber & Tubiello, 2007). Moreover, the toll of undernourished people will increase by 5–26 per cent in 2080. The studies also reveal that 170 million additional people will be at risk of hunger by 2080. Increase in temperatures would result in the increase of food poisoning cases in temperate regions. Warm seas have increased the cases of reef fish poisoning in tropical regions. Diarrhoeal disease in adults and children is often registered. A global mean temperature increase enhances the epidemic capacity of the mosquito population in tropical regions double-fold and more than 100-fold in temperate climates. Increased risk of malaria with insufficient resources to cope in the affected areas may affect the health seriously in the next century. Increasing oceanic temperatures with increased atmospheric CO_2 concentrations pose a serious threat to ecosystems such as coral reefs. They are pushed into negative carbonate balance. There would be a certain shift towards the demand for electric power. Solar powered cooling seems attractive. There would be an increase in the total building energy use where the heating load tends to be lower than the annual cooling load (Li, Yang, & Lam, 2012).

Impact on Biodiversity and Ecosystem Services

Climate change cannot be considered as an isolated issue. It is the mother of all issues with several aspects and inter-linkages namely, science and technology, economy and trade, diplomacy and politics. These features and the devastating impacts make it yet another issue in this complicated world of proliferating issues. Today, climate change is considered as a significant driver of biodiversity loss leading to extinction of various endemic species through habitat destruction and fragmentation. Carr et al. (2013) found negative bearing of climate change on human-utilized species while combining climate change vulnerability and use assessments. It was found that many species were identified to be facing extreme threats from the changes due to global warming, and hence the preservation of these should become a policy priority.

Biodiversity as a result of global warming is declining at an alarming rate. If it is not mitigated now, we could witness a two-third decline in biodiversity while putting survival of other species and our own future at risk. Although, the effect on wild populations seems relatively moderate as of now, it is quickly accelerating and it could be decisive as far future of biodiversity is concerned. Climate change aggravates the situation further, adding to the traditional threats, which wild species face such as habitat loss and overexploitation. This in turn may worsen the situation further by compromising a specie's inability to respond to global warming. Thus, urgent cooperative mechanism should be adapted and sought in order to address these issues of climate change.

These wild species are highly essential for maintaining the ecosystem balance of our nature which has to be cautiously monitored to hamper catastrophic impacts on earth. The impact seems to continue and biodiversity loss is estimated to escalate in extent and ubiquity as the emissions of GHG, particularly CO_2, continue to rise, giving rise to extremity of heat and storms in frequency and intensity. Because of their life history, ecological, physiological, behavioural and genetic characteristics of certain species are highly vulnerable to the impacts of climate change compared to others. Species loss is also affected by huge climatic alterations and susceptibility to climate change. Factors that cause increased vulnerability to climate change have been identified into the following trait groups (IUCN, 2008): requirement of micro and/or specialized habitats; narrow environmental thresholds/ tolerances that are likely to exceed because of climate change; dependence on particular environmental initiatives that will get disrupted by climate change; dependence on interspecific interactions; and inability to disperse or colonize to a new suitable range.

In 2008, International Union for Conservation of Nature (IUCN) collected information regarding the five groups of traits for the world's birds (9,856 species), amphibians (6,222 species) and warm-water reef-building corals (799 species). It was found after the compilation of scores for birds, amphibians as well as warm-water reef-building coral species that up to 35 per cent, 52 per cent and 71 per cent of these groups respectively could be vulnerable to climate change (see Box 12.1). The results also found that 70–80 per cent of birds, amphibians and corals are vulnerable because of climate change, though already threatened. However, it is pertinent to mention that if species that have least resilience to threat are exposed to large climate changes, then the risk of extinction will be the greatest. Therefore, these species and the areas where they are concentrated must be prioritized in policies aiming at conservation.

Bellard et al. (2012) observed that climate change alters species distribution as well as their temporal and physiological niche to a great extent. Moreover, climate change impacts by modifying species distribution range while exposing and adapting new conditions or making extinction local as well as global. These factors in proximity

Box 12.1 Impact of Climate Change on Individual Species

An extensive study on climate change susceptibility in a chapter of *2008 (IUCN) Red List* claimed that 25% of birds, 28% of amphibians and 51% of corals were vulnerable to climate change. From around the world 31 volunteer biologists researched that there are 90 traits that would make the species likely to be negatively affected by climate change. They categorized these 90 traits into five broad categories that explain the species' environmental, biological and social vulnerability. A sample group of birds (9,856 species), amphibians (6,222 species) and warm-water reef-building corals (799 species) was tested to find out whether they are susceptible to climate change and whether they are currently threatened. Sea birds such as albatrosses, penguins, petrels and shearwaters are most likely to be hit hard by climate change. Thrushes, antbirds and sandpipers are also in danger. IUCN estimates that 19% of reef corals are currently threatened and susceptible, 51% are climate change susceptible and 71% of coral species are likely to be affected adversely by warmer waters. *Acropora gemmifera* and *Pocillopora Seydoux* are among the 'near vulnerable' species. The results show that 8% of amphibians, 3% of birds and 9% of corals are threatened, whereas 24% amphibians, 10% birds and 19% corals are threatened and susceptible to climate change. Moreover, 17% amphibians, 25% birds and 39% of corals are declared susceptible. It is a great work of environmentalists.

with other anthropogenic pressures threaten the very existence of biological diversity as well as the productivity, stability and sustainability of Earth's ecosystems (Bellard et al., 2012). Perrings (2010) termed climate change both a cause as well as an effect of change in biodiversity. It is also the chief driver as far as changes in the distribution of beneficial and harmful species is concerned. Biodiversity clinches all life forms on the face of earth. It contributes directly as well as indirectly towards enhancement of human well-being. From provision of foods, fibres and fuels to the sequestration of carbon, biodiversity enhances the capability of ecosystems to adapt to climate change. However, we lack measures so that the value of biodiversity can be taken into consideration as either cause or an effect of climate change. *Stern Review's* conjectures is that the effects of climate change on ecosystems (excluding forest, agriculture or coastal systems) and human well-being can be as high as 6 per cent of the world GDP, while raising the long-run cost to 11 per cent on an annual basis. Moreover, IPCC estimates maintain that a 25 net emission reduction can be achieved by halting the reduction in carbon sequestration in forests or mangroves and so on. This will further benefit in terms of averted losses of nearly three per cent of global GDP already estimated by *Stern Review*.

As far as climate change assessment is concerned, it is found that both biodiversity and ecosystems are already stressed. Due to these stressors, many species have altered their geographical ranges, introducing shift in habitat distributions at an alarming rate. Further, vivid changes occurring in plant and animal species cause shifts in the location as well as the extent of biomes, affecting structure of ecosystems and their functions. Also, evident is the decline in the population and extinction of prime species due to rising temperatures. It is pertinent to mention that changes in winter are having significant but surprising impact on ecosystem services. For example, changes such as soil freezing, snow cover and air temperature have greatly affected carbon sequestration, decomposition and carbon export, which influence agricultural and forest production. However, outbreaks in pests and tree mortality will be enhanced due to warm winters and long growing seasons making forest fires more intense. It is equally going to decelerate recreation value of biodiversity and ecosystems making high projected economic losses.

Currently climate change is posing severe threats to species, ecosystems and people's livelihood around the globe. Warming of oceans and ocean acidification can prove to be critical and challenging for our generation. Until now, oceans have shielded humankind from adverse impacts of climate change by absorbing significant amount of heat and CO_2. The capacity of oceans to absorb carbon dioxide, a significant ecosystem service, is declining overtime continuously with increasing emissions. In addition, projections of anthropogenic emissions show a decline from 55 per cent and 22 per cent for Representative Concentration Pathway (RCP) 2.6 and RCP 8.5, respectively. Together with oceanic acidification, it is equally jeopardizing food security, affecting shoreline protection and provision of income adversely, and endangering livelihood sources and sustainable economic development. By the end of the 21st century, it is felt that the risk of impact to ecosystem services provided by oceans like coastal protection will be higher, therefore aggravating the risks of floods, particularly in the low-lying areas. It is therefore imperative for the world community to chalk out plans or vision documents to mitigate the effects of ocean warming so that the movement towards an unsustainable future can be avoided. According to Mangan (2015), the impact of climate change on oceans can be addressed successfully in the following ways:

1. Mitigation of carbon emissions, reduction of non-climate stressors via creation of more protected areas (such as national parks, biosphere reserves and instruments that can regulate the exploitation of natural resources and can protect marine and coastal ecosystems).

2. Repair and adaptation of ecosystems that have been damaged; examples can be an abetted evolution of coral and coral farming as well as diversifying economic activities or seaside elevated zones. Nonetheless, the amount of possibilities and their effectiveness may narrow down because of ocean warming or ocean acidification. In other words, the focus of shift to attaining the desired 2 °C path can also limit the policy options. For instance, coral reef resilience is hard to manage if there are no healthy reefs remaining. Moreover, refurbishment and restoration of previously damaged coastal ecosystems will be expensive as well as less successful, hence worsening the adverse consequences for humans.

Positive correlation of temperature exists with grain harvests. There was a major negative correlation of temperature change with drought and peasant uprisings for the period from 210 BC to 1910 AD. There were more poor and normal harvests (70.7% of the total harvests), along with the occurrence of more moderate and severe famines (77.6% of the total famines) and decades with peasant uprisings (51.7% of all the decades) during this period (Yun and Chao, 2015). IPCC report of 2007 shows that in India, several districts of Assam were badly affected due to drought like situations in 2005 and 2006 due to climate change (IPCC, 2007). Crop failure caused a loss of ₹100 crores in Assam. In the strong drought conditions in 15 districts of Assam in the summer months of the year 2006, more than 75 per cent of the 26 million people were adversely affected. The rainfall was recorded below normal (nearly 40%). There was change in the phonological phases in plants owing to change in temperatures.

It is clear from the literature review that climate change has adverse effects on the flora and fauna. There is a serious need to combat climate change to avoid it invading the ecosystems and causing loss of civilizations in future.

Impact of Climate Change on Oceans

The impact of climate change on oceans in general is huge, mostly due to the two-way relationship between oceans and climate. On the one hand, oceans largely decide the climatic conditions and variations and on the other, they are at the receiving end of climatic changes. In addition to environmental and economic bearings, climate change has far-reaching geo-political repercussions on the oceanic waters. The Indian Ocean, which is at the realm of geo-political competition in the 21st century with the likely rivalry between the rising powers, India and China, and the Asian Pivot by United States is key to impact on climate change. Unlike other places, the Indian Ocean is largely sensitive due to the volatile political situation of its littoral countries.

Mitigation of Climate Change

Reducing GHGs called for global action and needed an international scientific consensus. It started with IPCC, a conglomeration of the world's governments and the world's leading scientists, in 1988. Again, in 1992, the United Nations Framework Convention on Climate Change (UNFCCC) coordinated the international negotiations on climate change. Furthermore, the Kyoto Protocol was adopted in Kyoto in Japan on 11 December 1997, which came into force on 16

February 2005. The Protocol committed developed countries to reduce their overall GHG emissions by at least 5 per cent below 1990 levels during the period 2008–2012. Ultimately, 191 countries ratified the treaty. Meanwhile, the IPCC released its third assessment report in 2001. In the aggregated market sector, there were negative effects in many developing countries due to global mean temperature increases. IPCC's fourth assessment report released in 2007 cleared that warming of the climate system is 'unequivocal' with increases in global average air and ocean temperatures.

Good policy should account for alternative risk reduction strategies—mitigation, adaptation and insurance. Mitigation involves investments to reduce the probability of damages due to carbon emissions. It is a public good determined by the sum of all nation's efforts to reduce carbon. Adaptation involves investments to reduce the severity of realized damages. Adaptation is a private good in which the benefits of reduced severity accrue to one nation and usually to certain sectors of this nation (World Bank, 2010). Insurance involves investments that transfer wealth from good to bad states of nature given a bad event has been realized. The 10-step approach (Sarkar, 2010) to addressing GHG and climate change impacts is as follows:

1. To explain the existing global context in which climate change occurs and is expected to occur in the future.
2. To refer to any relevant state law that addresses climate change.
3. To put forward any relevant GHG inventories to which the project contributes.
4. To measure the project's direct and indirect GHG emissions
5. To change the GHG emissions into carbon equivalents using a 'carbon calculator'.
6. To discuss about the attainment of applicable state GHG reductions.
7. To elaborate on the cumulative global climate change impacts.
8. To explain how the impacts of global climate change could potentially affect the project.
9. To propose alternatives in order to meet objectives and reduce GHG emissions.
10. To observe mitigation measures for reducing GHG emissions.

According to Smith and Lenhart (1996), the suggestions for adaptation of agriculture include the following:

1. Development of new crop types
2. Enhancement of seed banks
3. Avoid monoculture
4. Motivating farmers to plant a variety of drought resistant crops
5. Liberalize trade in agriculture

They also emphasized for adaptation of ecosystems and devised the following:

1. Integrated ecosystem planning and management
2. Protection of buffer zones
3. Enhance methods to protect biodiversity

Smith and Lenhart gave the following policy options for sea level rise:

1. Planning urban growth
2. Discouraging permanent shoreline stabilization.
3. Incorporating marginal increase in the height of coastal infrastructure
4. Preserving vulnerable coastal wetlands

The Challenge of International Coordination

The economists use the Game Theory as a tool to examine the coordination problem. Hanley, Shogren and White (2013), addressed it as a problem of prisoner's dilemma as it falls in the realm of public good. According to this, each participant has an enticement to diverge from the complaisant elucidation, that is, each country desires to take an unrestricted benefit on others' diminutive activities. These free riders capture all the benefits of climate protection and pay none of the costs. In this case, the Nash equilibrium—the outcome in which no one has a unilateral incentive to deviate—is for all countries to free ride. Good international climate policy should address the implementation of cost-effective risk reduction strategies such as carbon taxes or carbon emission trading. Carbon taxes fix the cost of carbon and allow the quantity of emissions to be determined by the private sector. The tax can be collected in various ways such as a severance tax on domestic fossil fuel output and an equal tax on imports, a tax on primary energy inputs levied on refineries, gas transportation systems and coal shippers, cars or truck owners. The appropriate tax on natural gas entering the pipeline system could account for leakage and the greater relative potency of methane.

Moreover, a tradable permit system also called cap and trade is followed. Tradable permits are attractive since they create mutual gains between trading partners and guarantee a fixed level of emission reductions (Hanley et al., 2013). Firms might reduce their tax exposure by reducing CO_2 emissions. Nordhaus (2008) makes the case for an internationally harmonized carbon tax over a permit system. His argument is that a carbon tax is likely to be a more efficient incentive device because of its conceptual simplicity. The tax will hold an advantage over permits if the goals are to maintain the flexibility needed to promote economic growth.

Economists have argued for a hybrid system, one that combines both taxes and permits.

The Benefits and Costs of International Cooperation

The conventional economics approach to assessing climate change policy is to calculate the benefits and costs of action or inaction. As noted by Pindyck (2011), most economic analyses of climate change policy compare costs and benefits in five steps:

1. Defining a 'business as usual' (BAU) carbon emissions benchmark against which we can compare any policy options
2. Potential temperature changes that might arise from staying on the BAU benchmark path, either at a global average or at a regional level

3. The estimated losses to the world economy (GDP) due to higher temperatures from the BAU path—some estimates include human adaptation some do not
4. The estimated costs associated with reducing BAU emissions to some reduced target level of emissions
5. Presumptions about how the society values these changes today and off into the future

The benefits from climate policy are determined by what losses we avoid with lower concentrations of carbon: less biodiversity, less potable water, loss of coastal areas and more infectious diseases such as malaria and cholera. Furthermore, climate change would benefit some parts of agriculture with longer growing seasons and more fertilization. However, Tol (2012) finds that most estimates suggest that a doubling of atmospheric concentrations would lead to moderate economic decline, a decrease of 1 or 2 per cent of GDP.

The way forward from this grim situation is cover cropping and carbon sequestration. The policy suggestions include agroforestry with multipurpose trees, crops and animal components for improving hydrology. The activities for mitigation of climate change can include popularization of technologies such as system of rice cultivation (SRI), aerobic rice cultivation for water saving and mitigation of GHG emissions, promotion of technologies reducing N_2O emission and dependence on non-renewable energy. Change in the planting dates and crop varieties are another mitigating ways to address climate change.

Conclusion

Climate change has put economic pundits in a fix due to its fast-track impact on human life and their economic well-being. The objective of this chapter was to analyse the present status and impact of global climate change, and ways to mitigate it. However, mitigation efforts towards increasing global temperature encompass the scientific, citizen and political communities, and national governments. The unanimous call by a great majority in the scientific community is for drastic reduction in GHGs particularly CO_2 as well as significant measures aiming at conservation of resources. Reduction in GHGs calls for alternate energy resources that are more secure, efficient and environment friendly. Therefore, it requires less coal-burning power plants, significant improvement in travel (perhaps greater efficiency in travel) and communication. A comprehensive list of actions, though non-exhaustive, would be required; however, there is an insufficient evidence and little tendencies towards change or alternatives. The release of GHGs particularly CO_2 would be reduced if conventional coal for power generation was substituted by use of natural gas, wind, nuclear or solar energy. Another alternative that policymakers think can assume significance in reducing CO_2 emissions is bioenergy or biomass energy.

The scenario of climate change vulnerabilities in the developing countries are studied extensively in the chapter and policy challenges are identified in specific relation with India as the problem of climate change has spread to India in the 21st century. The findings suggest advancement in the economic use of GHGs in developing countries and transference to increasing use of renewable energy. Through this study, we suggest the sustainable use of renewables as they are secure, efficient, environmentally justifiable and economically viable. The increasing population in these developing countries is another impetus to accomplish environmental sustainability at the earliest. If we replace the traditional petro-based fuels with bio fuels, potential dangerous impacts of GHGs can be avoided. IRENA data indicates that, for instance, renewables from India have sidestepped 180.1 million tonnes CO_2e in 2016 compared to 73.8 million tonnes CO_2e in 2000. In addition, renewable electricity generation in India in 2016 has replaced the fossil fuel emission by 181.8 million tonnes CO_2e. Total emissions avoided in India from bio-energy use were 2.405 million tonnes CO_2e in 2000, which increased to maximum of 34.24 million tonnes CO_2e in 2014.

This chapter attempted to study the impact of climate change on agriculture and to explore the consequences of such impacts on human security. It is concluded that there was a negative impact of climate change on global production of several food crops such as maize, wheat and barley. The increase in night temperatures had an adverse effect on the yield of irrigated rice in the dry season. In fact, the risk of crop failure on a year-to-year basis is expected to increase. Moreover, the ultimate effect of global warming on global average supply of calories is likely to be fairly close to zero over the next few decades, but it could be as large as 20 per cent to 30 per cent of overall yield trends. According to the UN Report 2018, using 2050 as the end year, farm yield could fall by as much as 2.9 and 2.6 per cent in West Africa and India respectively. According to *International Policy Digest*, the starving population of India has increased from under 800 million in 1996 to over 1 billion recently. United Nations population data and projections show the global population reaching 9.1 billion by 2050, an increase of 32 per cent from 2010.

One of the major objectives of this chapter was to evaluate the biodiversity loss and deterioration of ecosystem services in India. Because of climate change, it is found by IUCN that 8 per cent of amphibians, 3 per cent of birds and 9 per cent of corals are threatened respectively. As well as, 24 per cent of amphibians, 10 per cent birds and 19 per cent of corals are susceptible for destruction. Given these figures, it is sufficiently clear that climate change is posing serious threat to the biodiversity loss. To assist this data, the 2019 UN Study reports that the human history is undergoing the worst level of biodiversity loss in these recent epochs.

The scope of the chapter is wide and accommodates agriculture, biodiversity, food security, oceans and other ecosystems. This chapter attempts to deliver constructive recommendations towards policy creation to mitigate these wider concerns of humanity. This study is significant for both developing and developed countries, and it specially focuses on mitigating policy challenges in achieving sustainable development. It proves that economic growth could be achieved without triggering environmental destruction, and planned and sustainable use of natural resources ensures a bright future to generations to come. The Sustainable Development Goal number 13 denotes Climate Action, and mitigating the climate change with accurate measures is the need of the hour.

References

Dobell, L. B., & Gourdji, S. M. (2012, December). The influence of climate change on global crop productivity. *Plant Physiology, 160*(4), 1686–1697.

Gillingham, K., Newell, R. G., & Palmer, K. L. (2009). Energy efficiency economics and policy. *Annual Review of Resource Economics, 1*(1), 597–620.

Hanley, N., Shogren, J., & White, B. (2013). *Introduction to environmental economics.* Oxford: Oxford University Press.

Li, D. H. W., Yang, L., & Lam, J. C. (2012). Impact of climate change on energy use in the built environment in different climate zones-A review. *Energy, 42* (1), 103–112.

Lobell, D. B., & Field, C. B. (2007, 16 March). Global scale climate-crop yield relationships and the impacts of recent warming. *Environmental Research Letters, 2*(1). Retrieved from doi.org/10.1088/1748-9326/2/1/014002

Mendelsohn, R., Nordhaus, W. D., & Shaw, D. (1994, September). The impact of global warming on agriculture—a Ricardian analysis. *The American Economic Review, 84* (4), 753–771.

Nordhaus, W. (2008). *A question of balance: Weighing the options on global warming policies.* New Haven, CT: Yale University Press.

Pindyck, R. S. (2011). Uncertain outcomes and climate change policy. *Journal of Environmental Economics and Management, 63* (3), 289–303.

Sarkar, A. N. (2010). *Emissions trading and carbon management.* New Delhi: Pentagon Earth.

Schmidhuber, J., & Tubiello, F. N. (2007, 11 December). Global food security under climate change. *Proceedings of the National Academy of Sciences of the United States of America, 104*(50), 19703–19708.

Vitousek, P. M. (1994). Beyond global warming: Ecology and global change. *Ecology, 75* (7), 1861–1876.

World Bank. (2010). *Economics of adapting to climate change.* Washington, DC: Author.

CHAPTER 13

Exploring the Sustainability of Urban Sanitation Models

Zoya Khan

Background

Growth of cities and increased urbanization have presented many developmental challenges for policymakers. Tier 1 cities that boast of better services and opportunities for livelihood have a burgeoning population and the principal challenge for the urban local bodies (ULBs) remains provisioning of basic services such as housing, water, education, healthcare and sanitation. As per Census 2011, about 32 per cent of the population in India resides in urban settlements and contributes to more than half of the country's gross domestic product (GDP). While on the road to progress, many urban centres have cropped up but the challenge remains to sustain these centres as they will be the drivers of future growth.

Access to sanitation remains a basic service and a fundamental right which has drawn much traction in recent years. Despite severe public health and environmental concerns, sanitation was not a key focus area in the initial development policy. The 11th Sustainable Development Goal (SDG) relates to building cities and communities that are sustainable and take care of the inequalities that are undesirable outcomes of the process of urbanization. The rapid uneven and unplanned process of urbanization in India not only results in uneven development but lays pressure on the resources of the city as well. With the growing demand for basic services such as sanitation and proper end disposal, the city infrastructure is unable to meet the needs of the inhabitants.

In conjunction with this the 6th SDG which mandates that adequate and equitable clean water and sanitation facilities should be provided to all, the Government of India launched the Swachh Bharat Mission (SBM) in 2014. With more than 50 per cent of the population still practicing open defecation, SBM was a welcome policy response to tackle this issue. However, with increasing number of toilets, the issue of safe management of excreta becomes pertinent. Against this backdrop, this chapter seeks to explore the sustainability of urban sanitation models with reference to Delhi and deliberate upon what can be the future pathways, learning from the experiences of other countries.

Sanitation Policy: A Brief History

As was the dominant tradition among the lower-middle income countries in the late 1900s, the policy in India too majorly focused on industrialization and hence there was a strong urban–rural bias in the policy. The policy approach for the country was mostly concentrated around agriculture and industry, largely ignoring the problems of urban settlements and cities. Within the cities too, urban development funds were mostly utilized for addressing the issues of poor housing and settlements. As far as budgetary allocations are considered, during the Third Five-Year Plan in 1961, the National Water Supply and Sanitation Committee had estimated that 9 billion would be needed to provide adequate water supply and sanitation for urban areas; out of this, only 0.69 billion could be allocated for the same. Given the resource crunch, investments were made into avenues and channels that were of higher priority.

'Sanitation' is an umbrella term used for services pertaining to water supply which include: drinking water supply, water supply for other household uses, access to toilets, sewerage disposal and management of wastewater. Therefore, water supply gets more preference over sewerage and management of wastewater which are the later processes in the sanitation chain (Chaplin, 2011). Chaplin asserts this with political will: water supply and pipeline connections can easily be translated into votes and thus always received the lion's share in both efforts and funds.

In the year 1979, the scheme Integrated Development of Small and Medium Towns (IDSMT) was initiated. This was the first formal policy response wherein improvement of basic urban services such as housing and sanitation were exclusively given weightage and were one of the main objectives. This was a centrally sponsored scheme with a 60:40 funding ratio between the centre and state, respectively.

The 1980s were declared as the International Drinking Water Supply and Sanitation Decade by the United Nations. India being a signatory to it had targeted to provide 100 per cent coverage of sewerage and sewerage treatment for Tier 1 cities which had a population greater than 100,000 and 80 per cent coverage in other towns and cities using low-cost measures and schemes. In the subsequent Five-Year Plans, the policy focus on urbanization increased and more stress was laid on providing services to urban areas. However, these were mostly limited to the regularized and authorized colonies especially in the Tier 1 cities.

Apart from sufficient fund allocation and low priority in national policymaking, the sanitation policies mainly concentrated on building toilets. Less priority was given to disposal of faecal waste. India constitutes nearly half of the global population that defecates openly, therefore increasing access to toilets is a much needed policy measure. However, the sustainability of this model depends completely on the ability to dispose of the excreta in a safe manner. Nirmal Bharat Abhiyan concentrated on increasing the toilet coverage in the rural areas. While 70 per cent of the population resided in the rural areas, no such specific policy intervention existed for urban areas until 2005 when sanitation received increased funding under Jawaharlal Nehru National Urban Renewal Mission and in 2008, when the National

Urban Sanitation Policy (NUSP) was launched. In 2015, the government launched SBM with a wider perspective by including both rural and urban areas. SBM with its wider ambit aimed at increasing access to sanitation by building more toilets.

The central government launched the Atal Mission for Rejuvenation and Urban Transformation (AMRUT) in 2015. The main thrust of this policy was to ensure proper development of urban infrastructure through universal coverage of water supply, sewerage connections, septage and solid waste management, storm water drains, reducing pollution, building sustainable transport networks and developing open green areas to enhance the aesthetics of cites. AMRUT is a centrally sponsored scheme with the centre allocating 100 per cent funds for city-wide development along the thrust areas. An outlay of ₹5 billion was allocated in its initial five-year run (2015–2020) for 500 cities across India. AMRUT has a more decentralized approach where the planning is entrusted with the ULBs.

The Census 2011 estimated that over 47 per cent of the urban households rely on on-site facilities such as septic tanks and pit latrines—with this number rapidly increasing as more population is added to the cities. However, the main thrust area for this policy remained to create a centralized network for sewerage by placing new sewer lines in un-authorized colonies and towards management of sewerage which is generated from household toilets and community toilet complexes. It also aims to revive old sewerage treatment plants (STPs) and sewage pumping stations SPSs and work upon the maintenance of the so created infrastructure by undertaking activities such as timely de-silting of drains.

In its spirit this scheme makes the states an equal stakeholder in development of the cities by enabling them to prepare a state action plan as per the needs of the city. Each state is required to prepare a State Annual Action Plan (SAAP) according to which funds are allocated after due approval. At a disaggregated level, these plans are prepared by ULBs in the form of SLIPs, as mandated by the central ministry across all mission cities and are collectively put together to form a SAAP.

Even though previous policies had tried to be inclusive in nature, they failed to address the concerns of the urban poor. The rapid increase in urban population is notably characterized by an increase in the urban slums and various slum-like habitations.

As per the report of the committee on slum statistics, the slum population of Delhi was estimated to be 3.2 million in 2012, which was estimated to increase to about 3.8 million by 2017. This increasing population added pressure on the city infrastructure and basic services. Delhi always had an unequal provisioning of sanitation facilities. While networks were laid to connect Delhi through a sewerage network, these were only limited to central and regularized colonies in Delhi, ignoring the city peripheries. *"The SAAP exclusively asks the states to elucidate if financial prioritisation is done for areas that are characterised by more poor population." intended meaning: areas that have larger poor populations require more financial resources. Hence while allocating the funds certain pockets (with larger shares of poor populations) should be prioritised. Delhi has always had unequal sanitation service provisioning. and such is the case with most urban settlements. Sanitation provisioning is limited to planned colonies and mostly overlooks the unplanned settlements that come up. Therefore financial resources should be allocated making such spaces a priority.* This factor is essential and states are encouraged to prepare plans in accordance with these guidelines. In its initial plan for the year 2015–2016, Delhi authorities had allocated equal amounts to all ULBs without consideration to ULBs with higher proportion of urban poor. However, projects under financially weaker ULBs were prioritized over others. In subsequent SAAPs (2016–2017 and 2017–2018), ULBs with higher proportion of urban poor were given financial preference.

While the above stated policy initiatives discuss that end disposal must be a priority and should be taken care of while building toilets, in reality the sustainability of the toilets so built are questionable. Owing to this, the government realized that it required a specific policy on faecal sludge and septage management. In 2017, it rolled out the National Policy on Faecal Sludge and Septage Management (FSSM). This was an interim policy measure until the country achieved 100 per cent coverage of sewers. The FSSM policy states the urgency of management of raw sludge and how its neglect has led to creation of illegal and hazardous practices that pose serious health issues and environmental pollution.

Because of the absence of government policy in this area, a number of private contractors have established their businesses which seldom have any regard for environmental damage they cause by improper disposal. The policy seeks to leverage and engage all existing infrastructure including the private players. Many countries which rely on FSSM have successful public–private partnerships for sludge management.

The Sanitation Chain

To assess the gaps in the sanitation chain, it is imperative to understand what processes exist. A sanitation chain consists of mainly five steps: Containment, emptying, transportation, treatment and reuse/disposal of waste. Normally, in developed countries a proper network of sewers running through the cities exists; the containment systems are built underground and the sewage is transported through a network of sewers to the treatment plant, where this waste is treated accordingly and then either reused or disposed of. This is known as an off-site sanitation system. Contrary to this, in most developing countries the coverage of sewerage systems is very less, and hence the households mostly rely on on-site sanitation (OSS) systems. To support this kind of system, a faecal sludge management (FSM) service is required which aids in the transportation of the faecal waste. The faecal waste is contained in a septic tank, which has no sewer connectivity. Thus, when this tank is full, it is emptied with the help of vacuum trucks or any other technology and transported to (ideally) a treatment plant where it is accordingly treated and disposed of or reused. The problem in this chain mainly occurs when there is no proper provisioning of services at every stage which results in dumping of faecal waste out in the open.

Most of India is not connected through pipes or sewer system. Pit latrines or septic tanks are most common in places where there is absence of a sewer. As per the Ministry of Urban Development, 45 per cent of urban Indian households are dependent on OSS systems. This makes it a very large percentage of people who are dependent on this technology. While under the SBM, toilets and various types of containment systems were built, the proper disposal of the faecal waste was largely ignored. Even though the policies mentions that wherever possible the toilet facility should be connected to the nearby sewerage system, or a proper septic tank should be built to ensure FSM, this was largely unrealized.

A look at the stage-by-stage process explains what happens when a part of this chain breaks down. When toilets are built, they are piped or networked into a septic tank where the excreta flows into after flushing. The excreta is contained in this tank until it is completely filled. In many cases households do not empty the tank until it starts to overflow. Until now there is no emptying service provided by ULBs or municipalities in Delhi. This missing link created an opportunity for the private players to step in (left by no provision of public facilities) for emptying and transportation services. The motive of these private operators is to keep business viable and profitable. Thus, most of them provide the emptying service for a fee depending upon the size of the tank, the distance travelled to dispose of the waste and so on. Since the motive of the business is earning profit and not environmental safety or any public health concern, these private collectors dispose the faecal waste in storm drains, open lands in the outskirts of the city, city drainage systems, rivers or other water bodies and so on, whichever is more cost-effective to them. A study by Strande et al. (2014) suggests that a truck load of faecal sludge released into the environment is equal to 5,000 persons practicing open defecation.

The target of the government remains to achieve 100 per cent coverage of sewerage network and the FSSM policy is often viewed as an interim policy which will be in place until the target is achieved. While achieving this goal is realistic, the unplanned growth in urban cities leads to a rise in irregular and unauthorized colonies. It is often difficult to carry out development works in such areas as there is no proper measure or plan laid out for such areas and they continue to grow at a fast rate.

The Case of Delhi: Current Situation, Lack of Data and Policy Response

Delhi displays the case of unbridled urbanization. Needless to say, provisioning of public services presents many challenges for the

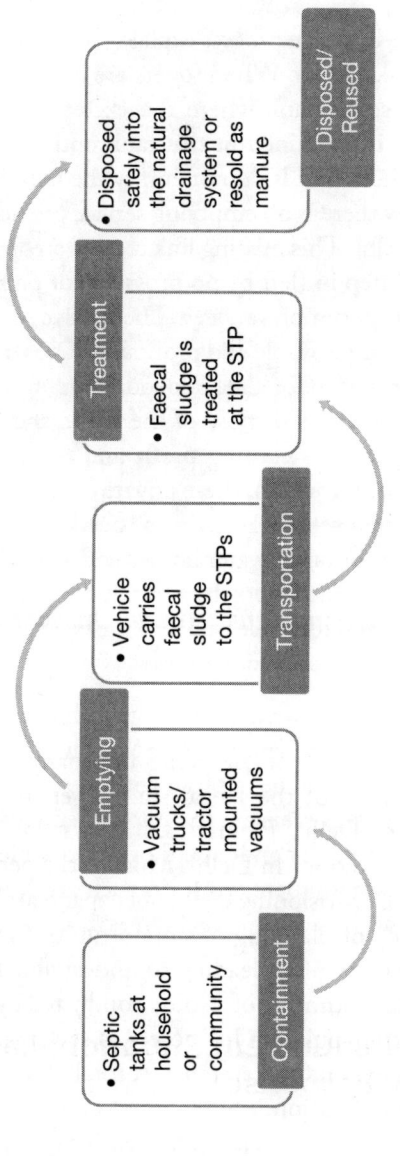

Figure 13.1 Sanitation Chain
Source: Author's own.

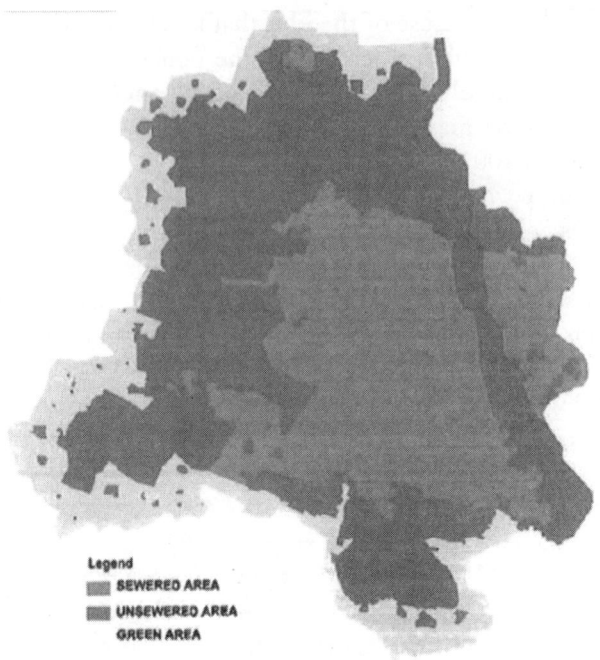

Figure 13.2 *Map Showing Sewered and Unsewered Areas of Delhi*
Source: Delhi Jal Board (2014).

ULBs and the state government. Among the many issues lies the problem of management of the faecal sludge generated from the unsewered colonies of Delhi. Figure 13.2 shows the network and reach of sewerage connections in Delhi. Most of the peripheral areas are unsewered. Service provisioning could not expand at the same pace as the city due to lack of planning. As opportunities grow, the city organically branches out—often leading to undesirable living conditions. According to the estimates of a study conducted by CSE, about 68 per cent of the city population has access to sewerage facility and 28 per cent is dependent on OSS systems. A total of 4 per cent of the people practice open defecation.

The sewerage connections of Delhi have been in place since the British era, and the city followed the European network model for sanitation plans. Because of the idea that a networked city is better able to help in service provisioning, the policy regarding disposal systems have largely been in favour of expanding the sewerage system. Even the master plan of the city for 2031 posits that the city will reach 100 per cent coverage in 15 years. While the idea of 100 per cent coverage is a good policy option, it may not always be viable or even be feasible in a city wherein living settlements grow unchecked. After much advocacy from various environment forums and civil society organizations, the government has seen FSM as an interim solution. However, the core focus remains on expansion of sewer lines. This is reflected in the Delhi Sewerage Master Plan document which lays stress only on investing heavily in underground pipelines connecting households and carrying city waste by way of sewers to STPs. The city sewage network is inadequate to cater to the current needs. In Delhi, only about 45 per cent of the sewage is managed safely (Susana, 2015). Estimates suggest that the city generates 3,800 MLD of sewage of which the STPs in the city have a capacity of 3,049 MLD. The treatment capacity however is 2,693.7 MLD (CPCB, 2015). While these estimates show that about 70 per cent of the sewage can be managed, only 45 per cent is treated and released safely.

Investments required for an elaborate network to be completed by 2031 includes an investment of INR 100,770 million (Delhi Jal Board, 2014) This project involves expansion of the sewage network to a length of 9,807 km in length, along with building pumping stations and treatment plants. The problem with such investments is that they are mostly categorized as sunk costs which cannot be recovered. Sunk costs are often the reason behind building up on the given infrastructure. Because Delhi already had a wide network of sewage with a wide expanse in comparison to other metropolitan cities, it was considered better to enhance the existing network. To choose an alternate mechanism for management of sewage would not be efficient. It is reasonable to consider that between expansion of the existing networks and building up an effective FSM chain, which method has more feasibility in terms of cost, coverage and more effective with regard to safe disposal.

The Sanitation Chain in Delhi

The FSSM policy is a national policy; however, its implementation is specific to each city and town. Given that 28 per cent of the population relies on OSS systems, it was mandated that the ULBs clearly delineate the roles of different bodies and stakeholders from various civil society organizations to private operators and citizens alike. The Delhi Jal Board (DJB) is the authority which looks into the management of sewers and the faecal waste generated. Since it does not have any infrastructure to collect the sludge from tanks, it invited applications from the already operating private players to register themselves with DJB, thereby leveraging the already existing network. The guidelines clearly state that only licensed operators will be allowed to operate and provide FSM services. The trucks should be leak proof/spill proof and shall be in an operational state and should be equipped with GPS tracking system. A small registration fee of 1,000 rupees will be incurred by the operator for this purpose. The guidelines also state that the sludge should be deposited in one of the 86 STPs of Delhi. The current scenario of the sanitation chain in Delhi is discussed further.

Containment: Various studies (CSE, 2016; Susana, 2014) have tried to map the kind of containment systems that exist in Delhi. The type of containment system a house is using depends on the income group. Lower income groups were found to have been using single chamber tanks. Due to constraints of space, houses build fully lined tanks which open into nearby open drains. The quality of these tanks/containment systems differs greatly. They vary according to the available space, cost, skills of the masons and the manner in which tanks are constructed in the neighbourhoods.

The major issue which arises in these cases is that often the standards are not followed in building these containment systems and there is no monitoring mechanism to keep a check on the quality. There is a general lack of awareness among the individual household members, masons and contractors about the sewage mechanism, and the environmental and public health ramifications of a poorly constructed containment tank.

While the new FSSM policy explains that ULBs must work towards creating awareness about proper FSM and involve all key stakeholders in the process, it is often difficult to do so and even if awareness is created, financial feasibility may often deter people from following the prescribed standard.

Emptying: In Delhi, FSM is dominated by private players and there has been no provision for a state sponsored or operated service. Around 350–400 vacuum tankers owned by private operators run in the city and offer emptying service (CSE, 2016). These are mainly of two kinds: a tractor mounted tanker and a truck mounted tanker with the former being more popular. It is imperative to note that the STPs that are operational in Delhi are designed to treat sewerage and not raw faecal sludge. To provide emptying services, the areas where OSS systems are dominant must be identified and a formal operational chain for the same must be designed with an appropriate user fee.

Most commonly in Delhi the containment tanks/septic tanks are emptied once they reach their saturation capacity. This is mainly because the individual households are not aware about how frequently the tanks should be emptied. Not emptying faecal sludge for longer intervals and improper maintenance of septic tanks may lead to deterioration of the tanks. Poorly built tanks may often leak and the waste may overflow, thus polluting the soil and groundwater. The groundwater in Delhi has also seen a rise in the levels of contamination caused by faecal waste (CPCB, 2008). The factors which lead to contamination of groundwater, soil and nearby areas are mainly difficult to monitor. In this regard the roles and responsibilities of the authority and ULBs are also unclear.

Another aspect of emptying service provided by private players is the user fee. This mainly depends upon the size of the tank and the cost incurred (travel cost) in disposing of the waste. This varies from 500 to 3,000 rupees (CSE, 2016). This cost would certainly go up in case there is a proper mechanism in place since it would account for proper disposal, which may require travelling greater distance to dispose the faecal waste and also include the cost of treatment of the sludge.

Transportation: For transportation of faecal sludge, households rely on private emptiers who charge a user fee accordingly. Previously there were no marked grounds where the sludge could be emptied, but recently DJB permitted licensed operators to empty the sludge in the operational STPs of the city. Often the sludge is dumped into storm drains or in the outskirts of the city. The lack of planning and absence of a monitoring mechanism make transportation and emptying difficult to check. The costs that the users pay for emptying their containment tanks is only reflective of the costs based on quantity of the sludge and the transport fee; there is no treatment cost or environmental cost factor added here. Mainly because of two points: No mechanism or policy so far has been put in place to ensure safe dumping/disposal of the sludge at the local level and there is a general lack of awareness among most key stakeholders. The people who work for the private operators are not fully aware of the perils of disposing raw sludge in the environment and the pathogens it carries. Households are mostly unaware of how or where the sludge is emptied and again about the serious repercussion this has on the environment. Through the ways of storm/open drains, this sludge finds its way into the natural drainage system of Delhi. One study revealed the levels of BOD were close to 90 per cent in the natural drains which makes is as good as domestic sewage (CSE, 2016).

Treatment and reuse/end disposal: Since it is being seen as an interim solution, the policymakers may not place priority on building a separate plant to treat raw sludge. The sewage master plan aims to achieve 100 per cent coverage by the year 2031 and requires huge investments. It is however puzzling to understand how will these cater to the needs of a city which grows unplanned and unchecked. In Delhi, there are no proper sites or plants where sludge can be disposed of safely. Therefore, the mandate by DJB is to dump the sludge in the STPs.

Treated sludge forms excellent manure and can be redirected in the market at some affordable cost. This is also an excellent substitute to the chemical fertilizers used. The generation of manure is much higher than its demand and is often made available on free of cost. The price is fixed at 7/KL rupees (CSE, 2016).

Challenges Associated with the Collection System

It must be noted that the mechanism so developed may not completely solve the problem of safe management of faecal sludge. The major problems associated with the model are the rising operational costs and therefore the user fee, lack of awareness among both the household owners and private players about the hazards of disposing raw sludge in the environment, lack of monitoring mechanisms to ensure the proper disposal of faecal sludge and lack of proper implementation of the FSM policy.

The cost of collection and disposal will sufficiently increase once the operators are prohibited from dumping the sludge anywhere. These will be reflective of the registration fee, GPS installation costs and the longer distance they travel to deposit the sludge at the STPs. The cost will also be reflective of the safety gear the operator is mandated to provide to its staff along with training, health benefits and insurance in case of accidents or sickness since it is a hazardous occupation. The onus of bearing the environmental cost and public health damage in case of accidents also lies with the operator. They will be responsible in case of leaks or spills. These added costs are reflective of the damage cost to environment. CSE in one of its studies found out that business owners take at least two trips in a day to keep business viable. They dispose of in nearby areas making short trips. If the travel involved here covers a longer distance, it may result in a single trip driving up the costs and increasing the fee for collection. The onus of ensuring whether the collector is a licensed also lies with the owner of the household. Since the registered owner may charge a higher fee, it is likely for them to employ the services of an unregistered collector and dispose it of in an unsuitable manner.

A general lack of awareness among the stakeholders is perhaps the biggest challenge which translates into a bigger challenge in terms of the implementation. Often individuals using OSS systems are unaware about how the waste they generate is disposed and ends up mostly in the natural drainage system of Delhi without any treatment. Efforts should be made to create awareness and build capacity of the stakeholders to ensure sustainability.

Lessons from Other Countries

Efficient models for FSM exist in many developing countries which can serve as a model for India and a city like Delhi. In Indonesia about 67 per cent of the urban population depends on OSS. The local governments have the role of a monitoring and regulatory agency while private companies operate in FSM after obtaining licenses. Indonesia is known to invest heavily in behavioural change and capacity building since it has a community-based decentralized model at the heart of its national sanitation policies (Dasgupta, Indonesia's Approach to Urban Sanitation: Lessons for India) (Centre for Science and Environment, 2011).

Malaysia too is a pioneer in FSM and has achieved 100 per cent septage treatment under Indah Water Konsortium. The country has a consolidated legal framework along with the institutional responsibilities to guarantee sewerage treatment services at the national level. The Sewerage Services Act and Water Services Industry Act were two such acts that ensure efficient management and monitoring of services.

In the capital of Philippines, Manila, 85 per cent households rely on OSS systems. The different agencies in the city manage the waste in an efficient way and add an environment fee of 10 per cent of water bill for desludging activities. The country has an inclusive law which mandates its local bodies to ensure proper disposal in areas that are deficient in sanitation infrastructure.

Conclusion

Various government policies targeted at providing basic sanitation services often have a very narrow focus. The much-acclaimed SBM which has various dimensions to it such as improving sewerage network, solid waste management and city cleaning has found its focus on meeting the targets of building toilets. The sustainability of extending the sewage network must be questioned given the nature of urbanization Indian cities witness. The FSSM policy is a step ahead in this regard. However, the government must recognize that a holistic sanitation policy must include proper disposal for OSS systems. It must not be viewed as an interim solution but demands focus as well.

For this purpose, proper investments should be made with efficient city-level planning institutions and ULBs. FSM infrastructure is also cheaper than building a network of sewers which involves huge costs that cannot be recovered.

There is immense lack of awareness about the hazards of dumping raw sludge in storm/open drains or city outskirts. The ULBs can play a major role in this regard by educating the key stakeholders in this. Capacity building of stakeholders such as masons, contractor, and common citizens must be adopted. Existing infrastructure, both private and public must be leveraged and enhanced to build a sustainable sanitation model. Inclusion of private players may have certain exclusionary effects, such as high user fee may deter some poorer houses to opt for unregulated operators. In this regard, the authorities must ensure a law which is inclusionary. Perhaps India could follow levying a surcharge to cover the costs of desludging. To ensure inclusion of the lowest rung, a review of the user fee model is a must.

For a sustainable sanitation model, the urban cities such as Delhi must not rely completely on sewage systems but invest in low-cost models. The sanitation model of Delhi is a supply-driven model instead of a demand-driven model. A mix of the two (off-site and on-site) systems can be permanently adopted as a policy measure to cater to the needs of the growing city.

References

Central Pollution Control Board. (2008). *Status of groundwater quality in India: Part II*. Delhi: Ministry of Environment and Forest, GoI.

Central Pollution Control Board. (2015). *Inventorization of sewage treatment plants*. Delhi: Ministry of Environment and Forest, GoI.

Centre for Science and Environment. (2011). *Policy paper on septage management in India*. Delhi: Centre for Science and Environment.

Chaplin, S. E. (2011). *The politics of sanitation in India: Cities, service and the state*. Delhi: Orient Black Swan.

Dasgupta, S. (n.d.). *Indonesia's approach to urban sanitation: Lessons for India*. New Delhi: Centre for Policy Research.

Dasgupta, S., Murali, R., George, N., & Kapur, D. (n.d.). *Faecal waste management in smaller cities across South Asia: Getting right the policy and practice*. Delhi: Centre for Policy Research.

Delhi Jal Board. (2014). *Sewerage master plan for Delhi—2031*. Delhi: Government of National Capital Territory of Delhi.

Dijk, Meine Pieter van, Etajak, S., Mwalwega, B., & Ssempebwa, J. (2014). Financing sanitation and cost recovery in slums of Dar es Salaam. *Habitat International, 43*, 206–213.

Government of India. (2017). *National policy on faecal sludge and septage management (FSSM)*. Delhi: Ministry of Urban Development, Government of India.

Government of National Capital Territory of Delhi. (2015). *State annual action plan*. Delhi: Government of National Capital Territory of Delhi.

Government of National Capital Territory of Delhi. (2016). *State annual action plan*. Delhi: Government of National Capital Territory of Delhi.

Government of National Capital Territory of Delhi. (2017). *State annual action plan*. Delhi: Government of National Capital Territory of Delhi.

Graham, S., & Marvin, S. (2001). *Splintering urbanism*. London: Routledge.

Johannessen, A., Rosemarin, A., Thomalla, F., Swartling, A. G., Stenstrom, T. A., & Vulturius, G. (2014). Strategies for building resilience to hazards in water, sanitation and hygiene (WASH) systems: The role of public private partnerships. *International Journal of Disaster Risk Reduction, 10*, 102–115.

Jueland, M., Kone, D., Strauss, M. (2004). *Private sector management of fecal sludge: A model for the future? Focus on an innovative planning experience in Bamako, Mali*. Dübendorf: Swiss Federal Institute for Environmental Science and Technology (EAWAG) , Department for Water and Sanitation in Developing Countries (SANDEC).

Ministry of Housing and Urban Affairs. (2017). *Guidelines of Swachh Bharat Mission: Urban*. Delhi: Government of India.

Parkinson, J., & Tayler, K. (2003, April). Decentralized wastewater management in peri-urban areas in low-income countries. *Environment & Urbanization, 15*(1), 75–90.

Peal, A., Evans, B., Blackett, I., Hawkins, P., & Haymans, C. (2013). *A review of fecal sludge management in 12 cities*. Washington, DC: Water and Sanitation Program Urban Glocal Practice Team.

Rohilla, S. K., Luthra, B., Varma, R. S., Padhi, S. K., & Yadav, A. (2016). *SFD report, Delhi*. Delhi: Centre for Science and Environment.

Thye, Y. P., Templeton, M. R., & Ali, M. (2011, August). A critical review of technologies for pit latrine emptying in development countries. *Critical Reviews in Environment Science and Technology, 41*(20), 1793–1819.

CHAPTER 14

CO_2 Emission, Energy Consumption and Human Development Nexus in BRICS

Hiranmoy Roy and
Tarun Dhingra

Introduction

Human development index (HDI) was conceptualized as an alternative to income in the form of gross domestic product (GDP) to measure economic development as a proxy to capture other important choices of the rational man such as social, cultural and political and emerged as a comprehensive index. It was well coined by United Nations Development Programme (UNDP) under the intellectual leadership of Mahbub ul Haq and Amartya Sen in 1990 and was based on arithmetic mean approach which was later revised to geometric mean approach in 2010 (UNDP, 2010). HDI is a more holistic approach than GDP to capture the effect of energy consumption (EC) and CO_2 emissions on quality of life since HDI is a better measure of quality of life than GDP. Meeting energy needs and climate change has an inherent trade-off as most of the energy sources are non-renewable and cause damage to ecology and environment. Thus, it requires significant government action related to promoting clean energy, pertaining regulations and making the sector attractive in terms of profit for investment by working on a conducive policy mix, rationalizing tax barriers and removing barriers to energy access and so on.

The implications of increased EC and CO_2 emission on human well-being in lower-middle income countries is a matter of debate in the sense that these countries need to achieve higher level of development and maintain better quality of life for people. This is a challenge for these countries since drive for higher economic development results in increased EC and CO_2 emission, thereby affecting quality of life (reflected by HDI). Thus, there is a need to analyse this complex relationship and take necessary policy actions to maintain better quality of life, along with achieving higher level of economic development and growth.

In this context, it is quite reasonable and worthwhile for nations to focus on the impact of CO_2 emission and EC on human development and quality of life. Thus, in this chapter we intend to analyse the impact of CO_2 emission and EC on HDI of Brazil, Russia, India, China and South Africa (BRICS) nations and requirement of policy intervention in this direction.

Literature Review

A study by Costa Luis and others about cumulative CO_2 emissions estimation of both developing and developed countries from year 2000 to 2050 had the basis of relationship between two variables: Per capita CO_2 emissions and HDI. This study took three assumptions for calculating per capita emission of individual countries. The first assumption was to fit and extrapolate HDI on taking country as unit by using logistic regression as function of time. This is because HDI falls between 0 and 1 and slows down as it approaches 1. To estimate country emission, extrapolated CO_2 per capita was multiplied with population taken from various scenarios of *Millennium Ecosystem*

Assessment Reports. As per the authors, countries with HDI value above development threshold reduce per capita CO$_2$ emission in proportion to rate of their HDI. The authors estimated the minimum proportionality constant so that the global emissions by 2050 meet the 1,000 Gt limit.

Costa, Rybski and Kropp, 2011 observed that there exists positive and time-dependent correlation between HDI and CO$_2$ emission emanating from fossil fuels. By following development as usual approach, cumulative CO$_2$ emission required for achieving specific GDP threshold of developing countries was estimated by taking specified correlation, HDI extrapolated figures and three population scenarios. By assuming sustenance of demographic and development trends, authors estimated that by 2050 approximately 80 per cent of the world population would live in countries possessing high HDI, that is, above 0.8. For development of 104 countries developing countries (year 2000), estimation of 300Gt of cumulative CO$_2$ emission was calculated for the period mentioned above. This estimated value lies between 20 per cent and 30 per cent of CO$_2$ budget earlier calculated which limits climate change in terms of global warming potential to 2 °C. All these findings and constraints were alternatively used as input for CO$_2$ reduction framework pertaining to related action for the concerned countries. A balanced emission way was proposed by this framework which indexed country context reduction of emission rates in proportion to HDI after hitting a threshold level, with an target of limiting 2 °C global temperature rise. By this approach estimation of global cumulative emission lies between 850 and 1100 Gt of emissions, although these value were within permissible limit.

The authors Serap et al., 2015 established a causal relation between logarithm of HDI and CO$_2$ emission in Organization of Economic Co-operation and Development (OECD) countries for the period 1992–2011. They used time series method based on regression and Wald test with bootstrapping value for specified countries. The Granger causality test supported growth hypotheses of countries such as Luxembourg, Poland, Japan, Korea, Ireland, Spain, Italy, Slovakia, Turkey, Denmark, Israel and USA. Conservation hypothesis of countries such as France, Greece, New Zealand, Finland, Estonia, Chile,

Mexico and Czech Republic was also supported. In addition to this, feedback hypothesis was supported for Norway, Portugal, Switzerland and Iceland and neutrality hypothesis of countries such as Austria, Australia, Slovenia, Sweden, Hungary, Canada, Belgium, UK and Netherlands also provided empirical evidence. Conclusion drawn can be stated that CO_2 emission reductions owing to conservation policies pertaining to different types of energy usage also reduce GDP growth and human living standards. Although negative impact of not implementing conservation policies is quite huge on environmental degradation which again affects human lining standards. Thus, there is a requirement for policymakers to meet reduction of carbon emission by developing a strategic plan that does not affect its constituents of Human Development negatively. One alternative way to do this is to augment for the energy efficiency in its usage. The study has observed that many scholars that have explored the relationship between HDI and energy assessed a strong relationship between HDI and EC by observing 120 countries. Based on these, three trends were highlighted: (a) poor countries witnessed steep rise in HDI in relation to EC, (b) in transitioning countries it is moderate and (c) in developed countries there is no rise in HDI.

There are few studies which state that improvement in EC will lead to a rise in human development for poor nations. Ediger, Hoşgör, Sürmeli and Tatlıdil (2007) recalculation of weights of HDI data by adding energy constituents for 173 countries is significant. Countries ranking saw major changes by doing this. Dias, Mattos and Balestieri (2006) by using 1999 HDI data and EC gave broad discussion on causality between HDI and EC. Another author, Pasternak has established strong correlation between HDI and also between HDI and consumption of energy and electricity in the year 1997. An electricity consumption limit for highest achievable level of HDI was also established in this study.

HDI contains three components: Education measured by its index, health measured by life expectancy and income measured by GDP per capita. The purpose of calculating HDI is to create an enabling environment for people to have long, healthy and creative lives. Therefore, income and economic growth are means and not end. The goal is to achieve high quality of living standards. Thus, human development was defined as a process of increasing people's choices by UNDP in its first report.

Thus, HDI has incorporated just a subset of indicators of human well-being; other important indicators which include EC have not been incorporated in UNDP methodology, which of course differ widely across countries. We must assess its impact on human development. HDI captures much more than GDP is the view of many authors because it denotes real quality of life as compared to measuring only income. Thus, we infer from the study of Costa et al. (2011) that though developing countries were invited for active engagement in emission reduction, efforts to evade pitfalls of global warming as the repercussions of such reduction programmes with respect to quality of life status of emerging nations are a cause of concern. These authors have shown that there is a unidirectional affirmative and time-dependent relationship between the quality of life indicators in terms of HDI and per capita emissions from energy usages. The authors have applied this pragmatic relationship and estimated the cumulative CO_2 emissions requirement for developing nations to achieve certain level of HDI. If the existing situation and trends continue for the developing nations, the projections by the authors reveal that in the year 2050 approximately 85 per cent of the global population will live in countries with high HDI, that is, above 0.8.

Thus, from the above discussion it is clear that CO_2 emission has a negative impact on HDI and EC impacts HDI positively. In this study, we shall use the panel regression technique to see the impact of CO_2 emission and EC on HDI.

The Methodology

The objectives of the study have necessitated the collection of published secondary annual data pertaining to HDI, CO_2 emission and EC of BRICS countries. The data on EC is collected from British Petroleum. The EC represents the primary EC (million tonnes equivalent) of the countries. The CO_2 data is taken from World Bank. HDI data is taken from UNDP. HDI is composed of three indexes: life expectancy index, education index and income index and is constructed as follows:

$$HDI = \sqrt[3]{\begin{array}{c} \text{Life expectancy index} \times \text{Education index} \\ \times \text{Income index} \end{array}} \tag{14.1}$$

$$\text{Dimension index} = \frac{\text{Actual value} - \text{Minimum value}}{\text{Maximum value} - \text{Minimum value}}.$$

The minimum and maximum values are taken as given by UNDP (1990; 2010) goal post. This empirical study has applied an econometric model to examine the effect of CO_2 emission and EC on HDI of BRICS countries using annual data for 11 observations from 2005 to 2015. This study explores the impact of CO_2 emissions and EC on BRIC's HDI over the years.

Econometric Model

In this analysis we intend to capture the influence of CO_2 emission and EC on the HDI that can be examined by running a panel data regression by taking the HDI as the dependent variable which is a function of multiple independent variables (CO_2 emission and EC).

$$HDI_t = \beta_0 + \beta_1 CO2P_t + \beta_2 EC_t + E_t \tag{14.2}$$

where t denotes time, HDI = human development index, $CO_2P = CO_2$ emission per-capita, EC = energy consumption and E = error terms.

The results of this regression would indicate that CO_2 emission is negatively related to HDI and EC is positively related to HDI. It is assumed from the theory that there is a relationship between past values of CO_2 emission, EC and the HDI. Thus, the results from this panel regression suggest that past values of CO_2 emission and EC do affect HDI of BRICS nations.

The study includes the following tools:

- Descriptive statistics
- Stationary test
- Hausman test
- Panel regression

Results and Discussion

This section details the results of different panel data analysis techniques used to estimate the role of CO_2 emission and EC on HDI among the BRICS nations.

Descriptive Statistics

Table 14A.1 (see the Appendix) summarizes the number of observations, mean value, standard deviations and maximum and minimum values of the dependent and independent variables used in this study. The maximum and minimum value of each variable indicates dispersion around mean value.

The results of summery statistics in Table 14A.1 show that there is a huge variation in minimum and maximum values of HDI, CO2P and EC. The distribution of HDI, CO2P and EC data is spread over the centre of their mean values.

The cause of the spread of HDI, CO2P and EC data over the time period in the panel of BRICS countries during 2005–2015 may be due to significant increase in HDI, CO2P and EC due to increase in economic activities in these countries. However, in the panel of countries CO2P emission increased gradually and EC increased sharply compared to HDI which is also reflected in the maximum values of CO2P emissions and EC in Table 14A.1 of the summary statistics.

The standard deviation values of EC and CO2P in Table 14A.1 of summery statistics reflect the spread of EC and CO2P emission from their mean. It is very clear from the summary statistics that standard deviations of EC and CO2P emission in the panel of countries are much higher than standard deviation of HDI.

Stationarity Tests

The stationary condition has been tested using all tests which are considered powerful tests. The unit root test results on the individual data series is shown further. The stationarity of the data has been checked by common unit root test through Levin, Lin and Chu (2002) test. And individual unit root tests have been done though Im, Pesaran and Shin (2003) W-stat, ADF–Fisher chi-square and PP–Fisher (1988) chi-square. These test results of HDI, CO_2 and EC in level as well as first difference are given in Tables 14A.2–14A.4.

From the above results, the common and individual unit root tests for HDI, CO_2 and EC confirms that there is no presence of unit root at first difference. Hence, all the selected variables are stationary at first difference. Unit root test suggest that all the variables are I (1).

Panel Data Regression Results

To investigate the impact of CO_2 emission and EC on HDI, this study used panel data regression analysis. The dependent variable is HDI and independent variables are CO_2 emission and EC by BRICS countries during the time period 2005–2015. Results of the Hausman test, fixed effects model (FEM) and random effects model (REM) of panel data regression are shown in Tables 14A.5–14A.7.

Two models of regression, FEM and REM for panel data were estimated. The Hausman specification test has not rejected the null hypothesis; therefore, random effect regression is appropriate. Hence, we have resorted to REM. The model analyses the relationship between three variables namely HDI, CO_2 emission and EC as mentioned in the methodology section.

The empirical results (Table 14A.7) obtained from panel OLS regression using REM shows that regression model explains 96 per cent (R^2) variation in HDI. This result indicates that the explanatory variables included in the equation explain 96 per cent variation in the dependent variable as per FEM model. The coefficient of CO_2 emission is negative while coefficient of EC is positive. Thus the estimated co-efficient has appropriate sign confirming the theory and literature about the relationship between HDI and CO2 emission and also between HDI and EC. The F statistics is 108.9076 and the probability of F statistics is 0.00 which shows that the result is statistically significant. Therefore, we have not used other models for the panel data analysis. Overall results explain that CO_2 emission affects human development negatively while EC affects human development positively.

Discussion

The panel data regression results of our analysis as shown in Table 14A.7 confirm the relationship between HDI, CO_2 emission and EC in the desired direction. The estimated co-efficient of CO_2 emission and EC have the appropriate sign as shown in Table 14A.7 showing a negative relationship between HDI and CO_2 emission and positive relationship between HDI and EC. There is substantial evidence in the literature that the standard of living and quality of life are negatively affected by CO_2 emission while it is positively impacted by EC. There is also evidence in the literature that presence of strong relationship between per-capita CO_2 emission and HDI as mentioned for most of the countries of the world that has also been confirmed by our analysis. Studies also revealed that improvement in EC would lead to rise in Human Development especially for poorer and developing nations showing a positive relationship between HDI and EC while CO_2 Emission reduces HDI that is further confirmed in our analysis.

Conclusion and Policy Implication

From the above analysis, it is clear that there exists an important relationship between human development patterns, CO_2 emission and EC of BRICS nations as evident from the past literature and further reinforced by our empirical analysis. It is proved that there exists a relationship among these variables from the panel data regression results. It is found that the BRICS HDIs are negatively related to CO_2 emission and positively related to EC which may be due to the following reasons.

1. The practices of energy efficiency and conservation have not been followed in developing regions properly as per the McKinsey Global Institute (Farrell & Ranes, 2009).
2. Environmental risks are the major issues faced by many developed and developing countries that reduce the value of HDI. Increasing EC without considering environmental risks like carbon emissions will adversely affect the HDI (as co-efficient of CO_2 emission is negative). Some of the countries which are having high amount of carbon emissions are the Russian Federation, China and India. Developing countries are severely affected by carbon emission which affects human development adversely. Hence, it is suggested that BRICS countries should be more careful as far as environmental risks are concerned which may increase the value of their HDI thereby achieving sustainable human development. Thus, there is an urgent need for policy intervention in this direction. Since environmental quality is affected by carbon emissions, it is suggested for the future studies relating to this area to incorporate the environmental quality as an additional indicator in constructing HDI.

References

Costa, L., Rybski, D., & Kropp, J. P. (2011). A human development framework for CO_2 reductions. *Plos One*, 6(12). doi: 10.1371/journal.pone.0029262

Dias, R. A., Mattos, C. R., & Balestieri, J. A. (2006). The limits of human development and the use of energy and natural resources. *Energy Policy*, 34(9), 1026–1031.

Ediger, V. Ş., Hoşgör, E., Sürmeli, A. N., & Tatlıdil, H. (2007) Fossil fuel sustainability index: An application of resource management. *Energy Policy*, 35(5), 2969–2977.

Farrell, D., & Remes, J. (2010, March). *Promoting energy efficiency in the developing world*. New York: McKinsey and Company.

Im, K. S., Pesaran, M., & Shin, Y. (2003). Testing for unit roots in heterogeneous panels. *Journal of Econometrics*, *115*(1), 53–74.

Levin, A., Lin, F., & Chu, C. J. (2002). Unit root tests in panel data: Asymptotic and finite-sample properties. *Journal of Econometrics*, *108*(1), 1–24.

Martinez, D. M., & Ebenhack, B. W. (2008). Understanding the role of energy consumption in human development through the use of saturation phenomena. *Energy Policy*, *36*(4), 1430–1435.

UNDP. (1990). *Human development report*. New York, NY: Oxford University Press.

UNDP. (2010). *Human development report*. New York, NY: Palgrave Macmillan.

Appendix A

Table 14A.1 Descriptive Statistics

	HDI	CO2P	EC
Mean	0.66937	6.306317	792.9372
Median	0.682	6.17249	520.5406
Maximum	0.804	13.6541	3005.9
Minimum	0.504	1.23315	113.5171
Std Dev.	0.078955	4.175919	855.5047
Skewness	-0.413472	0.208428	1.495508
Kurtosis	2.232393	1.574892	3.857527
Jarque-Bera	2.917422	5.052442	22.18684
Probability	0.232536	0.079961	0.000015
Sum	36.81538	346.8474	43,611.55
Sum Sq. Dev.	0.336626	941.6683	39,521,969
Observations	55	55	55

Table 14A.2 Unit Root Test Results for CO2P at Level

	At level		At first difference	
Panel Unit Root Test: Summary				
Series: D(CO2P)				
Sample: 2005-2015				
Test	*Statistic*	*P Value*	*Statistic*	*P Value*
Levin, Lin and Chu t*	1.11248	0.8670	-6.2249	0.000**
Im, Pesaran and Shin W-stat	2.06179	0.9804	-3.1489	0.0008**
ADF-Fisher chi-square	9.03627	0.5287	28.7166	0.0014**
PP-Fisher chi-square	22.9338	0.0110	35.7163	0.0001**

Note: *5% level of significance, **1% level of significance.

Table 14A.3 Unit Root Test Results for HDI at Level

	At level		At first difference	
Panel Unit Root Test: Summary				
Series: D(HDI)				
Sample: 2005-2015				
Test	*Statistic*	*P value*	*Statistic*	*P value*
Levin, Lin and Chu t*	2.2466	0.9877	-7.0901	0.000**
Im, Pesaran and Shin W-stat	4.0332	1	-4.4072	0.000**
ADF-Fisher chi-square	0.4348	1	37.9799	0.000**
PP-Fisher chi-square	0.4258	1	46.7653	0.000**

Note: *5% level of significance, **1% level of significance.

Table 14A.4 Unit Root Test Results for EC at Level

	At level		At first difference	
Panel Unit Root Test: Summary				
Series: D(EC)				
Sample: 2005-2015				
Method	*Statistic*	*P value*	*Statistic*	*P value*
Levin, Lin and Chu t*	-0.82190	0.02056	-3.1846	0.0007**
Im, Pesaran and Shin W-stat	0.96661	0.8356	-2.1961	0.014**
ADF-Fisher chi-square	8.70458	0.5603	23.0585	0.0105**
PP-Fisher chi-square	12.4639	0.2552	41.1981	0.000**

Note: *5% level of significance, **1% level of significance.

Table 14A.5 Results of Correlated Random Effects—Hausman Test

	Correlated Random Effects: Hausman Test		
	Test cross-section random effects		
Test Summary	*Chi-square Statistic*	*Chi-Square d.f.*	*Prob.*
Cross-section random	3.091936	2	0.2131

Table 14A.6 Results of Panel Least Squares—Fixed Effect Model

Variable	*Coefficient*	*Std. Error*	*t-Statistic*	*Prob.*
Dependent variable: HDI				
Method: panel least squares				
Sample: 2005-2015				
Periods included: 11				
Cross-sections included: 5				
Total panel (balanced) observations: 55				
C	0.697725	0.012222		
CO2P	-0.009639	0.002476	57.08632	0.0000*
EC	4.09E-05	6.86E-06	-3.89278	0.0004*

(Continued)

Table 14A.6 Continued

Variable	Coefficient	Std. Error	t-Statistic	Prob.
R-squared	0.99604	Mean dependent var	0.66937	
Adjusted R-squared	0.994372	S.D. dependent var	0.078955	
S.E. of regression	0.005923	Akaike info criterion	-7.171525	
Sum squared resid	0.001333	Schwarz criterion	-6.551077	
Log likelihood	214.2169	Hannan-Quinn criter.	-6.931593	
F-statistic	597.3469	Durbin-Watson stat	0.765995	
Prob. F-statistic	0.0000			

Note: *1% level of significance.

Table 14A.7 Results of Panel Least Squares—Random Effect Model

Dependent variable: HDI				
Method: Panel least squares				
Sample: 2005-2015				
Periods included: 11				
Cross-sections included: 5				
Total panel (balanced) observations: 55				
Variable	Coefficient	Std. Error	t-Statistic	Prob.
C	0.692994	0.011922	5.750030	0.000*
CO2P	-0.008602	0.002404	58.12643	0.0000*
EC	3.86E-05	6.72E-06	-3.57669	0.0009*
R-squared	0.968863	Mean dependent var	0.669370	
Adjusted R-squared	0.959967	S.D. dependent var	0.029985	
S.E. of regression	0.005999	Sum-squared resid	0.001512	
F-statistic	108.9076	Durbin-Watson stat	0.635265	
Prob (F-statistic)	0.000000			

Note: *1% level of significance.

CHAPTER 15

The Multidimensionality of Water Scarcity*

Jasleen Kaur and M. S. Bhatt

Introduction

Water is one of the most precious gifts of nature and an indispensable substance on which existence depends. It has many facets and many uses. Besides being a basic need and amenity, it is an essential input in the agriculture, industry and service sectors. It is a vital part of our ecological system, sustaining and being sustained by it. It is also a means of transportation and a significant part of our social, cultural and political lives (Iyer, 2011). These uses of water are nothing but drivers of the bigger concept of human development, of which water forms an indispensable part.

Development economics over the years has not only dealt with techniques of economic growth and development but also with improving human well-being. The process of human development

---

*The chapter is an outcome of the doctoral research of the first author under the guidance of the second author.

is concerned with whether people can live a healthy and long life, be able to escape illness, be able to read, write and participate, and have a decent standard of living (Sen, 1983). Pigou (1920) outlined what became the golden words in the 1970s, the 'basic needs', which were necessary to be fulfilled for human well-being and poverty allevia-tion. These needs traditionally comprised of food (including safe drinking water), clothing and shelter, and later, sanitation, educa-tion and healthcare. On similar lines, Scoones (1998) and Carney (1998) claimed that poverty was a result of lack of access to certain 'livelihood assets/capitals'. These capitals were social, financial, human, physical and natural. 'Sustainable livelihood framework' as it is known, was a concept woven to eradicate poverty by providing these entitlements, while at the same time respecting constraints of the earth.

In low-income countries, eradication of poverty, therefore, has meant looking beyond the variables of total supply of goods and population size, to include 'entitlements' of people (set of commodity bundles that can be demanded by an individual, provided the resources at hand) and the 'capabilities' generated by them (Sen, 1983). Desai (1995) broadly classified these capabilities into five: capability to live a long life, give birth, live healthier, build social relationships, and have freedom of expression and thought. Provision of adequate and safe water was, thus, one basic entitlement, which made the society healthy and productive, capable of contributing to development. Since availability of water is an important ingredient in development, water use patterns are known to be a function of the stage of development process that a region has embarked upon. In early stages of develop-ment, water supply for domestic use, livestock needs and irrigation is dominant. In later stages of development, water use becomes impor-tant for industry, energy and intensified agriculture (Falkenmark, 1977). Since water is central to development, the two cannot be isolated (Falkenmark, 1977).

It may, however be noted that water is not only a prerequisite for human survival and development; man also impacts water in the process. Man affects water in two ways: (a) directly, by withdrawal of water, disposal of wastes in water and by regulation of rivers; and (b) indirectly, by affecting vegetation and soil by land-use activities. For the first time, the adverse impact of human activities found its place in the *Brundtland Report* (WCED, 1987), which showed growing concern about the deteriorating environment and natural resources, including water. In the year 1987, the report gave birth to the concept of 'sustainable development'. This concept focused on the need to choose that path of development which fulfilled the requirements of the present generation while at the same time preserved the scarce resources for fulfilling the requirements of the future generations. The introduction of the *Brundtland Report* has generated worldwide attention for water scarcity.

Ever since the decade 1981–1990 was declared as the 'International Drinking Water Supply and Sanitation Decade' and the WHO–UNICEF Joint Monitoring Programme (JMP) established in 1990, the aim has been to improve water supply and sanitation across the globe (WHO & UNICEF, 2000). The indispensable role of water acting as a catalyst to human development was also formally recognized at the UN Millennium Summit in the year 2000 by the leaders of the world when they internationally agreed to a set of targets, bound by time, for reducing extreme poverty and widening human freedom for each nation. The Millennium Development Goals (MDGs) accepted in the year 2000 during the Millennium Summit have clearly linked water with human development. MDGs such as eradicating hunger and poverty, reducing child mortality, improving maternal health, combating HIV/AIDS, malaria and other diseases, and ensuring environmental sustainability are directly linked to the provision of clean water and sanitation (UNDP, 2006).

For understanding this link between water and development, economists have been prompted to define and measure water scarcity beyond the mere availability or unavailability of resources. The causes of water scarcity are seen beyond natural water endowments to extend to reasons such as population growth, accessibility, income poverty, inefficient use and environmental degradation. Therefore, water scarcity is now considered a multifaceted concept, a function of many variables rather than one. Given this and the fact that poverty has one of its important links in water, the term 'water poverty' is often used in place of 'water scarcity' to refer to the state of people with respect to water, rather than the state of water resources (Lawrence, et al., 2002; Sullivan, 2002). This recognition has made researchers develop composite indicators of water poverty, which link with human development. There is a large amount of literary work on the widening concept of development and the place water takes in it. Likewise, studies have also focused on the varying insights of water poverty and its determinants. The studies depict how we have come a long way from simple to composite indicators of water scarcity/poverty and how the composite indicators capture the multidimensional problem of this crisis. This chapter aims to study the widening idea of water scarcity and evolution of the water poverty index (WPI).

From Water Scarcity to Water Poverty

Scarcity is the fundamental economic problem of having infinite human wants in a world of finite resources. Water scarcity is said to occur when water resources fall short of the water usage demands. Scarcity can be demand-driven or supply-driven. This implies scarcity could be caused by the physical shortage of available freshwater resources or increasing demand due to increasing population and overuse. Water scarcity could also be the result of poor accessibility to water resources, a change in climate such as change in weather patterns causing floods and droughts and also because of increased pollution which deteriorates water quality, making it unfit for consumption. Broadly, water scarcity depends on three factors (Rijsberman, 2006): (a) the way people's need for water is defined, that is, whether it includes water requirements of the ecosystem, (b) the proportion of the water resources that can be made available and (c) whether scarcity is defined on a temporal or spatial basis. Molle and Molinga (2003) provide a clear and comprehensive bifurcation of different types of water scarcity. According to them, water scarcity can be divided into five categories: physical, economic, managerial, institutional and political. Water scarcity is *physical* when available water resources are naturally limited in supply, *economic* when people have insufficient human and financial resources to access water, *managerial* when water systems are ill-maintained, *institutional* when society is incapacitated to deal with the demand–supply imbalances of water, and *political* when people in a society are in a situation of political subservience, so cannot access a water source. Scarcity can be a combination of any of these and also vary in duration. It could be temporary or lasting. During the last 30 years, economists have defined water scarcity as a function of these variables, taking them individually or in combination.

One of the earliest attempts on defining the causes of water scarcity can be seen in the works of Falkenmark, Lundquist and Widstrand (1989). While analysing the supply side of water, the authors treated water available in a region as derived from the hydrological cycle. The hydrological cycle in turn depended on the geographical position of the country, which determined the level of precipitation and the amount of external water resources derived from countries which were upstream. So renewable freshwater resources were basically finite in nature. In this context, the authors add that absolute water scarcity was witnessed in countries where climates put them on the 'hydrological margin'.

With his main emphasis on the effect of growing population on finite water resources, Malin Falkenmark in the year 1989 introduced the first index on water scarcity, popularly called the Falkenmark index. It belonged to the category of first generation water scarcity index and was formally called the Hydrological Water Stress Index (HWSI). The HWSI originally dealt with studying the problem of water stress and its solution. The index was directly related to the flow of population per water unit. Using data from industrialized countries, it estimated that a flow unit of one million cubic metres of water supporting more than 2,000 people (500 cubic meters per capita) would mean crossing the 'water barrier' of manageable capability. The stress was much lesser and water management problems were limited when there were less than 600 people sharing one million cubic metres of water (i.e., approx. 1,700 cubic metres) (Falkenmark, 1989; Falkenmark et al., 1989). The Falkenmark index, in fact calculates available water resources per capita which is 'the ratio of the renewable water in the hydrological cycle to the number of people' (Falkenmark et al., 1989). Falkenmark defines 1,700 m³/capita/year water availability as the threshold level. Above this level, water shortage is considered to exist intermittently or locally. Below the threshold level, water scarcity occurs at different levels of severity as described further (Lawrence et al., 2002; Raskin, Gleick, Kirshen, Pontius, & Strzepek, 1997):

- For water availability between 1,000 m³/capita/year and 1,700 m³/capita/year, water stress is a regular phenomenon
- For water availability between 500 m³/capita/year and 1,000 m³/capita/year, water scarcity is a constraint to the development of the economy and to human health and welfare
- For water availability below 500 m³/capita/year, water is a main limitation to life

Falkenmark's index though simple to understand and easy to compute has some major drawbacks (Feitelson & Chenoweth, 2002). The index does not cater to water use patterns which are not the same across countries. It also overlooks the numerous in-stream uses of water and ignores the dependence on transboundary water, water quality aspects and 'virtual water' import options. It also does not include the economic capability of countries to manage and develop water resources (Raskin et al., 1997). Besides there are other issues such as the annual national figures hide reality at the micro level, infrastructure and water networks that make water available, are excluded, and international comparisons are deemed invalid, especially because water demand varies due to different lifestyles and weather patterns (Rijsberman, 2006).

Besides the limitations aforementioned one of the major drawbacks of the Falkenmark index is that floods and other renewable water resources, which are beyond control, are a part of 'renewable water' used in the index. The index was later refined to consider 'water withdrawals' (water diverted/abstracted) instead of renewable water (Raskin et al., 1997). Seckler, Amarasinghe, Molden, De Silva, and Barker (1998), however, note that water withdrawals and water effectively used is not the same. In most of the cases, only a small percentage (around 5%) of the total runoff reaches the downstream end of the basin. So regarding this index, the authors assert, there exists a serious problem and suitable changes in methodology are required before the index is used as a planning tool.

Based purely on the access and use of water, Gleick (1996) identified four 'basic water requirements' (BWR): drinking, cooking, bathing, sanitation and hygiene to arrive at the Basic Human Needs Index. According to the author, the minimum water required for all the uses was 50 litres/person/day. This included drinking (5 litres /person/day), cooking (10 litres /person/day), bathing (15 litres /person/day) and sanitation and hygiene (20 litres /person/day). These figures were recommended to be adopted irrespective of technology, culture and climate. Given this, the number of countries where the average domestic use of water was below the benchmark was found out. The index was criticized because collection of data on water usage at the domestic level was difficult. It was also criticized for ignoring water use by agriculture, industry and nature and for not taking into account the water quality aspect.

Salameh's (2000) water scarcity index is a reflection of Gleick's Basic Human Needs Index. Salameh computed the index of water scarcity as the share of the amount of available renewable water being used in the production of food and household consumption per person per annum under the existing climatic settings. This index was appreciated by Sullivan (2001) because of its emphasis on food self-sufficiency but criticized on the ground that it did not incorporate the water quality issues and the capacity of the people to access water for their food needs and household basic uses. It also did not take care of the non-food uses of water.

Considering the Falkenmark index as the basic measure of water scarcity, Ohlsson and Turton (1999) decomposed water scarcity into first-order and second-order scarcity. According to the authors, Falkenmark's natural resource shortage was the first-order scarcity. But water scarcity extended beyond physical shortage. It also included the lack of social resources to cater to the first-order water scarcity. The second-order scarcity was this lack of social adaptive capacity. In this context, factors such as equity in distribution, political involvement, access to health and education and the like determined how capable the society was in responding to issues related to water. According to the authors, these indicators were captured in the UNDP's Human Development Index (HDI). Thus, in a way, the capacity to access water and sustain that access, as a characteristic of water scarcity, was brought to light. Based on this notion, Ohlsson (1998) constructed the Social Water Scarcity Index (SWSI). To arrive at SWSI, the first generation water scarcity index of per capita availability of renewable fresh water (HWSI) was divided by HDI. Thus,

$$SWSI = HWSI \text{ divided by } HDI/2$$

According to Ohlsson (1998), the values of SWSI were to be interpreted as follows:

5	relatively sufficiency of water availability
6–10	water stress
11–20	water scarcity
>20	water scarcity beyond the barrier

According to the authors, the SWSI gave importance to society's social adaptive capacity in confronting water scarcity issues. At the same time, the index did away with certain inconsistencies associated with the Falkenmark index. However, there are many economists who believe Ohlsson's SWSI is open to further refinement. Feitelson and Chenoweth (2002) argued that by using the HDI, Ohlsson's index actually uses a proxy for what could be the direct means of assessing the social adaptive capacity; neither does it address the water quality issues nor the financial aspects of water provision. Turton and Warner (2002), on the other hand, identified five key indicators for refining second-order scarcity: (a) GNP per capita after adjusting to purchasing power parity, (b) The ability for data creation, indicating technical ingenuity,[1] (c) The ability for creation of 'coping strategies', indicating both technical and social ingenuity,[2] (d) The role of all stakeholders in negotiating and generating strategies to cope with the issue or developing institutions indicating social ingenuity and (e) the ability of a social entity to sustain institutions that are created, indicating both social and technical ingenuity. However, these works by Turton and Ohlsson produce discrepancies in the index, which have to be supported by additional considerations, thus making the index

---

[1] Technical ingenuity refers to society's capacity to adapt to changing circumstances though technological development and innovation.

[2] Social ingenuity refers to society's capacity to negotiate rules, develop institutions and to create the necessary incentives for technical ingenuity to occur in the first place.

not representative of a particular water situation and its complexity (Molle & Mollinga, 2003).

The solution to water scarcity can be found in Winpenny's (1994) 'economic view' of water scarcity. Winpenny explained water scarcity as the difference between water demand and supply, which could be solved only through a price mechanism, like the way commodity markets were cleared. He viewed water as a commodity and asserted that any increase in the demand for water relative to its supply should lead to escalation of the price of water. In this context, he added that it was important to set up an appropriate price mechanism or water market where prices can be determined. Biswas (1991) disregarded this theory much before the notion was given. The author opined that since in developing economies, subsidies were used to achieve their social and political goals, pricing of water to equate demand and supply had no role to play. Nevertheless, Winpenny's (1994) work does highlight the affordability to access water (or social adaptive capacity) as an important feature of water scarcity.

For assessing water stress at the level of a river basin, the World Resources Institute (WRI) as a part of their Pilot Analysis of Global Ecosystems (PAGE) (Revenga et al., 2000) developed an indicator called the 'Dry season flow by river basin'. This was computed by dividing the volume of runoff during the dry season with the lowest cumulative runoff by the population. Based on HWSI, a basin was considered water stressed when water availability was below 1,700 m^3/year/person. Amounts between 1,700 m^3/year/person and 4,000 m^3/year/person indicated adequate supply of water with a marked dry season. Basins with marked dry seasons were defined as those where less than 2 per cent surface runoff was available in the four driest months of the year. Like the Falkenmark index, this indictor too focused only on water availability without taking into account issues of access, capacity and water quality. However, its inclination towards the temporal variability of water gave a new and meaningful direction.

For measuring water scarcity in watersheds, Gleick (1990) developed five indicators for assessing what he called 'vulnerability of water systems'. He affirmed that the watersheds were vulnerable/endangered in the following cases: when (a) storage volume as a percentage to total renewable water resources was less than 60 per cent, (b) the threshold share of consumptive use in total renewable water resource was 20 per cent, (c) hydroelectricity was more than 25 per cent of total electricity (d) share of groundwater overdraft in total groundwater withdrawals was more than 25 per cent and (e) low variability of flow ensuring low occurrence of floods and droughts. The surface runoff exceeding only 5 per cent of the time was divided by the quantity exceeded 95 per cent of the time. A variability value above 3 indicated vulnerabilities.

As advancement over all the indicators which took into account only the supply of water resources, Meigh, McKenzie and Sene (1999) divided the water supply (surface and groundwater both) with water demand from all sectors—domestic, agriculture and industry—to compute the actual water available. As a part of their Global Water Availability Assessment model, the index, which was named the Water Availability Index (WAI), took into account the variability of water availability over a period of time. The WAI was normalized in the range −1 to +1, zero when demand matched supply.

Accordingly, WAI=(R+G–D) ÷ (R+G+D), where R+G=supply and D=demand, R=surface runoff, that is, average annual flow of rivers, G=groundwater resources and D=total demand of all sectors.

The United Nations (UN et al., 1997) gave one of the common measures of water scarcity, which was used by Vörösmarty, Green, Salisbury and Lammers (2000) This was computed as the share of water withdrawal per annum W in the annual water available Q. Heap, Kemp-Benedict and Raskin (1998) modified the ratio by subtracting the desalinated water resource S from W to arrive at, what he called the index of water scarcity R_{WS}. For countries like the UAE, desalinated water constituted 18 per cent of the annual abstractions. Thus,

$$R_{WS} = \frac{W - S}{Q}$$

where W is the annual freshwater abstractions,[3] S is the desalinated water resources and Q is the annual available water which is calculated by Q=R+α∑ D_{up} (where R is the internal water resources in

---

[3] abstractions is taking away water from any source

the country, D_{up} is the amount of external water resources and α is the ratio of the external water resources that can be used. The factor α is influenced by the quality of the transboundary water, the real consumption of water resources in the upstream region and the accessibility of water.

Water stress values were interpreted as under:

$R_{WS} < 0.1$ no water stress
$0.1 < R_{WS} < 0.2$ low water stress
$0.2 < R_{WS} < 0.4$ moderate water stress
$0.4 < R_{WS}$ high water stress

The increase in water withdrawals and hence water stress was directly linked to increase in population. This also demanded the need to put in place a better water management system.

One of the most popular indices capturing the environment aspect of water scarcity was the Environmental Sustainability Index (ESI). Ever since its introduction in the year 2000, the ESI has gained a lot of popularity. Environmental sustainability means to be able to preserve and sustain the valuable environmental resources for the next several decades and improve environmental performance (Esty, Levy, Srebotnjak, & Sherbinin, 2005). The ESI–2005 was constructed using 21 indicators and 76 variables. Values of the ESI for each country varied between 0 (least sustainable) and 100 (most sustainable). The ESI–2005 considered five important components: (a) environmental systems (air, water, land and biodiversity), (b) reducing environmental stresses (curbing pollution of the air, reducing stress on the ecosystem, dealing with population explosion and ensuring management of natural resources), (c) capacity index (CI, as a combination of per capita incomes adjusted for Purchasing Power Parity, under-five mortality rate, education enrolment rate and the Gini coefficient of income distribution), (d) social and institutional capacity (environmental governance, private sector responsiveness and science and technology) and (e) global stewardship (participation in international collaborative efforts and reducing transboundary environmental pressures).

Feitelson and Chenoweth (2002) also considered the environmental aspect while studying water poverty. Since man affects water in the course of development, it causes deterioration of quality of water and hence environmental degradation. This questions the sustainability of the scarce resource for generations to come. Inspired by the concept of sustainable development (WCED, 1987), the authors Feitelson and Chenoweth (2002) claimed that water usage cannot be limited to the viewpoint of the current generation. They also asserted that there were costs involved in making clean water available and preventing pollution of water sources with the purpose of internalizing inter-generational externalities. Hence, according to the authors, water poverty is a situation when the region cannot afford the cost of providing water (clean and sustainable) to its population. According to the authors, water resources for future generations should be as good in terms of quantity and quality as those with the present generation. To this end, the cost of water should be such that inter-generational externalities are internalized by the current generations. Accordingly, the new index, named the Structural WPI, computed the ratio of two elements as follows:

1. The first element (the numerator) was estimation of the cost of water provision (adequate and clean water) and sanitation to a nation's people. This would measure the financial magnitude of the water problem facing a nation.
2. The second element (the denominator) was GNP, which measures a nation's capacity to fulfil its basic domestic water needs and avoiding water poverty.

For water poverty to be absent, the water and sanitation cost estimates (numerator) should be a small percentage of GNP (denominator). A higher ratio implied that a higher percentage of the country's GNP was to be channelled towards the developmental aspects of the water sector. It can be said that Feitelson and Chenoweth's (2002) index takes a different and important course by focusing on the financial aspect of water provision, which is of national significance. At the same time, the index keeps the virtues of simplicity. However, it does pose problems of collection of new types of data, which is difficult.

All the water poverty concepts and indicators reviewed above cater to one aspect of water poverty or the other. The Falkenmark index

(Falkenmark, 1989; Falkenmark et al., 1989) calculates water scarcity by considering the shortage of water availability vis-à-vis increasing population; Gleick's (1996) Basic Human Needs Index defines water scarcity as occurring when the usage of water is below certain recommended thresholds; Meigh et al.'s (1999) WAI takes water scarcity as demand–supply imbalances; Ohlsson and Turton's (1998) SWSI considers water scarcity when social adaptive capacity is not enough to ensure water accessibility and to solve the problems related to it; Feitelson and Chenoweth's (2002) Structural WPI defines water scarcity as lack of a nation's affordability to provide water to both the present and future generations. These indexes are useful in focusing attention on a particular aspect of water poverty. However, they do not capture the multidimensional aspects of water scarcity which is well captured in the composite indicator of water poverty that has proliferated since the year 2002.

The Composite Water Poverty Index

The first comprehensive multidimensional perspective of creating an index of water scarcity was given by Sullivan (2002). Sullivan was one of the first to link water availability estimates with the socio-economic variables, naming the resultant index, the WPI. The author suggested three approaches to capture the essence of the water problem.

Sullivan's (2002) conventional composite index approach identified four variables for the WPI: availability of water, access to safe water, access to clean sanitation and time consumed in collecting domestic water. The WPI was to be computed as: $\text{WPI} = \frac{1}{4}$ $w_aA + w_sS + w_t$ $(100 - T)$, (where A = adjusted surface and ground water availability including seasonal variability, S = % of the population with access to safe water, T = time and effort taken in collecting water, a number between 0 and 100, and w_a, w_s and w_t as the arbitrary weights given to each variable such that $w_a + w_s + w_t = 1$). The higher the index, the better would be the water situation.

His second method of developing a WPI measure was the Gap Method, which compared the actual value of the variables with the set standard value. The variables were ecosystem health (measured by biodiversity, waste absorption and resource depletion), human health (measured by infant mortality rates and life expectancy), well-being of the society (comprising crime rates, education and political participation) and economic welfare (including per capita incomes, distribution of incomes and unemployment rates). Thus, larger the water poverty gaps, higher would be the water stress.

Sullivan (2002) also suggested a time-analysis perspective to water poverty. In this approach, water poverty was defined as the time needed to access a given quantity of water. Here $WPI = T/1000$ m³, where T is the time needed by a person to collect 1,000 cubic metres of water. In developed regions, this could mean the wage-earning labour time required to pay for the water provision. While this method focused on access, it completely ignored the supply side.

In the third and widely acclaimed approach, Sullivan (2002) conceptualized water poverty as the combinations of factors such as the physical quantity of water, access, ecological factors, water quality and capacity of the people to buy water. Based on this concept, Lawrence et al. (2002) developed a broad water poverty measure, called the WPI. The measure provided a method of combining physical and socio-economic factors, relating welfare of the household to water availability and assessing the impact of water scarcity on humans. The authors combined five measures: available water resources, access to water, capacity of people to buy water and manage its supply, water use for domestic, agriculture and industrial consumption and environmental management. It was designed on the lines of the HDI and for each location or area it gave a value between 0 and 100, where a maximum of 20 points was given to 5 different indices, which in turn comprised 17 indicators. The broad components were: (a) resource index (RI, as measured by sum of internal freshwater flows and external inflows divided by the population), (b) access index (AI, as measured by the % of population with access to clean water, % of population with access to sanitation and % of population with access to irrigation adjusted by per capita water resources), (c) capacity index (CI, as a combination of per capita incomes adjusted for Purchasing Power Parity, under-five mortality rate, education enrolment rate and the Gini coefficient of income distribution), (d) use index (UI, as measured by domestic water use in litres per day and share of water use by industry and agriculture adjusted by the sector's share of GDP) and (e) environment index (EI, as measured by water quality, water stress [pollution], environmental regulation and management, informational capacity and biodiversity based on threatened species).

Under each of the five components, the respective sub-component indices were averaged to get the component index or sub-index. Each of the five component indices were then averaged and multiplied by 100 to get the final index score for the WPI, which was in the range 0–100. The highest value 100 was taken to be the best situation (or the lowest possible level of water poverty), while 0, the worst. Equal weights were attached while averaging:

$$WPI = ([RI + AI + CI + UI + EI] \div 5) \times 100.$$

Over the last few years, there have been a lot of methodological improvements in the WPI methodology. This relates using multivariate techniques for dimension reduction, experimenting with geometric aggregation methods and devising objective weighting schemes. Dimension reduction involves the use of techniques like principal component analysis (PCA) for dealing with correlated variables and reducing the number of dimensions studied under the composite index. Such techniques also provide statistical ways of calculating weights for components/sub-components (OECD, 2008). The literature on this signifies the importance of reducing the number of variables and making the index more sensitive, while retaining virtues of simplicity (Cho, Ogwang, & Opio, 2010; Garriga & Foguet, 2010; Jemmali & Matoussi, 2012; Sullivan & Jemmali, 2014).

With growing concerns over climate changes and their impact on water resources, Sullivan and Huntingford (2009) produced a variant of the composite WPI of Lawrence et al. (2002), naming it the Climate Vulnerability Index (CVI). It assessed human vulnerability to the impact of global change on water resources. According to the authors, the global impact factors which made up the main components of the CVI were: geospatial variability (G), resource quantification (R), accessibility and property rights (A), utilization and economic efficiency (U), capacity of people and institutions (C) and maintenance of ecological integrity (E). The authors asserted that by bringing together the variables, vulnerability could be measured by the following formula in the context of globalization:

$$CVI = \sum_{i=1}^{N} r^i X_i \div \sum_{i=1}^{N} r^i$$

where r represents weights or rather degree of risks associated with each variable and X_i is the component i of the CVI structure. The values of CVI ranged between 1 and 100, higher scores indicating greater risk of being vulnerable to changing global conditions.

The composite indicator is, thus, evolving and economists are adding more dimensions to it. Yet the holistic WPI developed by Lawrence et al. (2002) occupies a prominent place in literary works which have experimented with its methodology including the retention of only principal variables or components and issues such as weights and aggregation methods.

Ever since its inception, studies have been done on the refinement of the WPI methodology. Lawrence et al. (2007) used its composite water poverty approach to calculate WPI for 147 countries. For the same data, using PCA, Cho et al. (2010) constructed a simplified version of WPI consisting of three components. He also experimented with objective weighting schemes. Garriga and Foguet (2010) used six different alternatives of combining sub-components and components of WPI to form the index. Using PCA, the authors also experimented with unequal weights. Sullivan and Jemmali (2014) used PCA at the sub-component and component level to create an Improved WPI for the governorates of Tunisia. Jolliffe's 'Method B4' based on PCA was used for extracting only the principal variables under each component (Jemmali & Matoussi, 2012).

The last decade has witnessed wide applications of the WPI. Some of the areas for which the index has been constructed are catchments in Nepal, Pakistan and India (Merz et al., 2003), communes and departments of Benin (Heidecke, 2006), local government areas in the Ondo state of Nigeria (Magagula, van Koppen, & Sally, 2006), Olifants basin in South Africa (Yahaya, Akinro, Mogaji, & Ologunagba, 2009), states of Mexico (Fenwick, 2010), a village of Nagaland (Sharma et al., 2010), districts of the Yellow river basin of China (Xin et al., 2011), governorates of Tunisia (Jemmali & Matoussi, 2012), middle east and north African Countries (Sullivan & Jemmali, 2014) and local government areas in the Oyo state of Nigeria (Awojobi, 2014).

Kaur (2017) in her thesis titled *Water Poverty Index: An Inter-State Analysis of India* (2017) constructed state-wise Falkenmark indices and composite WPIs for India for the year 2012. The Falkenmark index placed all the water abundant states with low population at the top. These were all the north eastern states (with per capita water availability over 30,000 cubic metres and comparatively less population), the coastal states of Goa, Odisha, Kerala, Karnataka and Maharashtra and the state of Chhattisgarh (with water availability between 1,700 and 3,000 cubic metre per capita, except Goa whose water availability was 5,800 cubic metre per capita).

The WPI computed, however, showed results different than the Falkenmark index because WPI was made up of a large number of factors (physical and socio-economic, both). When the HDI for each state was computed using the UNDP (India) HDI 2001 methodology, high correlation between the WPI and the HDI was found. The Karl Pearson's correlation coefficient was 0.67 (significant at 0.01 level), indicating that water and human development go hand-in-hand. Sikkim with its high level of accessibility to water resources, higher average income, better education and health status and better environmental factors, coupled with the abundant resources was found to have the first rank in terms of WPI. The top five states in WPI in India were also the top rankers in HDI. Conversely, the economically poor state of Jharkhand with low access to water for domestic uses and irrigation and with large-scale environmental degradation, including deteriorated water quality, was found to be most water-poor state in India.

Composite Indicators as Tools for Policy

Composite indexes have been known for their vast contribution to development theory. Such indicators (or indexes) are multifaceted and hence combine more than one variable to evaluate any macroeconomic aspect. The proliferation of these indicators shows their importance not only at the policy level but to macroeconomics at large (OECD, 2008). However, it has always been argued that any dimension of development and well-being is much deep-seated, rooted and comprehensive than what can be captured in any index or set of indicators (Streeten, 1994). This is also true for other indexes, like the WPI. It may also be argued as to why to 'catch a vector in a single number' (Streeten, 1994). However, it is done because the resulting index value provides a measure that is basic and simple. Indexes clearly put countries/regions on the same platform where one region's performance can be compared with the others as well as evaluated overtime. No matter how imperfect they look, they simplify the problem and focus attention. In comparison to a long list of individual indicators, composite indicators leave a bigger impact on the public and government.

Streeten (1994) also builds up a strong argument in favour of human indicators such as literacy rate and life expectancy, included in HDI as against the income per head component used. His arguments are as follows: (a) The distribution of human indicators is much less skewed than that of income. For instance, there is a maximum of 100 per cent literacy. Hence, human indicators are not affected by extreme values. (b) Since non-poor have access to public services before the poor, a move in a human indicator in the upward direction can be considered improvement. (c) Whereas high incomes for some individuals can lead to relative deprivation in others, this is not true for human indicators. Health and education benefits of any individual can benefit the community at large. (d) Looking at world development in human terms presents a more positive picture than in income terms. (e) Human indicators show the problems associated with overdevelopment, or rather, 'maldevelopment', as well as of underdevelopment. To exemplify, Streeten says that diseases of prosperity and wealth can kill just as diseases of poverty. The negative or 'destructive' impact of wealth, however, is not revealed by income. (f) Lastly, a simple indicator is politically more appealing because it relates well with the important objectives of the nation.

In context of the composite WPI the fact remains that it brings together several diverse indicators to form the index of water poverty

(Lawrence et al., 2002; Sullivan, 2002). The problem in the multifaceted character of composite indices is that they bring together diverse, disparate fragments of data with subjective weights, yielding interesting results (Feitelson & Chenoweth, 2002; Molle & Mollinga, 2003). However, the real information is found in the components, rather than the final score (Lawrence et al., 2002). Composite indicators are ordinal as far as distance in the index values are not interpreted meaningfully. Such indices of development are a précis of the complex aspects. They combine 'measures of ends and means'. In addition, the techniques of creating an index may be complex, but after the construction of the index there is room for enough flexibility in terms of changing the variables (their quantity and quality), aggregating techniques and weighting system. They can be used for cross-national and inter-temporal comparisons (Booysen, 2002).

Moreover, it remains a fact that the development on one index has paved way for the search for another one, which has not only increased the number and variety of composite indicators but also speaks of their success story. The reason behind the proliferation of composite/ multidimensional indices is the belief that development cannot be measured through a single variable (Wilson & Woods, 1982, p. 11).

Conclusion

Water is integral to all life on earth. Three-quarters of the human body is made up of water. Water is not only important for drinking and sanitation but is also a primary input in agriculture, which constitutes 70 per cent of the world demand for it. Increasing population, urbanization, industrialization and the accompanying consumerist culture have led to an unchecked growth in water demand, putting a pressure on this renewable but finite resource. Across the globe, there are now several signs that indicate human use of water has been extended beyond sustainable levels. Low river flows, depleting groundwater resources, increasing water pollution and environmental degradation are some of the main indicators of water stress in the world (Postel, 2000). *The United Nations World Water Development Report 2015* places water at the nucleus of sustainable development. According to the report, issues such as health, food security, energy security, urbanization, industrialization and climate change are some areas where policies pertaining to sustainable development can be reinforced or debilitated through water (WWAP, 2015).

With the dimensions of water scarcity becoming large, the way water scarcity is perceived and measured has seen a change since the late 1990s. The concept of 'water scarcity' has given way to the more comprehensive term 'water poverty', such that the latter covers all aspects of water scarcity, including physical and socio-economic both. Water poverty is a people-centric concept and covers all forms of deprivation of water. Water scarcity, however, is a resource-centric term, which only covers the physical estimates of resources available per capita. The growth of indicators measuring water poverty has seen immense proliferation, which is well documented in literature. Among these indicators, the one that has received the maximum attention and seen wide spread application is the WPI introduced by Sullivan (2002) and developed by Lawrence et al. (2002). The index aims to bring together the physical scarcity of water with the economic, social and environmental aspects to measure water poverty in a region. For an inclusive and balanced study of water scarcity of a region, the WPI is the way forward. It takes a different role when it is applied at the local and village community level. At such scales, data on the distance to the primary source of water, distance to alternate source of water, total time spent in water collected, members with secondary education, the uses to which water is put and the level of awareness of environmental degradation can be included for the computation of WPI and useful inferences for the village can be drawn. Besides, the index, like other human well-being indices, namely HDI and Multidimensional Poverty Index, should also be computed at regular intervals. To make it more effective, certain WPI-related questions can also be a part of the national census and other surveys. When applied at a gap of say every five years, such a tool would also help in assessing the effectiveness of policies across time.

References

Awojobi, O. N. (2014). Water poverty index: An apparatus for integrated water management in Nigeria. *International Journal of Innovation and Applied Studies*, *8*(2), 591–599.

Biswas, A. K. (1991). Water for sustainable development in the 21st century. *Water International, 16*(2), 219–224.

Booysen, F. (2002). An overview and evaluation of composite indices of development. *Social Indicators Research, 59*(2), 115–151.

Carney, D. (1998). *Sustainable rural livelihoods: What contribution can we make?* London: Department of International Development (DFID).

Cho, D, I., Ogwang, O. & Opio, C. (2010). Simplifying the water poverty index. *Social Indicators Research, 97*(2), 257–267.

Desai, M. (1995). *Poverty, famine and economic development.* Aldershot: Edward Elgar.

Esty, D., Levy, M., Srebotnjak, T., & Sherbinin, A. (2005). *Environmental sustainability Index: Benchmarking national environmental stewardship.* New Haven, CT: Yale Center for Environmental Law & Policy.

Falkenmark, M. (1977). Water and mankind: A complex system of mutual interaction. *Ambio, 6*(1), 3–9.

Falkenmark, M. (1989). The massive water scarcity now threatening Africa—why isn't it being addressed? *Ambio, 18*(2), 112–118.

Falkenmark, M., Lundquist, J., & Widstrand, C. (1989). Macro-scale water scarcity requires micro-scale approaches: Aspects of vulnerability in semi-arid development. *Natural Resources Forum, 13*(4), 258–267.

Feitelson, E., & Chenoweth, J. (2002). Water poverty: Towards a meaningful indicator. *Water Policy, 4*(3), 263–281.

Garriga, G. R., & Foguet, A. P. (2010). Improved method to calculate a water poverty index at local scale. *Journal of Environmental Engineering, 136*(11), 1287–1298.

Gleick, P. H. (1990). Vulnerability of water systems. In P. E. Waggoner (Ed.), *Climate change and U.S. water resources* (pp. 223–240). New York, NY: John Wiley and Sons.

Gleick, P. H. (1996). Basic water requirements for human activities: Meeting basic needs. *Water International, 21*(2), 83–92.

Heap, C., Kemp-Benedict E., & Raskin P. (1998). *Conventional worlds: Technical description of bending the curve scenarios.* (Polestar Series Report). Stockholm: Stockholm Environment Institute. Retrieved from https://www.energycommunity.org/documents/btctech.pdf

Heidecke, C. (2006). *Development and evaluation of a regional water poverty index for Benin* (EPT Discussion Paper 145). Washington, DC: Environment and Production Technology Division, International Food Policy Research Institute.

Iyer, R. (2011). National water policy: An alternative draft for consideration. *Economic & Political Weekly, XLVI* (26–27), 201–214.

Jemmali, H., & Matoussi, M. S. (2012). A multidimensional analysis of water poverty at local scale: Application of improved water poverty index for Tunisia. *Water Policy, 15*(1), 98–115.

Kaur, J. (2017). *The water poverty index: An inter-state analysis of India* (Unpublished PhD thesis). Jamia Millia Islamia, New Delhi.

Lawrence, P., Meigh, J., & Sullivan, C. (2002). *The water poverty index: An international comparison* (Keele Economics Research Papers). Keele University, Keele.

Magagula, T.F., van Koppen, B., & Sally, H. (2006, 1–3 November). Water access and poverty in the Olifants basin: A spatial analysis of population distribution, poverty prevalence and trends. In *7th Waternet/WARFSA/GWPSA Symposium*. Lilongwe, Malawi.

Meigh, J. R., McKenzie, A. A., & Sene, K. J. (1999). A grid based approach to water scarcity estimates for eastern and southern Africa. *Water Resources Management, 13*(2), 85–115.

Merz, J., Nakarmi, G., Shrestha, S. K., Dahal, B. M., Dangol, P. M., Dhakal M. P., ... Weingartner, R. (2003). Water: A scarce resource in rural watersheds of Nepal's Middle mountains. *Mountain Research and Development, 23*(1), 41–49.

Molle, F., & Mollinga, P. (2003). Water poverty indicators: Conceptual problems and policy issues. *Water Policy, 5*(5–6), 529–544.

OECD. (2008). *Handbook on constructing composite indicators: Methodology and user guide.* Paris: Organisation of Economic Co-operation and Development.

Ohlsson, L. (1998). *Water and social resource scarcity* (FAO issue paper). Rome: FAO.

Ohlsson, L., & Turton, A. R. (1999). *The turning of screw: Social resource scarcity as a bottleneck in adaptation to water scarcity* (Working Paper). London: School of Oriental African Studies, University of London. Retrieved from https://www.soas.ac.uk/water/publications/papers/file38362.pdf

Postel, S.L. (2000). Entering an era of water scarcity: The challenges ahead. *Ecological Applications, 10*(4), 941–948.

Pigou, A. (1920). *The economics of welfare.* Oxford: Macmillan.

Raskin, P., Gleick, P., Kirshen, P., Pontius, G., & Strzepek, K. (1997). *Water futures: Assessment of long-range patterns and problems.* Stockholm: Swedish Environment Institute/United Nations.

Rijsberman, F. R. (2006). Water scarcity: Fact or fiction? *Agricultural Water Management, 80*(1–3), 5–22.

Salameh, E. (2000). Redefining the water poverty index. *Water International, 25*(3), 469–473.

Scoones, I. (1998). *Sustainable rural livelihoods: A framework for analysis* (IDS Working Paper No. 72). Falmer: Institute of Development Studies, University of Sussex.

Seckler, D., Amarasinghe, U., Molden, D., De Silva, R., & Barker, R. (1998). *World water demand and supply, 1990 to 2025: Scenarios and issues* (IIMI Research Report 19). Colombo: IIMI.

Sen, A. K. (1983). Development: Which way now? *The Economic Journal, 93*(372), 745–762.

Sharma, B.R., Riaz, M.V., Pant, D., Adhikary, D.L., Bhatt, B.P. & Rahman, H. (2010). *Water Poverty in the Northeastern Hill Region (India): Potential Alleviation through Multiple-Use Water Systems - Cross Learnings from Nepal*

Hills. New Delhi, India: International Water Management Institute (IWMI-NAIP Report 1).

Streeten, P. (1994). Development: Means and ends. *American Economic Review, 84*(2), 232–237.

Sullivan, C. (2001). Comments on redefining the water poverty index by elias salameh. *Water International, 26*(2), 292–293.

Sullivan, C. (2002). Calculating a water poverty index, *World Development, 30* (7), 1195–1211.

Sullivan, C. A., & Huntingford, C. (2009). Water resources, climate change and human vulnerability. In *18th World IMACS/MODSIM Congress*, Cairns, Australia.

Sullivan, C. A., & Jemmali, H. (2014). *Towards understanding water conflicts in MENA region: A comparative analysis using water poverty index* (Working Paper No. 859). Economic Research Forum.

Turton, A. R., & Warner, J. F. (2002). Exploring the population/water resources nexus in the developing world. In G. D. Dabelko (Ed.), *Finding the source: the linkage between population and water, environmental change and security project (ECSP)*. Washington, DC: Woodrow Wilson Center.

UN, UNDP, UNEP, FAO, UNESCO, WMO...SEI. (1997). *Comprehensive assessment of the freshwater resources of the world*. New York, NY: World Meteorological Organization, 33.

UNDP. (2006). *Human development report*. New York, NY: Author.

Vörösmarty, C. J., Green, P., Salisbury, J., & Lammers, R. B. (2000). Global water resources: vulnerability from climate change and population growth. *Science, 289*(5477), 284–288.

WHO & UNICEF Joint Monitoring Programme for Water Supply and Sanitation (2000). *Global water supply and sanitation assessment 2000 report*. Geneva, Switzerland: World Health Organisation.

Wilson, R. K., & Woods, C. S. (1982). *Patterns of world economic development*. Melbourne: Longman Sorrett.

Winpenny, J. (1994). *Managing water as an economic resource*. London, NY: Routledge.

World Commission on Environment and Development (WCED). (1987). *Our common future*. Oxford: Oxford University Press.

WWAP. (2015). *The United Nations World Water Development Report 2015: Water for a Sustainable World*. United Nations World Water Assessment Programme, Paris: UNESCO.

Xin, L., Jun, W. & Jielin, J. (2011). Application of the water poverty index at districts of Yellow River Basin. *Advanced Materials Research, 250–253*, 3469–3474.

Yahaya, O., Akinro, A. O., Mogaji, K. O., & Ologunagba, B. (2009). Evaluation of Water Poverty Index in the Ondo State, Nigeria. *ARPN Journal of Engineering and Applied Sciences, 4*(10), 1–10.

About the Editors and Contributors

Editors

Mohammad Younus Bhat is currently working as an assistant professor in the Department of Economics and International Business, University of Petroleum and Energy Studies (UPES). Prior to this, he was associated with Jamia Millia Islamia and Amity University. He did his PhD in environmental economics from Jamia Millia Islamia. His area of research is economic valuation of biodiversity. He has published his work in many national and international journals. He has participated in various national and international conferences and workshops within and outside India on environment and natural resource economics.

Hiranmoy Roy has been engaged in teaching and research since the last 20 years. His areas of research interests are development economics and energy studies. Earlier, he worked with Assam (Central) University (2001–2004), Karimganj College (2005–2008) and IBS— Hyderabad (2008–2010). At present, he is the Head, Department of Economics, School of Business (SoB), UPES, Dehradun. He has written four books and presented 40 papers at national and international conferences. He has also published 25 research papers in national and international peer reviewed journals. He has completed two research project sanctioned by University Grants Commission (UGC) and UCO Bank in the years 2003–2004 and 2007–2008. He has also completed energy policy-related projects of the NITI Aayog in 2016. Five scholars have completed their PhD under the supervision of Dr Roy. and currently six PhD scholars are registered under him. He has been a visiting faculty at the Institute of Technology Management under DRDO, Mussoorie, and has also taken guest sessions in IIM Kashipur.

M. S. Bhatt is former professor of environmental economics and head of the Department of Economics, Jamia Millia Islamia, New Delhi. He has been associated with the University of Kashmir, Srinagar; Jawaharlal Nehru University (JNU), Delhi; the Institute of Economic Growth, Delhi; African–Asian Rural Development Organization (AARDO), Delhi; The Indira Gandhi National Open University (IGNOU), Delhi; the Institute for Social and Economic Change, Bangalore; and the Centre for Rural and Industrial Research, Chandigarh, among others. His main areas of specialization are, development economics, agrarian economics, environmental economics, research methodology and Kashmir studies. He was a member of the expert committee for economic reforms (Godbole Committee) appointed by the Government of Jammu and Kashmir. He has completed 10 major research projects and acted as a principal investigator in a number of research projects. He coordinated two UGC-sponsored special projects (DRS-I SAP, for five years) on environmental economics (DRS-I, SAP) and computer application programme (under emerging Area Programme of UGC, for 10 years). He has a rich experience of teaching and research spanning over a period of 40 years. He has guided 19 PhD scholars and 5 MPhil dissertations. He has authored/co-authored seven books and published more than 100 articles in national and international journals. He has participated in more than 50 seminars and presented papers in many national and international conferences organized in India and abroad. He has extensively written on Jammu and Kashmir's economy and economic evaluation of wetlands of north-western India. He has acted as a resource person, member of selection committees, member of boards of management to many national, international universities and research organizations such as AARDO, IGNOU, Central University Jammu, JNU, Central University Orissa, Central University Uttar Pradesh and University of Kashmir. As Head, Department of Economic Jamia Millia Islamia, Bhatt through hard work, dedication and introduction of new academic programmes raised the academic profile of the department which was formally recognized by the University's Academic Council through a formal resolution and by the eminent scholar professor Musheer-ul-Hassan who was the then Vice-Chancellor of the Jamia Millia Islamia. He has served as full-time elected member of Jamia Academic Council for nine years.

Contributors

Afkar Ahmad is an assistant professor (selection grade) in School of Law, UPES, Dehradun, Uttarakhand. He has an extensive experience of teaching undergraduate and postgraduate courses of law. He completed LLM with specialization in criminal law from Aligarh Muslim University. He was awarded with PhD from Chanakya National Law University, Patna, for his research on the topic 'Trafficking in Women and Children in India: A Socio-Legal study with special reference to the States of Bihar and Jharkhand'. He has a number of publications and academic presentations in various national and international seminars and conferences to his credit. His areas of interest are criminal law, family law and constitutional law.

Aounkar Anand is the co-founder and COO of RostrumLegal. He did his LLM from National University of Study and Research in Law, Ranchi. He is perusing PhD in Law from School of Law, UPES, Dehradun, Uttarakhand.

Aparna Radhakrishnan is an assistant professor, Agricultural Extension, Kerala Agricultural University, with masters and PhD in Agricultural Extension. She did her PhD from National Dairy Research Institute with DST-INSPIRE fellowship. She has two and a half years of post-PhD experience in research related to social sciences. She worked with IIT Delhi and S. M. Sehgal Foundation as a researcher post PhD. She is also a reviewer of many high-impact international journals with seven high-rated publications, three book chapters and paper presentations at five international conferences.

Arfat Ahmad Sofi is currently working as an assistant professor in the Department of Economics, BITS Pilani, K. K. Birla Goa Campus. His research interests include economic growth, development economics, public economics and applied spatial econometrics. Prior to joining BITS Pilani, Goa, he worked at IIT Madras as a post-doctoral fellow for two years. He was also associated with Rajiv Gandhi National Institute of Youth Development, Tamil Nadu (India) where he constructed India Youth Development Index. He has published his research in internationally acclaimed and accredited journals. His research focused on the development of spatial interactive models for public policy interface and endogenous growth suitable for developing countries. Currently, he is working in the areas of economic growth, urbanization and inequality. Sofi did his PhD in economics from Pondicherry University, Puducherry. He received his BA and MA Economics from University of Kashmir, India.

Aswani R. S. is an assistant professor in the Department of Economics & International Business, Uttarakhand. She did her PhD in maritime security in Indian Ocean Region. Her areas of interest include maritime security, Indian Ocean, Sino-Indian relations and climate policy.

Atri Nautiyal is working as an assistant professor in the Department of Economics and International Business, UPES, Dehradun. Atri has been in the academic domain for over seven years. He holds a master's degree in international economics and finance from Ryerson University, Canada. His areas of interest are in the fields of developmental economics, finance and international business. He has worked at University of Toronto and Ryerson University, Canada, as a research assistant. He has a corporate experience of over 12 years. Prior to academics, he has worked in major North American financial institutions such as Canadian Imperial Bank of Commerce and TD Canada Trust in Canada as a financial advisor. He is currently pursuing PhD in management from UPES, Dehradun, India.

Bhartendu Kumar Chaturvedi is currently working as an assistant professor in Department of Economics and International Business, UPES, Dehradun. Bhartendu has been in the academic domain for over six years. He holds a PhD in economics from Banaras Hindu University, India. His areas of interest are in the fields of developmental economics and industrial economics. He has published several research papers in national and international journals. He has also conducted and attended several training programmes on research.

Debasis Poddar is an associate professor in Xavier Law School, St. Xavier's University, Kolkata. A social science researcher, he has had disciplinary exposure in diverse domains, for example, literature, political science and education, besides his expertise in juridical science. Before joining St. Xavier's University, he served in several premier institutions such as National Law University, Jodhpur (NLUJ), National University of Study and Research in Law, Ranchi (NUSRL), and UPES, Dehradun, to name a few. An interdisciplinary researcher vis-à-vis public law, his core areas of interest include, yet are not limited to, environment, human rights, labour and the like. In this occasion, he has explored major flip sides of prima facie unproblematic eco-economic positions extended in line of arguments advanced by post-colonial polemics of the global south, thereby interrogated the grandeur of intergenerational equity with counterclaims of intragenerational equity. Indeed, hitherto ignored by the developed hemisphere, intragenerational equity voices basic human rights for those in extreme poverty, a concern reflected in the first Millennium Development Goal (MDG).

Indrani Roy Chowdhury worked as an associate professor in Department of Economics at Jamia Millia Islamia, Central University at New Delhi before joining at Centre for the Study of Regional Development, JNU. She was also an economist at National Institute of Public Finance and Policy, New Delhi. She has also worked as an associate fellow at Council for Social Development, New Delhi. Her research interests include applied game theory and quantitative methods, environmental economics, health economics and industrial organization. She completed her MA from University of Calcutta, MPhil from Jadavpur University and PhD from Centre for International Trade and Development (CITD), JNU. She has also been an active member of many committees including IGNOU, New Delhi. Her expertise knowledge in applied game and industrial organization attracted many educational institutions to invite her for delivering lectures. Apart from these, she has published many articles in international and national journals, and has presented several research papers at international and national conferences also.

Jasleen Kaur is an assistant professor of economics in the University of Delhi with a teaching experience of more than 12 years at the undergraduate level. She studied BA (Hons) in economics from Kamala

Nehru College, University of Delhi. Thereafter she completed her masters in economics from Jamia Millia Islamia with first division. She holds a PhD in the field of environmental economics from Jamia Millia Islamia. The topic of her thesis is 'The Water Poverty Index: An Inter-State Analysis of India'. She has published her research works in various national and international journals and has also participated in many conferences, both national and international.

Jaweriah Hazrana is currently a researcher at the Indian Council of Agricultural–National Institute of Agricultural Economics and Policy Research (ICAR–NIAP), New Delhi, India. She holds a doctoral degree in economics from Jamia Millia Islamia University, New Delhi, India. Her doctoral research focuses on the application of state space models to determine whether scarcity trends have placed a dominant role in Indian markets for metals and land resources. In addition to her dissertation, her current research focuses on environmental and resource economics, development economics and applied econometrics. Within the arena of environmental economics, she works extensively on the impact of extreme climatic events and adaptation strategies with reference to developing countries and trends in energy markets. Development issues include factors determining agricultural growth and the role of spatial spillovers, and the role of farmer choices and cropping patterns on risk in the agricultural sector.

Karthick Radhakrishnan is currently a doctoral student (PhD) at TERI School of Advanced Studies, New Delhi, and holds an MSc in environmental economics from Madras School of Economics, Chennai. He has an experience of more than six years in research. Prior to this, he worked with Sehgal Foundation, M. S. Swaminathan Research Foundation, TERI University, Madras Institute of Developments Studies, Ashden India Collective and TARU Leading Edge. His areas of interest lie in developmental economics, environmental economics, and monitoring and evaluation.

Md Hafiz Iqbal is an interdisciplinary researcher. He has conducted research activities in Bangladesh, Malaysia, Japan and Norway. He has extensive analytical expertise in health hazards of population, poverty/environment nexus, setting priorities in pollution control, deforestation and ecosystem valuation, impacts of climate change on coastal zone and adaptation to climate change. He began his career in banking and moved into Bangladesh Civil Service in 2005. He did his bachelor of social science (BSS) from Rajshahi University, Bangladesh, and master of social science (MSS) in economics from the same university. Later, he did his MS in development economics from Hiroshima University, Japan; MSc in climate change from Independent University, Bangladesh (IUB); and PhD in health economics from Bangladesh University of Professional (BUP). Currently, he is pursuing MA in education from Nottingham University. He is working as an assistant professor (economics) at Government Edward College, Pabna. He has written book chapters, journal papers and presented his work at several conferences worldwide.

Mohammed Yaqoot is currently working as an associate professor in the Department of Energy Management, UPES, Dehradun. Prior to joining the university, he worked with Voltas Ltd for four years followed by one and half year stint with Reliance Energy Ltd. His areas of interest are power generation technologies, renewable energy technologies, sustainable development and energy policy. He has published several research papers in top-notch international journals namely *Energy for Sustainable Development, Renewable Energy*, and *Renewable and Sustainable Energy Reviews*. He has also conducted several training programmes on clean development mechanism and renewable energy technologies. Currently, he is working on the linkages between Sustainable Development Goals and energy access.

Narendra N. Dalei is an assistant professor at SoB, UPES, Dehradun. Before joining UPES, he held various research and teaching positions at the University of Delhi, IGNOU, and the Ministry of Statistics and Programme Implementation (MoSPI), Government of India. He is the alumnus of UN's SDG Academy. He obtained his PhD in business economics from the University of Delhi. His research focuses on the interactions between energy, environment and climate change in the context of India and the rest of the world. He has published extensively in the *Journal of Quantitative Economics, Journal of Air Transport*

Management, Economics and Policy of Energy and Environment, International Journal of Ecological Economics and Statistics and *Utilities Policy.* He is the recipient of the Outstanding Reviewer Award in 2015 and 2017 for *Energy Policy,* Amsterdam, The Netherlands. He is also the recipient of Best Research Paper Presentation Award in 2018 at 20th International Conference on Climate Change and Global Warming held at Paris, France.

Niti Saxena has over 13 years of development research experience in Asia while working across sectors for non-governmental organizations, the United Nations and international donor agencies. Her expertise includes conducting independent evaluations of programmes focusing on agriculture development, water security, gender mainstreaming, women empowerment, collective action and issues of social justice. She is also an active contributor to academic research and is associated with academic institutes of repute as a guest faculty. She was recently awarded a grant to undertake feminist evaluation of a women empowerment programme in India's most backward district. Her interest lies in using mixed methods approach in every research she undertakes. Through her work, she attempts to link scientific evidence generated at the grassroots with relevant policies to further the movement of evidence-informed policy making in south Asia.

Rakhi Dawar is an assistant professor of economics, Centre of Continuing Education, UPES, Dehradun. She holds PhD in economics from HNB Garhwal University. She has nine years of teaching experience. Her fields of specialization include economics and management decisions; power sector economics and planning; infrastructure economy and planning; transport economics; business economics; business communication and marketing communication.

R. Balasubramanian is currently a professor of agricultural economics at the Tamil Nadu Agricultural University, Coimbatore, where he has been working for the past 31 years. His research interests include natural resource and environmental economics, and economics of climate change. He has handled several research projects funded by national and international agencies such as Indian Council of Agricultural Research,

State Planning Commission, National Bank for Agricultural and Rural Development, The Ford Foundation, World Bank, South Asian Network for Development and Environmental Economics (SANDEE), and the International Union for Conservation of Nature (IUCN). He has been a post-doctoral visiting scholar at the University of Wisconsin-Madison, United States, from 2001 to 2002. He has taught at Konkuk University, Seoul, South Korea, for two years from 2009 to 2011. He has published a number of research papers and book chapters, and presented papers at national and international conferences.

Shakir ul Hassan is currently working as an adjunct faculty in the Department of History and Culture, Jamia Millia Islamia, New Delhi. He has taught history of early complex societies, early modern empires and formation of literary cultures. His areas of interest are environment and early social formations. He is also pursuing research from University of Delhi. He has participated in various national and international conferences. He has also published on early social formations in west Asia and India. He has been a contributor to IGNOU text course preparation.

Sulakshana Rao C. is currently working as an assistant professor in the Department of Economics at Christ Deemed to be University, Delhi NCR, India. Prior to this, she was a research associate with ICAR–NIAP based in New Delhi, India. Her areas of research are resource economics, ecosystem valuation and sustainability assessments. She is a doctorate in economics and completed her PhD in the subject area of natural resource economics from Tamil Nadu Agricultural University, Coimbatore, in 2018. She is the recipient of the prestigious INSPIRE doctoral fellowship by the Department of Science and Technology. Dr Sulakshana completed her master's degree in Agricultural Economics from Punjab Agricultural University, Punjab, India, in 2014 and graduated in agriculture from Kerala Agricultural University, Thrissur, India, in 2012. She has several academic laurels to her credit including ICAR-JRF, ICAR-SRF, ICAR-ASRB NET, UGC NET with JRF.

Tapaswini Nayak was a lecturer in economics at Kendrapara Autonomous College, Odisha, before joining into PN Autonomous

College. She has worked as an assistant professor in Gyana Bharti College of IT and Management, Bhubaneswar. Her research interests include environmental economics, health economics and gender economics. She has published her research work in peer-reviewed national journals. She has also presented many research papers at international and national conferences including Indian Society for Ecological Economics (INSEE). She completed her MA from Ravenshaw University; MPhil from North Orissa University; and PhD from Jamia Millia Islamia, Central University, New Delhi. She has also worked in a research project on 'Health Impact of Air Pollution and Water Pollution in Proximity of Mining Belt.'

Tarun Dhingra has around 21 years (3 in industry) of experience in research, teaching and industry. Currently, he is working as a professor of strategic management in the SoB, UPES, Dehradun. He completed his doctorate from MNNIT, Allahabad, as an ICSSR doctoral fellow. He was Associate Dean—Research, for 3.5 years for promoting funded and non-funded research in SoB with 95 faculty members. Professor Dhingra has published many papers in reputed refereed academic journals (Scopus and ABDC list). He has six PhD-awarded and six research scholars in the domain of Strategy, Energy and Transportation, etc. He has been resource person in UGC refresher course and FDP/MDP conducted in various universities of eminence. He has won the Best Paper Award thrice at different reputed platforms such as IIMA, IISC, Bangalore, and K. J. Somiya, Mumbai. He has conducted strategic management (mainly) and research methodology classes for more than 2,000 managers for over 40 person-days at various energy companies such as OIL, GSEB, IOC, BPCL and HPCL.

Yamini Gupt is an associate professor in the Department of Business Economics, and Deputy Dean, International Relations (Social Sciences and Humanities) in the University of Delhi. Her recent research has been on the waste sector (economics of formal and informal, hazardous waste, impact on climate change), degraded ecosystems and change in livelihood patterns. She has completed international and Indian research projects on: 'Environmental Biotechnology—Restoration Ecology', 'Economic Aspects of Informal Sector Activity in Solid Waste', 'A Study of the Extended Producer Responsibility based Deposit-Refund System for Recycling Lead-Acid Batteries in Delhi', 'Policy Measures and Incentives for Green Recycling of Lead in India' and 'Modeling Studies on GHG Emission and Emission Intensity of Indian Economy'. She has published in journals such as *Southern Economic Journal, Environment and Development Economics, International Journal of Ecological Economics and Statistics, Journal of Quantitative Economics, Economic and Political Weekly, Waste Management and Research, Journal of Health and Pollution*, and *Arthaniti*.

Zoya Khan is currently working as a researcher at Institute of Economic Growth, New Delhi. She has studied economics at JNU and her current research interests are urbanization, sanitation and sustainable development. She has studied economics at JNU and her current research interests are urbanization, sanitation and sustainable development.

Index